Diamond

The Ultimate Gemstone

Authors

Emma S. Bullock, James E. Butler, John Chapman, Katherine Dunnell, Boris N. Feigelson
M. Tyler Funk, Eloïse Gaillou, Viktor K. Garanin, J. Michael Howard, Bram Janse, John A. Jaszczak
John I. Koivula, Galina Y. Kriulina, Claire Mitchell, Nick Norman, George R. Rossman
Elise A. Skalwold, James Shigley, Gloria A. Staebler, and Terry C. Wallace, Jr.

with

John H. Betts, Maximilian Glas, Jeff W. Harris, John Rakovan
R. Peter Richards and Alexander G. Schauss

Editors

Jeff W. Harris and Gloria A. Staebler

Illustrators

Alisa Abrahamson, Stepanov Aleksandrovich, Doris Antony, Amy Ashcraft, Bill Bachman
Michael Bainbridge, Anetta Banas, William W. Besse, John H. Betts, Gerhard Brandstetter
Henri Cartier-Bresson, Paul Bruins, Joe Budd, James E. Butler, John Chapman, Chip Clark, Adam Cohn
Alessandro Da Mommio, Jean-Michele Derochette, Mia Dixon, Andrew Edmonds, Berend G. Escher
Boris N. Feigelson, Kirk Feral, Paulo Fernandes, Eloïse Gaillou, Edmund B. Gerard, Jurgen Glinnerman
Victor Goldschmidt, Richard P. Goodbody, Theodore Gray, Marco Gubka, Francois Guillot
Tino Hammid, Craig Hazelton, Christopher Herwig, Eureka Hyman, Eric James, John A. Jaszczak
Kevin Jones, Dan Kile, Leo Klemm, John I. Koivula, Hansueli Krapf, Jesse La Plante, Billy "Pai Lai" Law
Matt Lee, Maria Letizia, Johnny and Tony Leung, Yves Logghe, Adam Mansur, Paul May
Scott Michelich, Sergeï Mikhaïlovich, Mark Mooney, Corey Neumeier, Imke de Pater, Tony Peterson,
Ping Yu Poon, R. Peter Richards, Josh Ryan, Vic Rzonca, Sean M. Sabatini, Jeff Scovil, Lidija Sekaric
Nick Thomas, Hans van Dyk, Harold and Erica van Pelt, Alexander von Fersman, Eric Welch
Robert Weldon, Michael Wong, Ben Yagbes and Michael Zolensky

Lithographie LTD • Arvada, Colorado

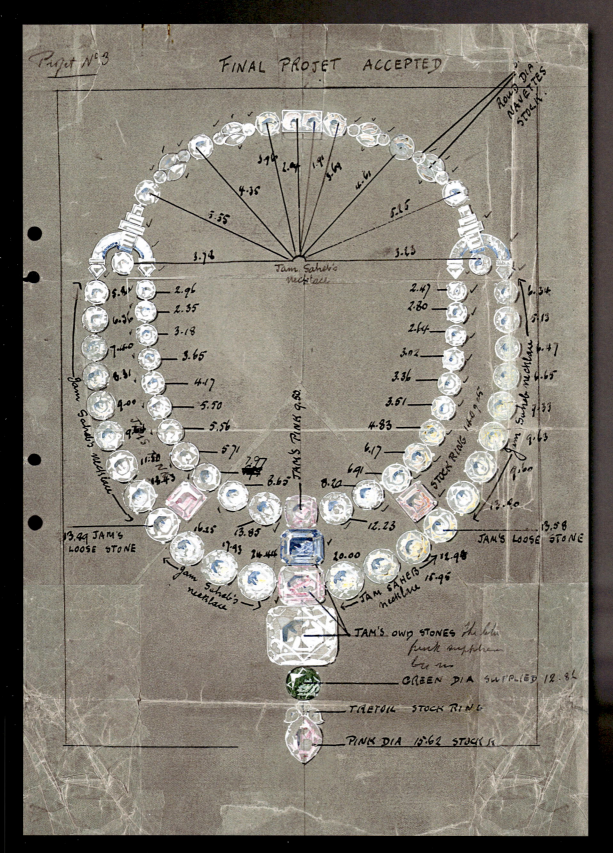

Above: In 1931, Jacques Cartier mounted the 136.25-carat *Queen of Holland* diamond on a ceremonial necklace destined for the Maharajah of Nawanagar, an Indian prince. Image © Cartier.

Facing Page: Heiress Evalyn (Walsh) McLean is sporting a Cartier necklace set with the 44.25-carat, blue Hope Diamond (see page 6). In her hair, the 94.8-carat pear-shaped Star of the East is set as an aigrette, replete with exotic features, on a diamond bandeau. Mrs. McLean was the daughter of Thomas Walsh, owner of the Camp Bird Gold Mine, and wife of publishing (*The Washington Post*) heir Edward Beale McLean. Library of Congress collection, Harris & Ewing photo, 1914.

CONTENTS

PAGE 4
Lands Immemorial
GLORIA A. STAEBLER AND CLAIRE MITCHELL

PAGE 10
Geology of Diamond
DR. BRAM JANSE

PAGE 24
The Magnificent Mineralogy of Diamond
DR. JOHN A. JASZCZAK AND KATHERINE DUNNELL

PAGE 36
Diamond Studies
MAXIMILIAN GLAS

PAGE 40
On the Beauty of Defects
DR. ELOÏSE GAILLOU AND DR. GEORGE R. ROSSMAN

PAGE 54
Diamond: Intimate Portraits
JOHN I. KOIVULA AND ELISE A. SKALWOLD

PAGE 62
Diamonds as Gemstones
DR. JAMES SHIGLEY

PAGE 70
Diamonds in Africa — A Tribute to Tom Clifford
NICK NORMAN

PAGE 86
Crater of Diamonds — The Natural State's Gem of a Park
J. MICHAEL HOWARD

PAGE 94
Diamonds in Russia
DR. VIKTOR K. GARANIN AND DR. GALINA Y. KRIULINA

PAGE 104
Argyle Diamonds
JOHN CHAPMAN

PAGE 110
Colorado Diamonds
DR. TERRY C. WALLACE, JR.

PAGE 114
Laboratory-Grown Diamonds
DR. JAMES E. BUTLER AND DR. BORIS N. FEIGELSON

PAGE 128
Diamonds in the Sky
DR. EMMA BULLOCK

PAGE 132
Diamond Heists
M TYLER FUNK

PAGES 138–152
Literature and Cited Works

Lands Immemorial

by Gloria A. Staebler and Claire Mitchell

Tangled in the narratives of foreign lands and ancient tongues, of oral tales and forgotten cultures, are the strands of humanity's first encounters with diamond. Archeological remains, scant documentation, and the diamonds themselves evidence that our infatuation with diamonds was born more than two millennia ago, in India.

Diamonds (*vajra* in Sanskrit) were a known commodity by 327 BCE when Alexander the Great invaded northern India. At the urging of his troops and lacking the resources to effectively rule, Alexander withdrew, leaving the territory in the hands of his satrapies (governors), who were forced out by Chandragupta Maurya (340–298 BCE) a few years later. Emperor Chandragupta went on to unify and rule the Mauryan Empire, which covered a major portion of present-day India during the fourth century BCE.

In his Sanskrit treatise *Arthaśāstra* ("Rules for Prosperity"), Chandragupta's Minister Kautiliya (ca. 350–283 BCE) discussed, among other things, some of the attributes of *vajra* (Kangle 1972, p. 100) noting, that it is "capable of bearing blows, with symmetrical points, [ability to scratch] a vessel, revolving like a spindle and brilliantly shining, is excellent. That with points lost, without edges and defective on one side, is bad." This short passage reveals not just an ancient familiarity with diamond and its properties but also that ancient gem enthusiasts were not unlike their modern counterparts in preferring complete, lustrous crystals.

In Ancient Rome, Pliny the Elder (23CE–79CE) wrote of *adamas*, which was interpreted by a number of translators and historians to be "diamond." Nineteenth-century mineralogists, Edward S. Dana (1850, p. 2) among them, were skeptical, however. They argued that Pliny referred to a number of minerals with a variety of properties as *adamas*, and there was no known source of diamond in the Ancient Roman Empire.

Anthropologist Berthold Laufer (1915) countered these comments, citing Pliny's initial remarks on the subject, "The most highly valued of human possessions, let alone gemstones, is the 'adamas,' for which long was known only to kings, and to very few of them" (Eichholz 1962, p. 205). Laufer argued that Pliny was familiar with many minerals and would not have presented quartz or even corundum in such superlative terms: "The ancients were not so narrow-minded that almost any stone picked up anywhere in nature could have been regarded as their precious stone foremost in the scale of valuation." And while Laufer admits that Pliny may have used *adamas* to refer to a number of different minerals, Pliny clearly recognized that the variety from India was in a class by itself.

Evidence that diamonds had reached Rome in Pliny's lifetime comes from knowledge of the sea and land diamond trade routes from India during the first to the third century BCE (Lenzen 1970). Also, twentieth-century excavations of a necropolis in the southern outskirts of Rome (Bedini et al. 2012), and of one marble sarcophagus in particular, revealed an octahedral diamond crystal set in a gold ring. The tomb, which dates to the second century CE, belonged to a young woman. Objects found in this grave evidence ties to the Syrian community, which in turn had connections to the Silk Road.

Finally, during excavations at Pompeii, destroyed by the volcanic eruption of Vesuvius in 79 CE (which was the cause of Pliny's death), an Indian ivory figurine has been recovered (Beard 2015). Thus trade routes and specific discoveries offer plausible evidence that commerce, either directly or indirectly, was carried out across the more than 9,700 kilometers (6,000 miles) that separate Rome and Golconda (present-day Hyderabad) in India.

As the printed word became more prevalent so too did musings celebrating diamond's origins and physical properties. In his encyclopedic *Brahat Samhita*, sixth century CE author Varāhamihira made reference to some eight historic diamond occurrences, noting that "diamonds got from the banks of the Venā river are of the purest kind" (Bhat 1987, p 738). *Venā* may refer to the present-day Waingaṅgā River, a tributary of the Godavari River, an historic alluvial diamond source. Varāhamihira later wrote (p. 740), "A diamond is said to be beneficial to the owner, if it cannot be cut by any other substance, is light, cleaves through water like a ray of light, is glossy and similar in luster to lightning, fire or the rain-bow."

Other writers echoed Varāhamihira's list of diamond occurrences, and geographer Carl Ritter (1836) framed those ancient sources in modern terms. He ultimately identified five diamond-producing regions on the eastern part of the Deccan Plateau in southern India. All of India's historic diamond sources were alluvial, and fittingly the mine groups defined by Ritter are associated with river systems. And archeologists have found evidence of old diggings in all five regions. The best known of these, the Golconda mines, worked the gravels concentrated by the Penner, Krishna, and Godavari rivers. Many of India's legendary stones are thought to have come from the Golconda group, which includes the famous **Kollur Mine**. Though found far south of the trading and administrative center of Golconda, diamonds from this group are misleadingly said to have come from "Golconda."

Zahiruddin Muhammad Bābur's (1483–1530) sixteenth century autobiographical *Bāburnama* ("Letters of Bābur") has succeeded in both illuminating and confounding India's diamond legacy with its mention of a remarkable stone, the history of which dates to before the rise of Emperor Bābur and the birth of the Mogul Empire. According to Bābur (Beveridge 1912), the great jewel was part of an offering that Rajah

Above: The fortified Indian port city of Goa in 1509. Courtesy of the Hebrew University of Jerusalem & The Jewish National & University Library.

Right: The 55.23-carat *Sancy* diamond was found in 16th century India. It belonged to Nicolas Harlay de Sancy, Superintendent of Finance for King Henry IV. It changed hands and was ultimately presented to French King Louis XIV in 1661. The diamond is unique in that it was cut with back-to-back tables and has no pavilion. It was placed at the top of Louis XV's coronation crown (pictured on page 132) and is among the French Crown Jewels. Photo © Musée du Louvre.

Below: Gold and diamond ring discovered at the 2nd century Vallerano site, outside of Rome is believed to belong to a woman with connections to Syria and indicates that Ancient Rome had at least limited access to diamonds from India. Maria Letizia photo.

Bikermājīt's family made to Bābur's son Humāyūn after the family was captured in Agra during the 1526 Battle at Panipat, which signaled Bābur's rise to power.

The history of Bābur's diamond both before and after it was given to Humāyūn is speculative. The mines certainly produced numerous significant stones through the centuries, but there is no way to determine which specific modern gems, if any, are the subjects of historical mentions. The fact that the Bābur's diamond warranted a digression from the narrative on his victory at Panipat, however, is a clear indication that it must have been extraordinary.

The era of European colonization and mercantilism brought global change. In 1498 a direct sea route between India and the Portuguese capital Lisbon was established, and Portugal gained control of the European distribution of Indian diamonds, dominating the trade for some 200 years. Lisbon emerged as a major diamond trading, cutting, and polishing center. In April 1500, Portuguese fleets also began arriving in Brazil to lay claim to its bounty, which for two centuries was a bonanza of brazilwood (source of red dye) and sugar.

Early in the sixteenth century, Portuguese travelers Domingo Paes and Fernão Nunes (Sewell et al. 1900) each visited southern India (the *Vijayanagara Empire* in those days) and bore witness to the mining of diamonds as well as the wealth of the Hindu kings. Their accounts, confirmed by many who followed, indicated that diamonds and other gems were mined on a royalty basis with a tax imposed, and all stones weighing more than 10 carats were sent to the kings for their personal use. Given the descriptions of lavish noble treasuries, the mines did well for their masters.

The Governor and Company of Merchants of London trading into the East Indies — the East India Company — was established in 1600 to gain British trading ties to the Mogul Empire. That company sent merchants including William Methwold, Nathaniel Cholmley, and Streynsham Master. Opportunities for adventure and riches brought India travelers from other European countries as well. Flemish gem trader Jaques de Coutre and his brother Joseph, French gemologist Jean-Baptiste Tavernier (1605–1689), and French physician François Bernier also spent considerable time in India in the seventeenth century, and all of these men provided invaluable insight into the heyday of India's diamond trade and culture.

Tavernier is probably the best known of these adventurers. From 1636 to 1662, he made six voyages to India, and buying gems was among his primary purposes. He visited many of the mines and in 1676 published a compilation of his experiences

Hope's Journey

by Dr. Jeff W. Harris

The 45.52-carat *Hope Diamond*. India. Smithsonian Institution collection, Photo by Robert Weldon © GIA.

The story of the *Hope Diamond*, one of the most famous jewels in the world, dates to seventeenth century French traveler, Jean Baptiste Tavernier. This engraver's son and jeweler first traveled to India in 1631. He returned five times to the country, buying diamonds from the Mogul Emperors and keeping detailed notes and sketches of the best of the diamonds, jewels, and other marvels he encountered.

The rudely cut *Tavernier Blue* was included in a large parcel of diamonds that King Louis XIV acquired from Tavernier shortly after he returned to France from his final trip to India in 1668. Tavernier had recorded the stone's weight as "112$\frac{3}{16}$ carats," but as it is uncertain whether this weight was in French or Florentine carats, it is not known whether the gem weighed 115.3 or 110.5 metric carats (respectively). In either case, the diamond was recut in 1673 and its weight reduced to 69.03 carats.

The newly cut stone was referred to as the *Blue Diamond of the Crown* or sometimes the *French Blue*. It became part of the French Crown Jewels of France, and in 1749, Louis XV had the stone reset in a *Golden Fleece* — a symbol of authority and kingship. Upsetting the regal apple cart, the decade-long French Revolution resulted in the ousting of the monarchy and the installation, on July 9, 1789, of the National Constituent Assembly, which ordered an inventory of the Crown Jewels and had them moved to the not-too-secure *Garde Meuble* ("Treasury Museum"). And on the night of September 16, 1792, virtually the whole of the Crown Jewels were stolen. While many of the diamonds in the collection were subsequently recovered, but the French Blue was not among them.

The gem resurfaced in London in 1812, when lapidary John Françillon described and sketched a large dark blue diamond he had recently seen. This stone was similarly described and drawn by Mawe (1813), who noted that it weighed 44 carats. Ten years later, in the second edition of his book, Mawe suggested that the stone belonged to diamond merchant Daniel Eliason. Though it is not known exactly when banker Henry Phillip Hope purchased the stone, it was included in a posthumous 1839 inventory of his jewels in which the *Hope Diamond* was described as being "44.5 cts, deep sapphire blue, brilliantly cut and of the highest purity."

Hope's nephew Henry Thomas Hope purchased the gem from his uncle's estate and it remained in the Hope family until 1884 when Henry's wife Anne Adele died. She bequeathed a *life interest* (not to be sold without court permission) in her estate to her proliferate younger grandson, the eventual 8th Duke of Newcastle, issue of 6th Duke and Mrs. Hope's only daughter. The 8th Duke was bankrupt by 1896, and in 1899 he unsuccessfully petitioned the Court of Chancery to sell the family jewels.

A 1901 petition was granted, however, and the Hope was sold to Adolf Weil of Hatton Garden, London. The diamond changed hands a number of times over the next several years before winding up with the Sultan of Turkey, whose estate put it up for auction in Paris in June 1909. Mr. Rosenau, a French dealer, bought the Hope and sold it a year later to Cartier.

Evalyn Walsh McLean purchased the gem in its Cartier setting in 1911. The Hope Diamond necklace was the heiress's trademark for the rest of her life. Harry Winston purchased Mrs. McLean's collection from her estate in 1949, and in 1958, he presented the Hope to the Smithsonian Institution where it resides today.

This special diamond was removed from its setting in 1974 and found to weigh 45.52 and not 44.5 carats. Then in 2007, the National Museum of Natural History in Paris came across a lead cast of the original Blue Diamond of the Crown. Three-dimensional imaging of the cast and Hope put to rest any question as to whether it had been derived from the French Blue. The 45.52-carat Hope Diamond was cut from the Blue Diamond of the Crown, and remarkably without cleaving the original gem.

Note: *Our "journey" was compiled principally from the book by Balfour (1987) with additions from Farges et al., (2009) and Sucher (2009).*

in a sort of merchant's guide; an English translation was published in 1678. Tavernier's writings have been translated, parsed, and studied as an uncommon source of information on seventeenth century Turkey, Iran (Persia), and India. His work contains impressions of many of the things he encountered during his more than two decades as a trader.

Two plates depict notable diamonds, among them the legendary *Great Mogul*, which on his final journey to India, Tavernier had occasion to examine. At the invitation of Emperor Aurangzeb, Tavernier stayed for two months in Delhi and spent considerable time at the palace assessing the extensive gem collection of Shah Jahān, Aurangzeb's father and predecessor, who lived in the Red Fort, under house arrest.

Uncut, Tavernier's Great Mogul is said to have weighed 793 "carats," but to the emperor's displeasure, in grinding away the flaws, Venetian cutter Hortensio Borgio brought the weight down to 279 9/16 carats (it is unclear whether Tavernier was using French or Florentine carats; thus the exact weight is unknown). Tavernier handled and sketched the cut stone, writing that the diamond had been found in the **Kollur Mine** and was presented to Shah Jahān by Mir Jumla II, Golconda's brazenly corrupt Prime Minister and later an important figure in the Imperial Court. Inconsistencies in Tavernier's account are however enough to cast doubt on the stone's provenance and give credence to those who believe that this clearly remarkable stone was in fact Bābur's diamond (see above).

As neither of these diamonds in their original form have surfaced in modern times, theories as to their fates abound. The Bārbur diamond appears to be lost to history; the Great Mogul is thought to have been plundered along with the immense Mogul treasury in 1739, when Persian Nadir Shah sacked Delhi. Some think that at that point, the stone was named the *Koh-i-nûr*, again recut and is today part of the British Crown Jewels. Others consider that Tavernier's drawing of the Great Mogul bears a resemblance to the famous *Orlov* diamond (pictured on page 94), which is part of the Kremlin Diamond Fund. Still others believe that the Great Mogul, like many of the gems enriching the famous Peacock Throne, which Nadir Shah is known to have looted, were reworked into obscurity and sold.

Tavernier also sketched a 112 3/16-carat diamond, which he described in his caption as "cleane of a faire violet." He sold this remarkable stone along with 14 other large Indian diamonds in 1668 to King Louis XIV of France; yet the only reference to it in his book are three drawings. Such scant details about the acquisition of the *Tavernier Blue*, (certainly among the most remarkable of Tavernier's purchases), raises questions as to the circumstances under which the author came to possess it. As all diamonds larger than 10 carats were the property of the Sultanate of Golconda, Tavernier may have been sold the stone illegally, perhaps by Mir Jumla, the aforementioned corrupt Prime Minister. The *Tavernier* or *French Blue* is the stone from which the 45.52-carat *Hope* diamond was cut (see sidebar, facing page), and Tavernier's sparse drawings and descriptions were key to unravelling the history of the Hope.

On the heels of the publication of Tavernier's celebrated work and prior to its release in English, Henry Howard, Earl Marshal of England (1677), published an account, thought to have been written by British merchant Nathaniel Cholmley, who had worked in Golconda for years. The report begins with

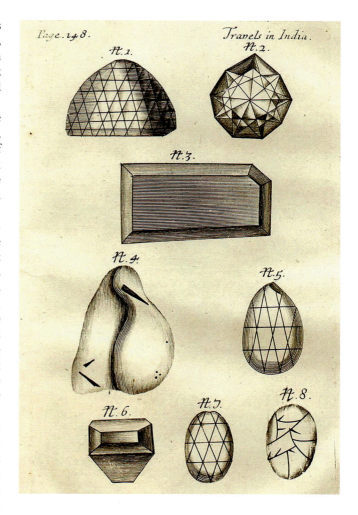

Above: Page 248 from the English-language version of Jean-Baptiste Tavernier's epic *Travels in India*. The top three stones are N. 1, the *Great Mogul*; N. 2 the *Florentine*; N. 3 *Great Table*.

Below: This 5-carat, 1-cm wide diamond is from Dawei, Myanmar (southern Burma). The Island of Pegu in present-day Myanmar was the only known source, outside of India, of diamonds in the ancient world.
Jon and Max Sigerman collection, Robert Weldon photo.

an overview of the world's seventeenth century diamond deposits: "The parts of the World known to contain Diamonds, are the Island of Borneo, and the Continent of India extra and intra Gangem [Indian territories east (extra) and west of (intra) the Ganges]." He goes on to say that deposits were reported on the Island of Pegu, (part of modern day Myanmar), but that the King had opted not to exploit (and therefore not to defend) them. So up to the early eighteenth century India was the source of most of the world's diamonds, but by then traders were beginning to realize that India's seemingly unending supply of diamonds was drying up.

On the other side of the globe, rumors of diamonds in Brazil had been circulating since at least 1587 (Albuquerque 1989), but it was not until the early 1700s that they coincidentally were brought to the attention of Lisbon. The luster and shape of the diamonds are said to have caught the eyes of Brazilian gold miners, who recognized them only as curiosities and would pick them up to use as game pieces (Joaquim Felício dos Santos' memoirs, as cited in Cornejo & Bartorelli 2009). Whether or not the Portuguese colonists knew what those novelties were and had been shipping diamonds to Lisbon via India to avoid the notice of the Crown is not known.

What is known is that in 1730, King Dom Joao V received colonist Bernardo da Fonseca Lobo, who bestowed upon His Majesty a bag of diamonds he had found in the Corrego Mountains of Brazil (Cornejo & Bartorelli 2009). That first formal find was celebrated and spurred bands of Portuguese fortune-hunters to the New World. As noted by Cornejo & Bartorelli (2009, p.180), "In 1732, the discovery of virgin 'potholes' and the reprocessing of gold mining waste-rock yielded more than three hundred thousand carats of diamonds, a surplus supply that made the price plummet".

John Mawe (1816) described his visits to the diamond deposit of Brazil's *Distrito Diamonaion* ("Diamond District"). Mawe had been given unprecedented (for a foreigner) access to the mines and provided a lucid account of, among other things, the workings at Mandanga, situated on a curve in the river Jigitonhonha, near Cerro do Frio in Minas Gerais.

The river, Mawe explained, was diverted into a canal to enable access to the diamondiferous alluvium, which was not uncommonly buried under various sterile sediments, sometimes more than one meter deep. African slaves worked the deposits, laboriously digging and hauling the overlying sand and gravel out of the riverbed until they reached the *cascalhão*, the diamond-bearing gravel.

The gravel was washed manually. Overseers looked on as slaves raked and washed the gravels. The slaves rotated positions to prevent them from accumulating diamonds in their troughs, and theft was punished. But the slaves also had incentive to turn in the diamonds they found (Mawe p. 232):

When a negro is so fortunate as to find a diamond of the weight of an octavo (17 ½ carats,) much ceremony takes place; he is crowned with a wreath of flowers and carried in procession to the administrator, who gives him his freedom, by paying his owner for it. He also receives a present of new clothes, and is permitted to work on his own account. When a stone of eight or ten carats is found, the negro receives two new shirts, a complete new suit, with a hat and handsome knife. For smaller stones of trivial amount proportionate premiums are given.

A female slave named Rosa found the 261.38-carat diamond in 1853 in Minas Gerais. Having handed the diamond over to her master, Casimiro de Tal, Rosa was granted her freedom with a pension for life. Unfortunately, de Tal was unaware of the diamond's true value and sold it for just £3,000.

Right: A Mogul, silk necklace containing five flat-cut diamonds, ranging from 16 to 28 carats; the largest diamond is 2.43 cm wide. The gems were cut in the 17th century and very few diamonds worked during this period exist intact. The 18th century, fluted Colombian emerald drops were added later. Photo courtesy of Bonhams.

Facing page, left: "View of Negros washing for Diamonds at Mandango on the River Jigitonhonha in Cerro do Frio Brazil," an etching by T. Webster that was based on a sketch by John Mawe.

Facing page, right: Maharani Sita Devi of Baroda (India) dressed for her husband's 40th birthday celebration. The necklace she is wearing includes the 128.48-carat *Star of the South* and the 78.5-carat, pear-shaped, *English Dresden* diamonds, both were recovered in the mid-1800s from the Bagagem mines, Minas Gerais, Brazil. Henri Cartier-Bresson photo, 1948.

Its savvier buyer received an advance to secure it of some £30,000. The diamond changed ownership several times, and was eventually cut in Amsterdam by the important firm of Coster, which had previously faceted the famous Koh-i-nûr. It was given the name *Star of the South* by the French owners, and Bagagem, the town in which the diamond was found was renamed *Estrela do Sul*, "Star of the South" in Portuguese.

For a century until Brazil gained independence in 1834, Portugal tried to harvest and control the colony's diamond and metal resources. The Crown claimed as its property all of the diamond- and gold-rich land in Brazil, and families who had been living (and often mining) in those areas were driven off. Thus were born independent *garimpeiros*, who prospected watercourses abandoned by nature and furtively worked the bends and cavities or "potholes", where diamondiferous gravels might have accumulated.

According to Mawe (1816), each month the largest diamonds from the many official mining areas in the district were delivered to the treasury in Rio de Janeiro under military guard. An estimated 20,000 to 25,000 carats of diamonds were shipped to Rio annually (p. 240). The king in Portugal would select the finest diamonds in a parcel and the rest were sold. Thus in time, the Portuguese royal family's collection of diamonds was said to rival that of any other kingdom.

Wallis Cattelle (1911 p. 185) described how the lesser size diamonds were sorted into grades and sold locally,

> "Bons" are crystals of good shape and colour; "fazenda fina" are small tinted but fine; "melee" are imperfect and off color; "vitrie" or "vidrilhos" are very small bright stones of various colors; "fundos" are broken or defective crystals mixed with second quality carbons.

Cattelle also discussed how Brazilian diamonds were shipped to Europe via ports in the Indian state of Goa, where they were mingled with Indian diamonds. Such melding may have been a means of obscuring production and thus avoiding taxes, although Cattelle suggested that markets had the impression that Brazilian diamonds were inferior to those from India. To combat that prejudice, some of the Brazilian production was shipped to Goa and on to Europe, where it was sold as "Indian."

Edwin Streeter (1898), however, had a different take on the practice of admixing (p. 106):

> *The European merchants, who up to that time had obtained their Diamonds from India, were frightened lest this discovery should cause a fall in the price of gems in their possession. They consequently spread the report that the Brazilian Diamonds were only the refuse of the Indian stones, forwarded to Goa and then to Brazil ... The Portuguese, however, turned the tables, and sent the Brazilian Diamonds to Goa and thence to Bengal, where they were offered for sale as Indian stones, and obtained at Indian prices.*

And diamonds were not the only New World gems passed off as being from Old World mines. Oxygen isotope analyses (Giuliani et al. 2000) have shown that high-quality emerald cut in India in the eighteenth century originated in mines in Colombia thought to have been discovered in the 1900s, but it turns out the Spaniards had been supplying lapidaries in India with Colombian emerald since the sixteenth century!

The discovery of the diamond fields of South Africa in 1868 revolutionized the global diamond market, and while India and Brazil continue to produce diamonds for the gem, industrial, and occasionally the collector markets, the focus is on the prolific deposits in other countries. Giant, efficient, industrial mine complexes in Australia, Russia, Africa, and Canada have rendered Indian and Brazilian diamond deposits more or less inconsequential. Nevertheless, those kingmaker gravels and the souls who worked them have had a monumental hand in shaping the world, sparking the imagination, and infusing diamond with lasting romance.

Diamond in kimberlite, approximately 5 carats, field of view 2.6 cm wide.
Russia
Bill Larson collection (ex William Pinch), Harold and Erica Van Pelt photo.

Geology of Diamond

by Dr. Bram Janse

Diamond deposits have been outlined and investigated on every continent except Antarctica, and this is only because an international treaty has placed a moratorium on mineral exploration. Diamonds have been mined for centuries from places such as India (beginning circa 800 BCE), Borneo (about 800 CE), Brazil (1720s), Russia (1830s), USA (1840s), and New South Wales, Australia (1850s).

Diamonds from all of these places are found along rivers and creeks, in alluvial placer deposits, or *wet diggings*, as they are called in South Africa. Placer diamonds were often byproducts of gold winning.

The discovery of diamonds in May 1870 in places well away from watercourses gave rise to the term *dry diggings*, which in 1872 were recognized as the surface expression of intrusive chimneys or pipes (Cohen 1872). Emil Cohen was the first person to recognize this, but as he published his comments in German, E. J. Dunn (1873) who published in English, usually gets the credit for this insight as well as for coining the term *pipes*. Carvill Lewis, Professor of Mineralogy at the Philadelphia Institute of Natural Sciences, was first to use the term *kimberlite*, which he mentioned in 1887 during a lecture to the British Association for the Advancement of Science in Manchester. He used the term in print the following year (Lewis 1888).

In contrast to the placer deposits from which diamonds are recovered by washing and sieving wet sands and gravels, dry diggings tend to contain much higher concentrations of diamonds, which are recovered by sieving dry sand and loam (Janse 1995). That historic first dry diggings discovery, made on the De Beer brothers' farm in South Africa, forever changed the diamond industry.

Diamond deposits are today categorized as: primary (kimberlites and lamproites) or secondary (alluvial and marine). The primary designation, however, can be misleading as diamonds do not form *in* kimberlites or lamproites, the primary *host* rocks for diamonds. The *source* rocks for diamonds are deep-seated ultrabasic rocks including peridotites and eclogites that are found in the lithospheric (rigid) part of the Earth's upper mantle.

FORMATION AND EMPLACEMENT

Experiments synthesizing diamond and associated species such as olivine, garnet, and clino- and ortho-pyroxene have shown that these minerals crystallize at pressures of 40 to 50 kilobars or 4 to 5 gigapascals and temperatures of 900 to 1200 degrees Celsius — conditions similar to those that occur in the Earth's upper mantle, at depths of 120 to 150 kilometers (Shirey & Shigley 2013).

Once formed, diamonds and other minerals are transported to the surface by fluid systems generated from within or below the diamond formation zone. The magma must ascend rapidly and cooling must be quick otherwise the diamonds convert to graphite, or when oxygen is present, form carbon dioxide (CO_2). Deep-seated fluid systems are rich in magnesium; thus the transporting medium is an ultrabasic fluid composed of solids and molten rock (magma) that is propelled to the surface by high pressure gas through self-propagating cracks and fissures.

For the cracks to propagate, the surrounding rocks in the diamond formation zone must be rigid. In certain areas, the crust–upper mantle boundary — the lithospheric-asthenospheric boundary (LAB) — dips into the mantle to form a trough or keel, the geothermal gradient of which is cooler or lower than that of the surrounding asthenospheric upper mantle. These cool geotherms are found under old, stable parts of the Earth's crust known as *cratons*, particularly beneath the oldest parts of the cratons — the Archean nuclei or *Archons* (Janse & Sheahan 1995).

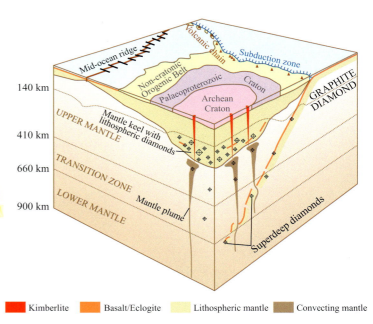

This block diagram depicts the basic relationship between a continental craton, its lithospheric mantle keel (the thick portion of the lithospheric mantle under the craton), and diamond stability regions in the keel and the convecting mantle. Under the right conditions of low oxidation, diamonds can form in the convecting mantle, the subducting slab, and the mantle keel.

William W. Besse graphic, after Stachel et al. (2005), Tappert and Tappert (2011), and Shirey et al. (2013).

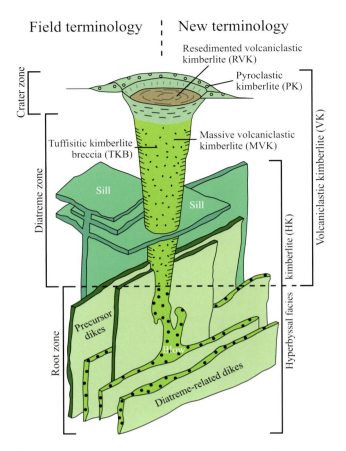

A perspective diagram of a kimberlite pipe with the surrounding country rock removed shows dikes and sills related to different levels of intrusion of kimberlitic magma and kimberlite types. Shown here is the terminology used by field geologists to understand what part of the kimberlite is exposed at the surface or sampled in drill core. Diamonds can potentially be distributed through all the types of kimberlite shown. William W. Besse graphic, after Kjarsgaard (2007).

Near the surface, fluidized systems commonly encounter water-saturated rocks, and the resulting mixture of steam and inherent gases causes an explosion that creates a funnel- or bowl-shaped crater. Gas and steam are vented off, and the sudden release of pressure reduces the temperature of the mixture, which consolidates into a kimberlite or lamproite — a mixed, hybrid rock composed of breccias, tuffs, and unevenly grained rocks (resembling porphyrites) — that plugs up the chimney. Confirming the rapid ascent and cooling model, kimberlites show little or no thermal affects at their contacts with surrounding rocks — in contrast to many other intrusive rocks, kimberlites do not "eat" their way to the surface.

The open crater fills with water, tuffs, epiclastics, soil, debris, and country rock fragments. Thus the rocks and minerals contained in a kimberlite pipe may include many fragments of upper mantle derived ultrabasic rocks ("mantle xenoliths" or "mantle nodules") including peridotites such as garnet-harzburgite (olivine, pyrope, and orthopyroxene), garnet-lherzolite (olivine, pyrope, and clinopyroxene), and eclogites (almandine and clinopyroxene). In addition the pipe may contain accidental, deep-seated, crustal fragments of basement rocks including granite-gneiss, migmatite, schist, as well as regional country rocks, which predate the age of intrusion and were brought up from below. Adding to the mix, surrounding country rocks, which postdate the age of intrusion but are often eroded and no longer present in the surrounding area, may have fallen in from above and sunk into the volatile-rich mixture. As a rule, the deeper their origin, the more rounded the fragments in a kimberlite pipe are; a fragment's shape thus provides a clue as to it source, which can be helpful when reading a kimberlite pipe.

Kimberlite pipes are vertically zoned as follows: crater zone (top), diatreme zone (middle), and root zone (deepest). In the shape of a funnel or shallow bowl, the crater zone can be hundreds of meters deep. These craters are typically filled with sediments of mixed volcanic and sedimentary origin that derived from both the extruded kimberlite and the surrounding country rock. The diatreme zone is the actual pipe or chimney. It is filled with kimberlite tuffs and breccias, which grade to less brecciated, more fine-grained, massive rock with depth. In the lowermost root zone, the kimberlite's chimney-like shape transitions into one or more fissures that are filled with massive, fine-grained rock.

Petrographers have recently changed the simple structural division of crater, diatreme, and root zones and now recognize volcaniclastic and hypabyssal kimberlite rocks instead (see diagram on the left). Volcaniclastic kimberlite (VK), which occurs in the crater and is layered as a result of successive pulses, may be resedimented due to slumping. Resedimented volcaniclastic kimberlite (RVK) becomes more massive with depth graduating to non-layered, massive volcaniclastic kimberlite (MVK), which is often referred to as *tuffisitic kimberlite breccia* (TKB). This is the general kimberlite breccia present in many specimen collections. Hypabyssal kimberlite (HK) is a dense *aphanitic* (evenly fine-grained, non-breccia) rock occurring in the root zone. However, in many pipes the VK and HK facies overlap in the depth profile; that is, some parts of the pipe are filled with VK and other parts with HK at the same depth level in the pipe. For a detailed discussion on this not-yet-resolved matter, see Kjarsgaard (2007a, 2007b).

The degree of erosion in the general countryside can expose these rocks at different levels in the vertical zoning pattern. Because crater sediments are easily eroded, with the exception of the very young (1.7 my) Igwisi Hills volcano in Tanzania, no distinct crater has ever been found with its upper portion and surrounding ring wall or tuff ring of ejecta intact. Barry Hawthorne (1975), citing personal communication with Egbert Gerryts, mentioned that the Kasama pipe in Mali has a tuff ring, but because the age of intrusion of the Mali pipes is considered to be Early Proterozoic or at least Early Cretaceous (Chirico, Barthélémi & Koné 2010) the preservation of a tuff ring is unlikely.

PRIMARY HOST ROCKS

Until the 1980s it was believed that kimberlites were the exclusive host rocks of diamond. However, economic concentrations of diamonds have since been found in lamproites, which resemble kimberlites but have a distinct mineralogy and chemistry (Jaques et al. 1986). Primary diamond host rocks are categorized as kimberlites, orangeites, and lamproites. Diamonds also are found in lamprophyres (e.g., Wawa, Ontario, Wilson 2006); in meteorites and cosmic dust, where they are of pre-solar origin (Clayton & Nittler 2004); and as micro- and nano-diamonds in orogenic zones (see Dating

Diamonds on page 19), but these occurrences are minor and are considered curiosities. Small to micro (less than 0.5 millimeters in largest dimension) diamonds also occur in carbonaceous rocks impacted by meteorites (e.g., Popigai, Sakha (Yakutia) Republic, Russia); and in metamorphic rocks that were subjected to ultrahigh pressures by deep burial (e.g., Kokchetav, Kazakhstan; DeCorte et al. 2000). These two last mentioned occurrences contain huge quantities of diamonds — up to billions of carats — but being tiny and brittle, they are not of economic interest.

Kimberlite, *sensu stricto* (i.e., without the usual included fragments of deep-seated rocks, basement gneiss, and regional country rock), is a volatile-rich, potassic, ultrabasic, igneous rock. It has an inequigranular texture resulting from the presence of large crystals (*macrocrysts*), which are quite visible to the naked eye. These macrocrysts consist of minerals including olivine, phlogopite, pyrope, chromium-rich diopside, enstatite, ilmenite, and chromite, which are derived from the disintegration of deep seated mantle rocks such as peridotite and eclogite. Such crystals constitute the *kimberlite indicator minerals* which can be recovered from the *regolith* (surface outcrop atop a pipe or dike) or from an alluvial stream sample. The presence of any or all of these indicators in a concentrate of *heavy* (or dense) minerals mean that a kimberlite (or orangeite or lamproite) is near or upstream.

The macrocrysts (phenocrysts and xenocrysts) are contained in a fine-grained matrix, or *groundmass*. The groundmass of kimberlite is essentially composed of olivine that has more or less altered to serpentine, with lesser amounts of phlogopite, calcite, and monticellite, and accessory minerals such as apatite, ilmenite, perovskite, and chromite. Kimberlite was at one time characterized as "basaltic" kimberlite, which was a misnomer as kimberlite does not contain plagioclase, an essential component of basalt. In South Africa, these typical kimberlites are categorized as Group I Kimberlites, but in many other countries they are referred to simply as *kimberlites*.

Orangeite, previously categorized as micaceous kimberlite and named after the type locality in the Orange Free State, South Africa, is sometimes referred to as *Group II Kimberlite*, while many diamond geologists, particularly those outside of South Africa, consider these rocks a South African variety of lamproite. Orangeites contain less olivine and more phlogopite, calcite, and serpentine than do Group I Kimberlites. But unlike their Group I counterparts, orangeites contain neither ilmenite nor monticellite. They do, however, contain deep-seated peridotite and eclogite fragments. Their heavy mineral concentrates contain all of the usual indicator minerals including a wider variety of garnet and clino- and ortho-pyroxenes. (Mitchel 1995).

Hypabyssal facies kimberlite from the east side of the Udachnaya Pipe (Mirninsky District, Sakha (Yakutia) Republic, Russia) as seen under the petrographic microscope in crossed polars, showing xenoliths and olivine macrocrysts. Field of view is 7 mm wide. Alessandro Da Mommio specimen and photo.

Essential Mineral Components of Kimberlites and Related Rocks

Primary Host Rock	Primary Minerals	Groundmass Minerals	Xenocryst Minerals	Examples
Kimberlite (Group I)	Olivine, +/- Phlogopite	Serpentine, Calcite, Monticellite, Perovskite, Apatite	Pyrope, Cr-Diopside, Enstatite, Ilmenite, Chromite, Diamond	Kimberley (Big Hole), South Africa Cullinan, South Africa Mir-Udachnaya-Jubilee, Russian Federation Ekati-Diavik, Canada
Orangeite (Group II)	Phlogopite, Olivine	Serpentine, Calcite, Diopside, Perovskite + REE Apatite + F + REE K-Ba-titanates Zr-silicates, Barite No Monticellite	Pyrope, Cr-Diopside, Enstatite, Diamond, No Ilmenite, No Chromite	Finsch, South Africa Voorspoed, South Africa
Lamproite	+/- Olivine, Leucite, Diopside, +/- Sanidine, Richterite	Leucite, Diopside, Priderite, Jeppeite, Wadeite, Apatite	+/- Garnet, +/- Cr-Diopside, Chromite, Diamond, No Ilmenite	Argyle Mine, Western Australia Crater of Diamonds, Arkansas, USA
Lamprophyre	+/- Olivine, Amphiboles, Pyroxenes, Micas	Melilite, Calcite, Serpentine, Amphiboles, Pyroxenes, Biotite, Sericite	same as kimberlites or lamproites, +/- amphiboles, +/- pyroxenes, +/- biotite, Ti-garnet, +/-diamond	Aillikite dikes, West Greenland Alnoite dikes, Alno, Sweden Dikes at Wawa, Canada

Lamproites range from non-diamondiferous leucite- to diamondiferous olivine-lamproite. Lamproites in general contain less olivine than do kimberlites but more phlogopite and diopside. Many also contain leucite, amphibole, and sanidine, but it is olivine-rich lamproite (olivine-lamproite) that has the potential to contain economic quantities of diamond. Lamproites also contain fluorapatite and many rare potassium- and barium-rich titanates, the most characteristic being priderite and wadeite. However, relative to kimberlites or orangeites, lamproites generally contain fewer or even no macrocrysts and therefore their heavy mineral concentrates can be poor in indicator minerals, the grain sizes of which are generally smaller (0.3 to 0.5 millimeters) than those in kimberlites (0.5 to 2 millimeters). The only mineral in lamproites indicative of diamond is chromite.

Lamprophyres are ultrapotassic, igneous rocks, which in general are not breccias or tuffs. They commonly contain large crystals of pyroxenes, amphiboles, and mica. Their groundmass is dark and contains melilite, dark colored garnets (melanite, schorlomite), mica, and perovskite. Ultramafic, olivine-rich, alkaline lamprophyres may contain small amounts of diamond, as for instance, in West Greenland (Larsen & Rex 1992, Steenfelt et al. 2009) and near **Wawa**, Ontario (Wilson 2006).

For a general overview and specific details on the petrologies and mineralogies of these rocks, see Mitchell (1988, 1995) and Mitchell and Bergman (1991).

DISTRIBUTION AND PROSPECTING

Dikes, which are defined by the rocks that they contain, usually occur in vertical or near vertical swarms and can be tens of kilometers in length, but are usually less than one meter and often only tens of centimeters wide; thus kimberlite dikes (*kimberlite fissures* in South Africa) are in many places uneconomical to mine as too much sterile wall rock has to be moved before the kimberlite can be extracted.

Pipes, on the other hand, range in size from 1 to 50 hectares but can flare out into craters as large as 150 hectares. Pipes and dikes often occur in the same general area, although dikes tend to contain fewer fragments of country rock and other debris that may be present in pipes. Dikes are usually older than pipes, but younger dikes within pipes and younger radial dikes also occur around pipes. When the pressure of the magma is insufficient to break through to the surface, the magma moves sideways intruding as *sills* along sediment boundaries.

Kimberlites occur in clusters, and although no standard terminology has been adopted, *provinces* generally cover hundreds of square kilometers while *fields* tend to span smaller areas, generally some tens of square kilometers. Pipes and dikes are often found in crude concentric zones in which the largest and richest pipes are at the center of a field and the incidence of dikes increases toward the periphery (Garanin et al. 1993). On a larger scale, zonal distribution is seen in districts or provinces with true kimberlite pipes containing diamonds and abundant dark red to purplish-red pyrope occurring in the center; whereas the incidence of barren lamprophyric dikes (no diamonds, little to no garnet) increases toward the periphery of the province or district.

Clifford (1966) recognized that in Africa diamondiferous kimberlites are restricted to the older cratons while non-diamondiferous kimberlites tend to occur in younger cratonic belts surrounding the older cratons, which are welded together into large tectonic blocks distinct from the younger orogenic belts that make up the African continent.

In most geological dictionaries, *cratons* are defined as parts of the continental crust that have been stable for a long time, generally for about 1.6 billion years. Later tectonic forces or thermal events have not affected them; they are thus neither folded nor deformed, although they may have cracked, suffered

Right: The Pikoo Project logged plenty of core samples while evaluating the PK150 kimberlite, in east-central Saskatchewan, Canada. The drill cores are stored on site in the core shack where kimberlite samples are prepared for shipment to an Ontario lab for testing.
Nick Thomas/North Arrow Minerals, Inc., photo.
Facing page: Abhishek Pandey stands for scale beside a kimberlite dike in Beitbridge, Zimbabwe. Josh Ryan photo, July 2013.

faulting, or tilted slightly. In some cases, such as in Canada, cratons are uplifted and now exposed as shields formed by basement granite-gneiss and migmatites which include long narrow greenstone belts, made up of schists, metavolcanics and quartzites. Alternatively, cratons such as those in South Africa or Botswana may have been partly or entirely down-warped and covered by younger Paleozoic to Tertiary sediments.

Most cratons contain a nucleus of Archean rocks, which are more than 2.5 billion years old and are made up of granite-greenstone terranes. These old nuclei are surrounded by Early Proterozoic rocks, which are more than 1.6 billion years old and consist of belts of high-grade poly-metamorphic gneisses. Many of these belts contain highly contorted layers of banded gneiss and are thus referred to as *mobile belts* which is a misnomer as these belts have been cratonized, having become rigid at least 1.6 billion years ago. The only truly mobile belts are the much younger (late Precambrian and Paleozoic) orogenic belts that uphold present day mountain ranges.

In South Africa all of the diamondiferous kimberlites occur within the Kaapvaal Archean nucleus, which is referred to as the *craton*. In contrast, the non-diamondiferous kimberlites occur in the surrounding Proterozoic Namaqua-Natal mobile belt. Thus was created *Clifford's Rule*, which has guided diamond prospectors around the world and which states that one must be *on craton* to find a diamond mine.

This rule still stands, there are no exceptions: all *kimberlite-hosted* diamond mines occur on an Archean craton (Janse 1994). To find a diamondiferous kimberlite by field methods, one must first outline an Archean craton, collecting heavy mineral stream and loam samples, searching for kimberlite indicator minerals in the 0.5- to 2-millimeter range (often including those in the 2- to 4-millimeter range), and by using airborne magnetic surveys usually followed by ground-based geophysical surveys to search for distinct anomalies or kimberlite signatures. After locating a kimberlite, it must be outlined by trenching and drilling and then evaluated by further drilling, geochemical analysis of drill cores, and counting the number and size of diamonds recovered.

In 1979 Clifford's Rule appeared to have been broken when diamonds were found in the non-kimberlitic rock in non-Archaean rocks that surrounds the Archean Kimberley Craton in northern Western Australia. This diamondiferous non-kimberlite is an olivine lamproite located in the Halls Creek mobile belt. The occurrence was ultimately exploited as the open pit of the **Argyle Mine** and since 2013 as an underground mine (see page 104–109). Clifford's Rule, however, applies only to kimberlite-hosted diamond deposits.

Olivine lamproite-hosted diamond deposits can occur in Early Proterozoic belts surrounding Archaean cores of cratons. The Mesoproterozoic (1185-million-year-old) diamondiferous Argyle olivine lamproite, for example, occurs in the Early Proterozoic (1800-million-year-old) Halls Creek belt, which is situated along the northeastern margin of the Archaean Kimberley Craton; whereas, the Miocene (20-million-year-old) non-diamondiferous Ellendale leucite-diopside lamproites and the diamondiferous Ellendale olivine lamproites of the same age occur together in the Early Proterozoic King Leopold belt, located along the southwestern margin of this craton. The leucite-diopside lamproites stand out as hills and pinnacles; while the more easily eroded olivine lamproites are similar to kimberlites and form negative or flat landforms.

Field prospecting lamproites is more difficult given that the grain sizes of the indicator minerals are smaller than those found in kimberlites, and indicator minerals are often restricted to chromite and diamond. (Prospectors were tipped off to the existence of the Argyle deposit when they found small diamonds in stream samples). Geophysical signatures of lamproites are often absent or non-distinctive.

Left: Polished peridotite containing pyrope, diopside, olivine, and pyroxene, field of view about 11 cm wide. Kimberley Mine dumps, North Cape Province, South Africa. Bruce Kjarsgaard collection, Tony Peterson photo.

Below: Indicator minerals from a kimberlite sample are sorted to assist with classification and evaluation of the sample. Photo courtesy of Debut Diamonds, Inc.

KIMBERLITE MINERALOGY

In addition to rare diamonds, kimberlites contain many large single crystals, which range in size from 0.5 centimeter to tens of centimeters. As it is often not known if these are *phenocrysts* (crystals that grew in the magma in which they occur) or *xenocrysts* (crystals foreign to the magma), the non-generic terms *macrocrysts* (0.5 to 1 centimeters) and *megacrysts* (1 to 10 centimeters) have been introduced. Such crystals include dark red to purple pyrope; orange to red eclogitic garnet; bright green chromium-rich diopside (chrome-rich clinopyroxene); black, magnesium-rich ilmenite; dark brown chromite; dull green orthopyroxene; rare zircon; and last but not least, diamond.

These minerals constitute the diamond satellite or indicator minerals, which may be found in the kimberlite rocks in the pipe, on the surface outcrop, and in the derived alluvial deposits. Being heavy and resistant to weathering, the crystals may have traveled great distances from their primary occurrences and can become concentrated in fluvial trap sites. In general chromite is most resistant, garnet and ilmenite less, and pyroxene is the least resistant to weathering. Travel distances tend to be longest in cold and dry climates and shortest in hot and wet climates, probably because higher temperatures and the presence of water favor the decomposition of minerals. I have observed that in the dry and cold climate of Siberia garnets travel several hundreds of kilometers downstream; whereas in Brazil, they tend to weather and disappear within ten kilometers.

Some of the minerals present in the rocks in a kimberlite pipe or on surface outcrops may have been derived from the breakup of deep-seated rock fragments or from shallower derived crustal and country rock fragments; thus, concentrates may also contain non-kimberlitic minerals such as pink almandine; red to brownish-red garnet (titanium-bearing and chromium-poor); dull green to dark colored pyroxenes; amphiboles; black (non-magnesian) ilmenite; and hard, sharp-edged octahedral spinel.

Several pulses of deep-seated mixtures may be propelled through the same chimney system, which may thus contain different mineralogies and diamond contents. Thus, the distribution of diamonds in a kimberlite can appear random, but the often intricate geometry of the different phases has the potential to create rich pockets or layers. The combination of different phases and the "nugget effect," the statistical distortion of value per tonne of ore caused by the incidence of a large stone, makes kimberlites very difficult to evaluate by sampling. Each phase has to be outlined in three dimensions, and each has to be drilled and sampled separately in order to accurately assess the overall diamond contents of a pipe.

Left: Diamond-rich alluvial gravels buried beneath several meters of sediments are exposed in a mine in Lunda Norte Province, Angola. Diamonds in this deposit were identified using sonic diamond sampling technology. Eijkelkamp SonicSampDrill photo, Aug 2013.

Below: The diamond specimens that originally appeared on Plate I in Bauer's *Edelsteinkunde* (1896). They are described as (clockwise from the top): Diamond crystal in matrix (Brazil), Diamond (Carbonado), Diamond crystal in matrix (South Africa), Diamond (bort). Carlos Cornejo collection.

SECONDARY DIAMOND DEPOSITS

Crater zone sediments are easily weathered and eroded. And given millions of years, so are the rocks in the diatreme zone. This destruction of the original pipe gives rise to secondary or alluvial accumulations of diamond and other likewise resistant satellite minerals. Secondary deposits often have expansive horizontal geometries, making them difficult to define and control. The two types of secondary deposits are broadly categorized as alluvial and marine.

Alluvial deposits formed as water, wind, or frost action eroded the primary deposit and distributed the resistant minerals in streambeds, river terraces, or riverbanks. Alluvial deposits are commonly overlain by sterile sand and gravel, the diamonds being found in buried meanders or hidden potholes. Alluvial diamonds form large to small economic deposits in many countries, notably South Africa, Namibia, Angola, Democratic Republic of Congo, Central African Republic, Ghana, Sierra Leone, Guinea, India, Brazil, Guyana, Venezuela, and recently Zimbabwe.

Eluvial deposits are those formed on the weathered surface of the outcrop of primary host rocks which remain more or less in place. Those that are *colluvial* moved downslope away from the outcrop. Eluvial and colluvial diamonds of note are found in the Democratic Republic of the Congo in the **Mbuji Mayi** area where the eluvial weathered tops of kimberlite pipes and their colluvial downslope debris was mined (Demaiffe et al. 1991). In desert areas, diamonds may be moved by wind. The most notable of these *aeolian* deposits is in the Namib Desert of Namibia. Finally, diamonds can be moved and deposited by *glacial activity* and deposited in eskers, moraines, and periglacial rivers as happened in the Great Lakes area in Michigan, Wisconsin, and Indiana (Gunn 1968, Vierthaler 1961).

GEOLOGY OF DIAMOND 17

Above: A 4 mm diamond crystal still embedded in a quartz conglomerate was recovered from the alluvial diamond deposits in Sierra Leone, Africa.
Specimen and photo courtesy of Crystal Classics.

Below: DeBeers' *Debmar Atlantic* "vacuums" the floor of the Atlantic Ocean off the coast of Namibia in search of diamonds. Robert Weldon photo, 2003.

Marine sand and gravel deposits formed by the action of ocean currents and waves create *raised* (above present sea level), *tidal* (at present sea level), and *drowned* (below present sea level) diamond-bearing beaches (Corbett 1996). Additionally, diamonds are found on the sea floors adjacent to these deposits. Such occurrences form large economic deposits, as testified by those found along and off the coast of Namibia and Namaqualand (west coast of South Africa). Large-scale earth-moving equipment is required to mine the raised beaches, and small diving and "vacuum cleaner" equipment is used to clean riffles and potholes in the tidal zones. Submarine diamondiferous mud, sand, and gravel deposits further offshore, require highly specialized ships equipped with remotely controlled underwater equipment for diamond recovery.

Most alluvial deposits can be traced to their host kimberlite or lamproite. The main non-marine alluvial recoveries worldwide have come from Tertiary to recent alluvial sand and gravel deposits in the beds, bars, flats, banks, and terraces of modern streams as well as from older cut off meanders, which are often covered by more recent sands. The origin of the diamonds in these deposits can in some cases be traced to host rocks further upstream. Well known examples include the deposits in the **Vaal-Orange** river drainage in South Africa, which have been traced to kimberlites in the Kimberley and Free State areas (De Wit 1999, Helgren 1979, Wilson et al. 2007); the **Lunda-Quango** (Kwango) rivers in Angola have been traced to kimberlites in the Lunda and Lulo areas (Delville 1980, Wilson 1982); the **Sewa River** in Sierra Leone traced to kimberlite pipes and dikes in the Koidu area (Laan 1965, Hall 1970, Greenhalgh 1985); the **Bow River** traced to the Argyle lamproite in Australia (Fazakerly 1990); and the **Vilyuy River** in Siberia traced to kimberlites in the Mirny area (Bardet 1965, Polutof 1965, Benson and Sussex 1990, Strnad 1991).

There are, however, many alluvial deposits for which the diamonds cannot be traced to primary host rock. These include the lower **Krishna River** in India, the alluvial fields in New South Wales and South Australia, and those in eastern, western, and central Borneo. Recent research (Philips et al. 2004, Tappert et al. 2009) suggests that the Australian alluvial diamonds may have been derived from kimberlites in Antarctica and distributed in Permian glacial sediments. No Antarctic kimberlites were known at that time, but kimberlites have recently been found in Antarctica (Yaxley et al. 2013).

The alluvial fields in the western (**Carnot-Berberati**) and eastern (**Mouka Ouadda**) fields of Central African Republic can be traced only to Mesozoic conglomerates and sandstones (Censier 1996), and the sandy alluviums of the **Marange** Field in Zimbabwe can be traced to the Meso-Proterozoic Umkondo conglomerate, but the origin of the diamonds found in these deposits is unknown (Janse 2012, Mugumbate 2012).

Another problematic diamond deposit is located in Ghana, where the erosional detritus of Precambrian greywackes are mined on watersheds and in valleys of the upper **Birim River**. There diamonds occur as small, clear, sharp-edged crystals which suggests short surface transport. Lenses of very altered ultrabasic rocks containing diamonds (Janse, personal observation) occur in several places and Stachel & Harris (1997) ponder whether these may be the original host rocks.

Brazil's main placers are in the north, near where the Brazilian, Venezuelan, and Guyanian borders meet. The

Diamond "macle" twin with pyrope inclusion, field of view 1.2 mm wide. South Africa. John Koivula collection and photo.

diamonds in the rivers **Caroni** (Venezuela), **Mazaruni** (Guyana), and **Rio Branco** (Brazil) can be traced to the 1.7-million-year-old Roraima sandstone formation, which contains beds of conglomerates and which forms a high plateau. The origin of the diamonds is a mystery (Tappert et al. 2006).

The alluvial diamond in the **Jequitinhonha River** in Minas Gerais can be traced to the 1.5-million-year-old quartzites, conglomerates, and dolomites of the Espinhaço Mountains near Diamantina, but there the trail goes cold (Chaves et al. 2001). Also in Minas Gerais, the rivers in the **Coromandel** area contain many incidental and small deposits of alluvial diamonds, and the area is home to hundreds of kimberlites in pipes and dikes, but the diamonds and kimberlites are apparently unrelated. The alluvial diamond deposits in the rivers are slightly older than the age of intrusion of the kimberlites, and while there could be an error in the age determination, all of the kimberlites in the area are barren (Gonzaga et al. 1994). Several diamonds weighing more than 100 carats were found in **Rio Ribeirão Santo Antônio das Minas Vermelhas**, which drains the large Vargem kimberlite, but that kimberlite too is devoid of diamonds.

The origin of the diamonds in the marine deposits on and off the coast of Namibia and Namaqualand cannot be traced directly, but recent research (Philips & Harris 2009) concluded that the most likely source was the Cretaceous Group I and II kimberlites in the interior of the Republic of South Africa.

DATING DIAMONDS

A diamond's age of formation is determined by establishing the age of formation of its *syngenetic* (simultaneously formed) inclusions. Thus the age of formation of a flawless, inclusion-free diamond cannot be measured, but they are assumed to be of similar age to that of inclusions contained in diamonds in the same population. Some peridotitic or "P-Type" diamonds are more than 3 billion years old while more extensive measurements on eclogitic or "E-Type" diamonds show them to range from 3 billion down to 660 million years. Generally, diamonds are much older than their host rocks (see below), although recent analyses indicate that some kimberlites contain more than one population of diamonds and some diamonds date to within a few tens of millions of years of the age of intrusion (Pearson et al. 1998, Burgess et al. 2004).

The early idea that diamonds form in the chimneys in which they occur also had to be given up when Precambrian age diamonds where found in kimberlite pipes that intruded during the much later Cretaceous period. Diamonds are not phenocrysts, crystals grown early in the magma in which they occur, but are true xenocrysts, crystals foreign to the magma, grown somewhere else, that are much older than their kimberlite host rocks.

Most kimberlites are relatively young, having intruded less than 550 million years ago. There are very few economic Precambrian (greater than 550 million years) kimberlites, notable exceptions are the **Cullinan** (**Premier**) kimberlite (South Africa) and the **Argyle** olivine lamproite (Western Australia), both of which are 1.185 billion years old. The majority of kimberlites in South Africa and Botswana date to between 120 and 80 million years ago (Late Cretaceous), although **Jwaneng** in southeastern Botswana is 240 million years old, and **Venetia** in northern Republic of South Africa's Limpopo belt is 520 million years old. Most of the kimberlites in Siberia (Eastern Sakha Republic or Yakutia) are 380 to 325 years old (Middle Devonian). The majority of the kimberlites in western Canada are much younger, 50 to 54 million years

Diamond crystals recovered from the Mirny Mine, Sakha Republic, Russia, in November 2013. Photo courtesy of Alrosa.

old (Paleoeocene), although **Victor** in eastern Canada is 150 million years old. The **Mwadui (Williamson)** kimberlite in Tanzania is also 50 to 54 million years old. The youngest diamondiferous host rocks are the olivine lamproites of **Ellendale** in Western Australia; they date to the Miocene and are 22 to 20 million years old (Gurney et al. 2010).

While the model outlined above for diamond occurrence is widely accepted, it does not explain the source of the carbon atoms required to form diamond. This topic has been studied in detail both through understanding the mineralogy and geochemistry of inclusions in diamonds and by determining the carbon and nitrogen isotopes and nitrogen abundances of the diamonds from which the inclusions were obtained. As a result, and irrespective of the original environment, diamond formation occurs from chemical reactions either involving the reduction of carbon dioxide and carbonates, or the oxidation of methane. For reviews on this specific subject see Stachel and Harris (2008, 2009) and for a more general overview, Shirey and Shigley (2013).

WORLD DIAMOND PRODUCTION

Country	Year of 1st Recorded Diamond Find	Year of 1st Recorded Kimberlite Find	Year 1st Diamond Mine Started	Annual Production 1870-2015				2015 Production		Deposit Type %***
				Millions of Carats	% Global Production	Value in Billion USD	% Global Value	Millions of Carats	Avg price per carat (USD)	
Angola	1912	1952	1916	206	4	29	7	9.02	131	80p/20a
Australia	1851	1972	1981	863	16	15	4	13.57	23	100p
Botswana	1959	1967	1970	738	14	75	19	20.78	144	100p
Brazil	1721	1973	1727	36	0.5	3	<1	<1	46	100a
Canada	1971	1948	1998	175	3	26	7	11.68	144	100p
CAR	1914	not found	1930	24	0.5	4	1	<1	170	100a
China	1870	1965	1955	13	<1	0.3	<1	<1	37	50p/50a
DR Congo*	1903	1910	1913	1143	22	29	7	16.02	8	10p/90a
Ghana	1919	not found	1920	118	2	4	1	<1	44	100a
Guinée	1932	1952	1936	61	1	2	<1	<1	88	100a
Guyana	1887	not found	1890	8	<1	1	<1	<1	161	100a
India	antiquity	1829	antiquity	7	<1	0.4	<1	<1	208	100p
Indonesia	800	not found	800	2	<1	0.1	<1	<1	80**	100a
Ivory Coast	1928	1960	1958	8	<1	1	<1	<1	198	100a
Lesotho	1955	1939	1968	4	<1	3	<1	<1	931	100p
Liberia	1910	1952	1955	22	1	3	<1	<1	459	10p/90a
Namibia	1908	1909	1909	113	2	44	11	2.05	591	10a/90m
Russia	1829	1954	1960	1010	19	67	17	41.91	101	90p/10a
Sierra Leone	1930	1948	1932	61	1	14	3	<1	309	20p/80a
South Africa	1867	1870	1870	610	12	71	23	7.22	193	80p/20a
Swaziland	1973	1975	1984	1	<1	0.1	<1	<1	100	100p
Tanzania	1910	1925	1925	23	0.5	3	<1	<1	270	90p/10a
Venezuela	1883	1982	1913	17	0.5	1	<1	<1	100**	10p/90a
Zimbabwe	1903	1907	1913	53	1	1	<1	3.49	50	10p/90a
Total				5,316	100	397	100	127.4	135	

*DR Congo includes production from Gabon and Congo Republic
**estimates based on previous production   ***Deposit Type a=alluvial, m=marine, p=primary

HISTORICAL PERCENTAGES OF WORLD DIAMOND PRODUCTION

	1869	1889	1909	1929	1949	1969	1989	2009	2015
World Production in Millions of Carats	0.2	2.8	3.6	12.5	13.6	43.0	98.5	124.8	127.4
World Production Percentage by Continent									
Africa	15%	99%	99%	98%	98%	81%	49%	51%	47%
Asia (Russia)	2%	0%	0%	0%	0%	18%	13%	28%	33%
Australia	3%	0%	0%	0%	0%	0%	37%	12%	11%
North America (Canada)	0%	0%	0%	0%	0%	0%	0%	9%	9%
South America (Brazil)	80%	1%	1%	2%	2%	1%	1%	0%	0%
African Production Percentage by Country									
Angola	0%	0%	0%	4%	6%	5%	1%	11%	7%
Botswana	0%	0%	0%	0%	0%	0%	19%	14%	16%
Congo/CAR/Zim	0%	0%	0%	27%	71%	35%	21%	19%	15%
Namibia	0%	0%	10%	8%	2%	5%	1%	1%	2%
South Africa	15%	99%	89%	50%	9%	20%	9%	5%	6%
Tanzania	0%	0%	0%	0%	2%	2%	0%	0%	0%
West Africa	0%	0%	0%	9%	8%	14%	1%	1%	1%
World Production Percentage by Deposit Type									
Primary	0%	98%	88%	30%	9%	35%	77%	74%	80%
Alluvial	100%	2%	2%	62%	89%	60%	22%	25%	18%
Marine	0%	0%	10%	8%	2%	5%	1%	1%	2%

DIAMOND PRODUCTION

There is no official diamond production from the historical alluvial fields in India, nor from Brazil, where diamonds were recovered from the sericite-quartz schists of the Espinhaço Range (Burton 1869, Ball 1929). After the discovery of the primary diamond fields at Kimberley, South Africa, new productive diamond fields began coming on line at a rate of about one every ten years. At the same time production records started to be kept. In the first part of the last century and apart from the primary **Premier** (Cullinan) kimberlite pipe in South Africa, these were mainly alluvial and marine deposits. In the 1910s, the marine deposits on the coast of Namibia were found. In the 1920s, alluvial deposits in Western Africa, Angola, Congo, and the Lichtenburg area in South Africa as well as the marine deposits on the Namaqualand coast of South Africa were all discovered.

In the 1930s, with The Great Depression and the onset of World War II, most kimberlite mines were closed, but alluvial production greatly increased in Angola and the Congo (Janse 1995, 1996). Alluvial deposits can be developed quickly; the period between discovery and production varies from one to two years. Because alluvial deposits are relatively small and notoriously erratic in their diamond distribution, commercial interests prefer to develop large pipe deposits, but these can take up to ten to fifteen years to bring into production. The primary deposits began coming on stream in the 1950s with the development of **Mwadui** (Tanzania), the first large primary diamond mine outside South Africa. This was followed in the 1960s by the **Mir, International**, and **Udachnaya** pipes in the Sakha Republic, Russian Federation. Mining of the **Finsch** pipe in South Africa; and the **Orapa, Letlhakane**, and **Jwaneng** pipes in Botswana began in the 1970s. The **Argyle** pipe in Western Australia went into production in the 1980s and the **Venetia** pipe in South Africa in the 1990s.

The **Ekati, Diavik, Snap Lake**, and **Victor** pipes, all in Canada; the **Voorspoed** pipe in South Africa; the **Letšeng** pipe in Lesotho; and the **Arkhangelskaya** pipe in the new Lomonosov field in northwestern Russia all went into production in the first decade of the twenty-first century (Shigley 2010). That trend has continued in the second decade as Canadian deposits, **Gahcho Kue** in the Northwest Territories and **Renard** in northern Québec, came online, as did the **Grib** and **Karpinskogo** pipes in the Lomonosov field in northwest Russia, **Lace** in South Africa, **Kao** and **Liqhobong** in Lesotho, **Karowe** and **Ghaghoo** in Botswana, and the **Murowa** pipe in Zimbabwe. The large alluvial deposits of **Lulo** in Angola and **Marange** in Zimbabwe also began contributing to world diamond production in the 2010s.

The **Star, Taurus**, and **Orion** deposits in the Fort a la Corne field in Saskatchewan, Canada; the **Camafuca, Camatchia**, and **Luaxe** pipes in Angola; the **Upper Muna** kimberlites in the Siberian Arctic; as well as the **Melville Island** and **Baffin Island** projects in Arctic Canada are all in development and are expected to come online in the coming years.

The proportion of kimberlite (and lamproite) to finds of alluvial and marine deposits has changed dramatically over time. The table above shows, for example, the abrupt shift from the Brazilian alluvial production to that from South African kimberlites from 1869 to 1889; dominance of Congo/Central African Republic/Angola alluvial production from 1929 to 1969; the increasing importance of kimberlite production from Russia beginning in 1969, then from Botswana in 1989; the peak of Australian lamproite production in the 1990s which in 1993 reached up to 40 percent of global production (although

only 11 percent of the value of total global production); and the beginning of Canadian kimberlite production in 1999.

Global annual diamond production increased from about 13 million carats in 1948 to 120 million carats at the end of the twentieth century to reach a peak of 176 million carats, worth $12 billion in 2006. Yields dropped to 125 million carats, worth $8.65 billion in 2009, because of the global financial crisis. At present in 2015, production stands at 127.4 million carats, worth $14 billion. Interestingly, although the annual volume of diamond production is down, the value increased as the global price per carat rose from $69 in 2006 to $109 in 2015.

While production decreased when several large mines, including Argyle in Australia, and Mir, International and Udachnaya in Siberia moved from open pit to underground operations, several new mines came into production so that in the near future annual production will be flat at around 130 million carats. But early in the next decade annual production from mines that are currently in the development stage could reach 160 million, worth $20 billion. If, however, no new discoveries are made, production will be back down to 130 million carats.

Recent predictions (Bain & Company 2016) suggest that by 2030, diamond production will face an annual shortfall of $4 billion, which is equal to about 30 million carats. As it takes some 15 years from discovery to bring a diamond deposit on line, there is significant pressure on exploration geologists to locate new diamond sources and meet future demand. Much therefore hinges on the successful development of new mines in Angola, and the Siberian and Canadian Arctic. If these fail to come on line or are significantly delayed, the price of rough diamonds will likely increase dramatically (Read & Janse 2009).

COLLECTING YOUR OWN ROUGH DIAMONDS

Prospectors can forget about collecting in African countries. To obtain a prospecting permit one needs to be a citizen born in the country or have very deep pockets. Similar conditions are imposed in Russia, Brazil, and Venezuela. Prospecting permits for most minerals including diamonds are easy and cheap to obtain in Australia, but it is rare to find a promising area that is not already under claim. And the Madrid Protocol imposes a 50-year ban on mining activity in Antarctica. Diamond prospectors' efforts are thus best focused on Canada and the United States.

Prospecting in Canada can involve substantial costs, such as contracting helicopter services, but it is still possible to walk over bare gneiss basement rocks exposed above the tree line and find a new field of outcropping diamondiferous kimberlite pipes as Peregrine Resources geologists did a few years ago. The area is located on the southeastern peninsula of **Baffin Island**, 150 kilometers from Iqaluit, the administrative center of Nunavut. Peregrine's effort involved setting up a base camp and logistic support, but that's not to say that a lone prospector could not have located the kimberlite field.

I was involved in the initial discovery of the **Wawa** diamond deposit in central Ontario when the well know prospecting couple Sandor Surmacz and Marcelle Hauseux in September 1995 sampled a nodule-rich rock exposed in a road cut along Highway 17, 30 kilometers north of Wawa. I had spotted the road cut several years earlier, but unlike Sandor and Marcelle, I did nothing about it. As alluvial diamonds had been found in the general area earlier (Wilson 2006), the couple took their samples to a laboratory in Saskatchewan that found significant numbers of microdiamonds (19 micro diamonds in a 25-kilogram sample) in them. The couple then contacted me in Toronto, as I was an old friend and I had written a paper on an ultramafic lamprophyre dike near Wawa (Mitchell & Janse 1981). I introduced Sandor and Marcelle to KWG Resources, a junior mining and exploration company in Montreal, who applied for a diamond prospecting license in the area. Several other companies immediately jumped in, and the area quickly became covered in claims.

Quite a few interesting diamond deposits were outlined, but none so far have proven to be economically significant. Interestingly, purple and mauve-colored diamonds are among those that have been found in the area. The Ontario diamonds are enclosed in Archean alkaline lamprophyre dikes, which contain fist-sized nodules that stand out on the surface of the road cut. All of the minerals are metamorphosed and have been replaced by varieties of amphibole and sericite. As many of the claims have now lapsed, it is possible to collect samples of (micro) diamondiferous rocks. Some of the property remains under active claim, so be sure to check the claim status before digging and be aware of First-Nation issues of access.

In the United States sands and gravels in small streams are known to contain sporadic diamonds in **California** (Hill 1972), on the **Colorado-Wyoming** border (pages 110–113), in **Michigan** (Gunn 1968), **Wisconsin** (Vierthaler 1991), and **Indiana** (Hill & Blatchley 2005). Samples can be collected in many places, after checking with the owner of the land for access. Diamonds in Colorado and Wyoming, and in Arkansas can be traced to known primary host rocks, and those in the Great Lakes area to glacial transport from Canada (Hobbs 1899), but the origin of the Californian diamonds is not known.

The most promising place to find your own rough diamonds is the **Crater of Diamonds State Park** in Arkansas (pages 86–93). There, for a small entrance fee, you can dig for diamonds in the soft, plowed up lamproite breccia, using only simple tools, such as small spades or trowels, sieves, brushes, and keen eyes. Any finds can be identified and certified by a Park Ranger. The diamonds are yours to keep!

Dr. Bram Janse is an independent diamond exploration geologist, based in Perth, Western Australia. Dr. Janse studied Geology at the University of Leiden in the Netherlands, and upon graduating was employed by De Beers mapping coastal diamond deposits in Namaqualand (South Africa) and kimberlites, and the Gross Brukkaros (Geitsi Gubib) phreatic volcano in Namibia. After obtaining a PhD degree at the University of Leeds (England), he became assistant to the chief geologist of London-based Selection Trust, inspecting many diamond prospects in South Africa, Canada, the United States, Brazil, and Australia. Selection Trust merged into BP Minerals International where he was chief consultant (diamonds).

Facing page: A tiny crew drill sampling a newly discovered kimberlite, now being developed as Peregrine Diamond's Qilaq project, on the coastal fjords of Baffin Island, Canada. Mark Mooney photo, July 2011.

Diamonds from the Ekati Mine, Lac de Gras, Northwest Territories, Canada. The largest weighs 27.24 carats and is 1.95 cm wide; the faceted stone weighs 0.53 carats and is 5 mm in diameter.
Canadian Museum of Nature collection, donated by BHP Billiton Corporation; Michael Bainbridge photo.

The Magnificent Mineralogy of Diamond

by John A. Jaszczak and Katherine Dunnell

To understand diamond is to understand its structure — the knowledge of which sheds light on the myriad of amazing properties exhibited by this wonder of the mineral kingdom.

Although he is perhaps best known for his studies of the physics of motion, Isaac Newton (1643–1727) also devoted significant attention to studies into understanding the nature of light and its interactions with materials. His studies on dispersion, separating white light into its component colors using a prism, are well known and culminated in the second of his great works in physics, *Opticks* (1704).

Newton noted in particular that diamond could bend light more than one might expect based on its relatively low mass density[1], and he accurately measured its index of refraction for yellow light to within one percent of 2.44, the presently accepted value. Extrapolating his observation that "oily" materials tended to have higher refractive indices than might have been expected based on their density, Newton wrote that diamond was "probably an unctuous substance coagulated."

Ultimately, the true nature of diamond's composition came from experiments on combustibility. The "vaporization" of diamond was investigated as early as 1694 by Giuseppe Averani and Cipriano Targioni in Florence, Italy, who focused sunlight through a lens onto diamond samples. However, it was Antoine Lavoisier (1742–1794), working in Paris in 1772, who carried out key experiments on the combustibility of diamond. Although Lavoisier was primarily interested in the role of oxygen in combustion, he discovered that the gas produced in the combustion of diamond actually had the same properties as carbon dioxide, which was released by burning charcoal. Building on Lavoisier's work, Smithson Tennant (1761–1815) conducted similar quantitative experiments on diamond and read this insightful conclusion before the Royal Society on December 15, 1796:

> As the nature of diamond is so extremely singular, it seemed deserving of further examination; and it will appear from the following experiments, that it consists entirely of charcoal, differing from the usual state of that substance only by its crystallized form. (Tennant 1797)

---

[1] Here we distinguish between mass and atom densities. Diamond has an ideal mass density of 3.52 g/cm³, and the highest atom density of any known material at 1.77×10^{23} cm⁻³ at ambient conditions (Zhu et al. 2011). For comparison, the mass density of graphite is 2.23g/cm³, and its atom density is 1.14×10^{23} cm⁻³.

Because of the obvious and striking physical differences between diamond and charcoal, it was several decades before scientists agreed that both were made of the same element. Humphry Davy (1778–1829), for example, initially thought that diamond might also contain a small but vital concentration of another substance such as oxygen but ultimately found that diamond, "plumbago" (graphite), and charcoal all basically consisted of the same element, concluding that "the difference depends upon crystallization" (Davy 1840, p. 489). Indeed in its pure form, diamond consists simply of the element carbon.

All carbon is not the same, however, and diamonds can have different stable carbon isotope ratios of ^{12}C to ^{13}C. Interpreting the distributions of stable carbon isotope data for terrestrial diamonds is complex, but taken with studies of isotopes of other elements in impurities and inclusions in diamond, isotope research is helping to refine models of diamond genesis and hypotheses for the source of the carbon for different terrestrial diamond occurrences (Shirey and Shigley 2013, Ogasawara 2005).

DIAMOND STRUCTURE

Although the external shapes of diamond crystals are consistent with the symmetry of a cube-shaped unit cell, the determination of diamond's crystal structure only came about with the 1912 discovery by Max von Laue, Walter Friedrich, and Paul Knipping that crystals diffract X-rays. Soon after, William Lawrence Bragg and his father William Henry Bragg, who in 1915 jointly received the Nobel Prize in physics, began using X-ray diffraction to study diamonds. Remarkably, the crystal structure deduced by the father and son team is the same structure accepted for diamond today.

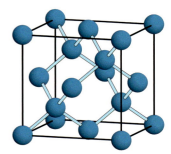

Diamond Unit Cell

The arrangement of the carbon atoms and the nature of their bonds give rise to the myriad of amazing properties that diamond exhibits. Ultimately, the unique versatility of carbon to form different types of bonds and crystal structures has its roots in the structure of the carbon atom itself. Although each carbon atom has six electrons, it is carbon's four valence

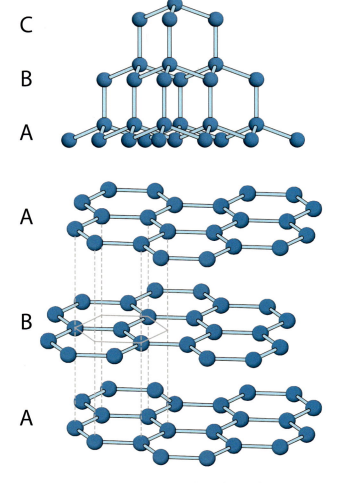

Ball-and-stick crystal structure models of (top) diamond and (bottom) graphite. The diamond structure, showing ABC stacking, is oriented with the [111] direction vertical as originally illustrated by Bragg and Bragg (1913). The graphite structure is oriented with its c-axis nearly vertically. Consecutive layers AB form the stacking sequence.
R. Peter Richards graphics.

electrons that participate in bonding. In diamond, the 2s electron orbital and three 2p orbitals of each atom hybridize[2] into four equivalent sp^3 orbitals that form strong covalent bonds, with each carbon atom bonding with four neighbors.

The quantum mechanical states, associated energies, and bonding geometry of the electrons in its crystal structure are ultimately what determine the optical, electrical, and mechanical properties of diamond. For example, since all of the valence electrons are involved in the three-dimensional network of strong covalent bonds, diamond is an excellent insulator with outstanding mechanical properties.

By comparison, in graphite only two 2p orbitals hybridize with the 2s orbital to form layers of covalent-bond-forming sp^2 orbitals. The remaining 2p electrons are effectively shared among all the carbon atoms in each layer leading to graphite's metallic properties. Adjacent layers of atoms in graphite are only weakly bonded to each other in an AB stacking pattern.

The minerals diamond, graphite, lonsdaleite, and chaoite are all composed solely of carbon. Having the same chemical composition but different crystal structures, the four species are considered *polymorphs* of one another. The structural differences between the polymorphs explain the differences in their appearances and physical properties.

Lonsdaleite and chaoite are formally recognized minerals and while a wealth of literature addresses both of these phases, their actual existence remains a topic of some controversy.

Lonsdaleite, named for crystallographer Kathleen Lonsdale (1903–1971), is commonly called *hexagonal diamond*. The stacking sequence of the zig-zag-bonded layers (perpendicular to the c-axis) of the structure differs from that of diamond as lonsdaleite has an ABAB sequence whereas diamond has an ABCABC sequence. This subtle difference results in distinct physical properties in addition to dramatically different symmetries between them.

Recent work by Németh et al. (2014), however, has called into question whether lonsdaleite is a distinct mineral species. These authors not only noted that this mineral has never been produced as a pure phase but also provide convincing evidence that lonsdaleite both from the Canyon Diablo meteorite, the type specimen, and synthetic material is actually heavily twinned and defect-riddled diamond. A significant body of work still attests to the existence of both natural and synthetic lonsdaleite, and recent work by Shiell et al. (2016) suggests that the case against lonsdaleite is not yet closed.

The story of chaoite, named for impact metamorphism pioneer Edward C. T. Chao, is also fascinating and controversial. Like lonsdaleite, chaoite's occurrence is linked to meteorite impacts. Its carbon atoms are strongly bonded in one-dimensional chains. Whether or not chaoite exists in nature or represents a distinct mineral species, remains a subject of debate; although work by Shumilova et. al. (2011) has made strides toward proving its existence.

THE GRAPHITE RELATIONSHIP

Selected properties of diamond and graphite are shown in the table on the facing page. The comparision illustrates some of the stark differences between these two crystalline forms of carbon. For example, while diamond is the hardest known natural material, graphite is one of the softest. Diamond also has 1.5 times the bulk modulus (a measure of a material's resistance to changing volume by compression) of graphite. While diamond is optically isotropic and transparent, graphite is optically anisotropic and opaque. Diamond is an excellent insulator with very high resistivity, whereas graphite is metallic and has an electrical resistivity many orders of magnitude smaller.

Diamond has an exceedingly sharp and intense diagnostic Raman peak at 1332 cm^{-1} indicating a very efficient coupling between the incident electromagnetic radiation (photons) and the creation of lattice vibrations (phonons). The particular type of vibration that corresponds to this peak is a relative motion between the two interpenetrating face-centered-cubic lattices that comprise the diamond crystal structure (see Prawer and Nemanich 2004). On the other hand, graphite has a diagnostic but much less intense peak near 1580 cm^{-1}.

---

[2]Hybridization is the quantum mechanical description of the mixing of atomic orbitals to form new orbitals that participate in the formation of chemical bonds. Orbitals are related to the probability of where electrons may be found in an atom or molecule.

Despite its apparent stability, diamond is actually not thermodynamically stable under ambient conditions and, relative to graphite, is only stable at relatively high pressures. However, the conversion to graphite under ambient conditions is extremely slow due to a very high energy barrier for the transformation. On the other hand, there are several interesting occurrences in southern Spain and northern Morocco in which pseudomorphs of graphite after diamond have been found (Slodkevich 1983, Pearson et al. 1989, Davies et al. 1993, El Atrassi et al. 2011). These remarkable pseudomorphs show many of the typical external morphologies of diamond, including octahedral shapes and macle twins, but are polycrystalline aggregates of graphite.

Of course the reverse transformation from graphite to diamond is also of interest. Diamond is only thermodynamically stable at very high pressure, but because of the extremely high activation barrier, this transformation requires pressures that are 40,000 times atmospheric pressure at the Earth's surface and temperatures in excess of 1,000 degrees Celsius. Probably the most remarkable synthesis of diamond was one conducted by the scientists at General Electric, who in 1963 "accomplished the ultimate culinary tour de force" by creating diamond crystals out of peanut butter (Hazen 1993)! The fascinating history of diamond synthesis is summarized in an article beginning on page 114.

Other natural occurrences of diamond that are believed to be conversions from graphite are so-called *impact diamonds*. They result from meteorite impacts that cause such local high pressure and temperature conditions that graphite crystals in the country rocks transform to diamond (see pages 128–131).

Selected Properties of Diamond and Graphite

Property	Diamond	Graphite
Mass Density	3.52 g/cm^3	2.23 g/cm^3
Atom Density	1.77×10^{23} cm^{-3}	1.14×10^{23} cm^{-3}
Mohs Hardness	10	1-2
Crystal System	Isometric	Hexagonal
Crystal Class (Point Group Symmetry)	Hexoctahedral $4/m\bar{3}2/m$	Dihexagonal Pyramidal $6mm$
Space Group Symmetry	*Fd3m*	*P6$_3$mc*
C-C bond length	1.54 Å	1.42 Å
Bulk Modulus[a]	442 GPa	286 GPa
Electrical Conduction	Insulator (wide-band-gap semiconductor)	Semi-metal
Electrical Resistivity[b]	Type I and most Type IIa: 10^{18} Ωm Type IIb: 10^3–10^5 Ωm	3000×10^{-6} Ωm along [00.1] 2.5–5.0×10^{-6} Ωm perpendicular to [00.1]
Band Gap[c,d]	5.5 eV (indirect) 7.3 eV (direct)	none
Thermal Conductivity[a,b,e,f]	600–2200 W/m.K at 293 K up to 15,000 W/m.K at 80 K	2–5 W/m.K along [00.1] ~390 perpendicular to [00.1]
Optical	Isotropic	Anisotropic
Luster	Adamantine	Sub-metallic
Diaphaneity	Transparent	Opaque
Tenacity	Brittle	Flexible
Cleavage	Perfect parallel to {111}, also on {221} and {110}	Perfect parallel to {00.1}
Magnetic Susceptibility	Diamagnetic	Strongly Diamagnetic

[a]McEnaney 1999, [b]Pierson 1993, [c]Stoneham 1992, [d]Partoens and Peeters 2006, [e]Field 1992, [f]Berman 1992b.

Upper: Graphite and diamond, xtl 10.50 ct from South Africa. GIA collection. Photo Robert Weldon © GIA.

Middle: Graphite, ~ 1 mm wide. Crestmore, California. J.A. Jaszczak collection and photo.

Lower: Impact diamond, 0.35 mm wide. Zapadnaya Crater, Ukraine. J.A. Jaszczak collection and photo.

Upper left: Diamond, 0.9 cm tall, 3.05 carats. Venezuela. Keith and Mauna Proctor specimen, Jeff Scovil photo.
Upper right: Diamond, 0.94 cm tall, 2.05 carats. Crater of Diamonds, Murfreesboro, Pike County, Arkansas. Jon and Max Sigerman collection, Jeff Scovil photo.
Lower left: Diamond, 1.3 cm tall, 37.31 carats. South Africa. Martin Zinn collection, Jeff Scovil photo.

DIAMOND MORPHOLOGY

Magmatic diamonds such as those found in kimberlites and lamproites are the most abundant and familiar. They have been transported to the earth's surface in environments dramatically different from those in which they formed. As a result, such diamonds can undergo complex episodic sequences of growth and dissolution of variable durations (Orlov 1977, Spetsius and Taylor 2008, Tappert and Tappert 2011). The variety and complexity of the formation and transport histories can result in diamonds, even those from the same mine, that may exhibit very different morphologies.

Attesting to diamond's rich variety of habits and types of aggregates, Goldschmidt (1916) presented 366 crystal drawings of diamond on 22 pages. Orlov (1977) describes and illustrates five different varieties of single-crystal diamonds based on morphology, texture, and associated genesis. He also describes an additional five varieties of polycrystalline aggregates: ballas, two varieties of bort, carbonado, and unnamed irregular aggregates of rounded octahedral crystals.

Tappert and Tappert (2011) present a simpler classification based on morphology and growth mechanism. The growth rate of the diamonds in each category increases from group 1 through 3, with polycrystalline aggregates growing the fastest:

1. Monocrystalline diamond, which includes twins and small numbers of individual crystals in intergrowths;
2. Fibrous diamonds, which are comprised of elongated microscopic fibers;
3. Polycrystalline aggregates.

Monocrystalline Diamond

The planar faces of most diamond crystals are octahedral {111} faces, and the octahedron is the dominant form for most magmatic diamonds. Monocrystalline cubic diamonds are relatively rare and typically have rough rather than planar faces. Fibrous (coated) diamonds (see below), on the other hand, commonly exhibit an overall cubic shape, often with octahedral and dodecahedral modifications.

At some localities, such as the Crater of Diamonds State Park in Arkansas (see pages 86–93), diamonds exhibit completely or almost completely rounded surfaces. Oxidation occurring as the diamonds were transported to the earth's surface are likely responsible for the moderate to extreme dissolution evidenced by the diamonds' rounded shapes.

Diamonds that, on the other hand, were protected in xenoliths (eg., eclogite) during their journey to the earth's surface commonly exhibit sharp octahedral shapes. Even slight to moderate dissolution will soften initially sharp corners and edges. With more extreme dissolution the diamond crystal can lose a significant fraction of its initial volume and become completely rounded giving rise to shapes that resemble a dodecahedron, tetrahexahedron, or hexoctahedron.

While diamond belongs to the isometric (cubic) crystal system, the symmetry of diamond has long been the subject of controversy, due in part to its occasional occurrence as apparently tetrahedral crystals (Orlov 1977, Davies 1984). Nevertheless, consistent with its crystal structure, diamond possesses the full symmetry of the isometric system's hexoctahedral class (point group), and its crystals can form any of the class's allowed forms and combinations of forms including the cube, octahedron, rhombic dodecahedron,

Right: Weighing 0.92 (**left**) and 0.977 carats, this pair of *Star of David* double macle twins represents a very rare diamond morphology. Africa. Diamonds courtesy of Trillion Diamond Company, NY. Photo Robert Weldon © GIA.

Middle: Geometric relationship between an octahedron and a flattened macle. The twin operation can be either a reflection about the contact plane (pink), or by a 180° rotation about the [111] axis.

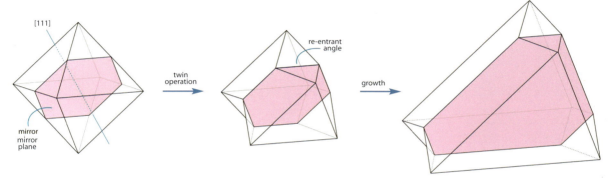

trapezohedron, trisoctahedron, and hexoctahedron (see pages 36–39). The tetrahedron, on the other hand, has lower symmetry than do the forms of the hexoctahedral class, and tetrahedral diamond morphologies have been shown to have been a result of natural cleavages or of twinning (Yacoot and Moore 1993).

Twinning

Diamond crystals have a propensity to form twins, which can create morphologically attractive, interesting, and complicated specimens. In general, two crystals are said to be *twins* when the two, either in contact or inter-grown, are related to one another by a crystallographic symmetry or twinning operation, such as reflection or rotation, that is not part of the symmetries of the individual crystals.

In the case of diamond, the individual crystals forming a twin are mirror images of one another, related by reflection across an octahedral (111) plane. If the crystals are octahedral in form, these growth twins are typically tabular and triangular in shape and are known as *macles*. Twinned crystals commonly have pairs of faces that form concave surfaces, with so-called *reentrant angles*. These can provide favorable sites for atom attachment during growth that lead to accelerated growth rates and ultimately morphologies that are distorted relative to single crystals, which in the case of diamonds, leads to the tabular triangular shape. *Star of David* double macle twins are very rare and highly prized by collectors, as are rare crystals showing a tabular hexagonal shape due to multiple twinning on parallel (111) planes.

Above: Macle twin diamond, 1.4 cm high, 9.3 carats. Locality unknown. Private collection, Jeff Scovil photo.

Diamond varieties: "gem," 6.14 carat, South Africa (left); "bort" 109.47 carats, DRC (middle); and "carbonado" 118.01 carats, Central African Republic (right).
GIA collection, photo Robert Weldon © GIA.

Multiple twinning on non-parallel {111} planes can lead to complex arrangements, sometimes with beautiful results, such as the pseudo-five-fold diamond clusters as illustrated by Goldschmidt (1916, figures 360–362). Because of diamond's high degree of symmetry, the twinning operation by reflection across (111) is equivalent to a 180-degree rotation about a [111] axis (i.e., a cube diagonal). Diamond crystals of cubic morphology commonly form *penetration twins* (see examples on pages 31, 36) whose component crystals can conveniently be visualized as being related to each other by such a rotation.

Fibrous and Polycrystalline Diamond

A particularly interesting class of diamonds is one referred to as *coated diamonds*, which when cleaved, show distinct differences between an older, gemmy, monocrystalline core region and an outer layer of a later-generation of diamond growth (coating) that may be fibrous in nature. If the growth is fibrous then its formation may be due to increased carbon supersaturation conditions leading to increased growth rates that result in the incorporation of impurities (Sunagawa 1984). Depending on the original morphology of the core and the thickness of the coating, a range of morphologies can include cube, flat-faced dodecahedron, and octahedron faces. The micron-scale textures and mineral inclusions in these coatings give clues about the geological environment(s) the diamond experienced as it developed (Spetsius and Taylor 2008, Shirey et al. 2013).

While monocrystalline diamond is the primary focus of the gem and jewelry markets, polycrystalline diamond varieties drive the industrial markets (Olson 2014). Informal and cultural terms for these types of diamond including *bort*, *ballas*, *framesite*, and *carbonado* are often applied inconsistently.

Bort generally refers to polycrystalline, non-gem grade diamond, which is primarily used in, indeed often crushed for, industrial cutting tools and abrasives. Bort is well suited for such applications not only because it has the same exceptional properties as monocrystalline diamond but also because its polycrystalline nature makes bort tough (i.e. resistant to breaking). An unusual but interesting banded form of bort is sometimes referred to as *hailstone bort*.

Ballas is a spherical polycrystalline variety of diamond that exhibits a radial texture aligned along diamond's <110> directions (Trueb and Barrett 1972). First discovered in Brazil, these diamonds have also been recovered in Russia and Africa. Ballas are important in industrial applications since, in contrast to single crystals, the fragmented grains lack consistently oriented cleavage planes and are thus quite durable, making them invaluable for use in abrasive tools.

Perhaps the "most enigmatic" (Haggerty 1999) variety of industrial diamond is carbonado, which is so unlike other varieties of diamond and is so restricted in its occurrence that it is believed to have been formed in a manner unlike most other diamond varieties. Carbonado is a porous, randomly oriented aggregate of sometimes euhedral diamond crystals (and sometimes twins) up to hundreds of microns across that are cemented together by micron-sized diamond grains — a natural micro-diamond ceramic (Heaney et al. 2005, Haggerty 2014). This variety of diamond occurs in Brazil, where it was originally discovered and mined, and in an almost certainly related occurrence, via the Gondwana supercontinent, in the Bangui Region of the Central African Republic. Carbonado seems never to occur with "normal" diamonds in kimberlite

Diamond Twins and Varieties:

Top left: Diamond, complex multiple twins, 1 cm wide.
Finsch Mine, South Africa
Arkenstone specimen, Joe Budd photo.

Second left: Diamond, reentrant-cube penetration twin, 1 cm wide.
Diavik Mine, Lac de Gras, Northwest Territories, Canada.
A. E. Seaman Mineral Museum collection, John A. Jaszczak photo.

Third left: Diamond, coated cubic penetration twin, 7 mm wide.
Mbuji-Mayi, DRC. John Betts photo.

Bottom left: Diamond, reentrant-cube penetration twin, 8 mm wide.
Finsch Mine, Free State, South Africa
Arkenstone specimen, Joe Budd photo.

Bottom center: Tabular, twinned diamond with pronounced hexagonal and rounded surface pits and a raised triangular growth that also appears to be a twin, 1 cm wide.
Argyle Mine, Kimberley Division, Western Australia, Australia.
Argyle Mine Visitor Centre collection, John Chapman photo

Top right: Diamond "hailstone bort," about 1 cm wide.
Courtesy of Lazare Kaplan International, photo Robert Weldon © GIA.

Second right: Diamond "ballas," 1.1 cm wide, Brazil.
Martin Zinn collection, Jeff Scovil photo

Third right: Diamond overgrown with a fibrous, fluid-included second generation of diamond, approximately 1 carat.
Jwaneng Mine, Botswana.
University of Alberta collection, Anetta Banas photo.

Bottom right: Diamond, 8 mm tall, with octahedral core and partial fibrous coating. Canada.
John A. Jaszczak collection and photo.

pipes or other igneous intrusions. Hypotheses of the origin of carbonado remain varied and controversial and include the possibility that they may be the result of meteorite impacts or are the result of modification of organic matter by intense irradiation.

Framesite, named for former Chairman of the **Premier Mine** in South Africa Ross Frames, is similar to carbonado. Unlike carbonado, however, framesite is found in association with kimberlites and is further distinguished from carbonado by its lighter color, more irregular surface, lower porosity, and a heavier carbon isotope ratio. Framesite and carbonado also have distinctively different sets of inclusions. As might be expected for mantle-derived kimberlitic diamond, the common inclusions in framesite include pyrope, almandine, chromite, and clinopyroxene; whereas carbonado's inclusions commonly include florencite-goyazite-gorceixite, xenotime, kaolinite, quartz, feldspar, zircon, and more exotic phases such as iron, iron-nickel, silicon carbide, silicon, and tin.

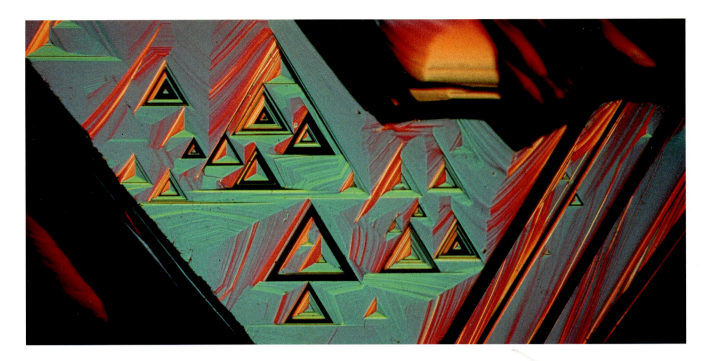

Above: Multiple trigons on the octahedral face of a diamond crystal. Interference contrast, field of view 3.6 mm.
South Africa.
John Koivula collection and photo.

Left: Etching on a diamond cube face surface under polarized light, crossed polars, field of view 4 mm.
South Africa.
John Koivula collection and photo.

Facing page, upper: Sector-zoned (asteriated) diamonds from Zimbabwe, the largest crystal is 1.3 cm tall. Impurity and defect concentrations vary among the cube and octahedral sectors of these crystals, whose surfaces have been polished to reveal the resulting patterns (Rakovan et al. 2014).
James Zigras collection, Jeff Scovil photo.

Facing page, lower: A 1 mm long polycrystalline graphite inclusion in a 3 mm wide diamond.
Panda open pit, Ekati Mine, Lac de Gras,
Northwest Territories, Canada.
Jeff Harris collection, Jurgen Glinnerman photo.

SURFACE FEATURES

Many crystals exhibit irregular surfaces, pits, triangular pits, striations, mosaic structures, or other rough surfaces. Triangular pits called trigons are particularly common on {111} surfaces, and are typically oriented upside down relative to the triangular octahedral face (photo above). Although they have been thought by some scientists to be due to growth processes, Frank and Lang (1965) have provided clear evidence that trigons on natural diamonds result from dissolution where crystallographic defects (dislocations) intersect the crystal surface. Six-sided etch pits also occur on some octahedral diamonds, and square-ouining etch pits (tetragons) can occur on cube faces. Layered growth on octahedral surfaces can form triangular plates that may be isolated or multiply stacked upon each other giving rise to a heavily stepped appearance (see drawings page 36, row 5, middle and right). Resorption of triangular plates can form rounded shield-shaped surface features. Dodecahedral faces and re-entrant cubes often show groups of elongated drop-shaped hillocks that result from resorption. Other surface features commonly observed on diamonds include pyramidal hillocks, corrosion sculptures, deformation lines, frosting, percussion marks, and abrasion.

LUSTER, REFRACTION, DISPERSION

Diamond's high refractive index theoretically gives it an adamantine luster (Correns et al. 1969, Orlov 1977). But luster also depends strongly on the smoothness of the surfaces, as highly smooth faces, such as those on nitrogen-rich Type I diamonds, are the most lustrous. Refractive index is dependent on the wavelength of light, a property known as *dispersion*, which gives refractive materials the ability to break white light into the spectral rainbow of colors. Over the visible spectrum, diamond's index of refraction changes from about 2.46 for blue light to about 2.40 for red light (Orlov 1977).

Because of its cubic symmetry, diamonds are ideally optically isotropic; however, various internal strains related to a diamond's growth history, structural defects, texture, and mineral inclusions invariably lead to a variety of anomalous birefringence effects that can result in informative and lovely patterns visible in polarized light (see Howell 2012).

INCLUSIONS

Diamond's refractory properties and high-pressure stability make it an ideal messenger of clues about the earth's interior, as diamonds can preserve mineral and fluid inclusions from its various growth environments, including the deep mantle, and transport them to the earth's surface. The study of inclusions in diamond and their implications for our understanding of how diamonds form and the varied geological conditions that they experience are topics of extensive current research (eg., Stachel and Harris 2008).

The common inclusions indicate that magmatic diamonds have two principal growth environments: peridotitic and eclogitic (Spetsius and Taylor 2008). The principal inclusions in the former include olivine, garnet, chromite, ortho– and clino-pyroxene. On the other hand, the common inclusions in eclogitic diamonds include omphacitic clinopyroxene, garnet, and sulfides. Lovely inclusions can also be found of the odd diamond crystal that is misoriented relative to the host diamond (see for example, photos on pages 57 and 59). While graphite is also a relatively common inclusion in diamond, one particularly interesting study found unusual oriented graphite single-crystal inclusions in several diamonds from the Panda pit at the **Ekati Diamond Mine**, Northwest Territories, Canada, suggesting that the graphite crystals formed before the diamonds grew around them (Glinnemann et al. 2003). More exotic inclusions such as ferropericlase and stishovite, among others, provide scientists unique opportunities to study the Earth's lower mantle.

Inclusions in diamond are not only scientifically significant, they can also be visually stunning, as evidenced by the gallery by John I. Koivula and Elise A. Skalwold, pages 54–61.

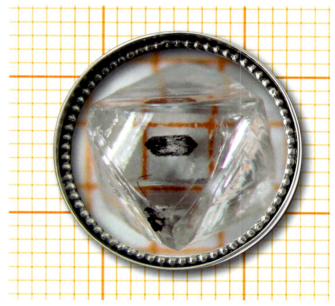

DIAMOND TYPES AND COLORS

As noted earlier, diamonds can be classified according to morphology (Orlov 1977, Tappert and Tappert 2011). Based on the presence or absence of nitrogen as an atomic impurity, diamonds can also be conveniently classified as Type I (nitrogen present) and Type II (nitrogen absent). Each of these types is further subdivided based on the configuration of the nitrogen in the diamond structure, or in the case of Type II diamonds, the presence of the atomic impurity boron. Due to potentially complex growth histories, any individual diamond crystal may have different impurity profiles in different zones and sectors (Rakovan et al. 2014). The different configurations of nitrogen and the presence of other specific impurities can profoundly affect how a diamond absorbs light, and thereby, its color (see pages 40–53). Impurities and crystallographic defects are also responsible for the fluorescence and occasional phosphorescence in diamond.

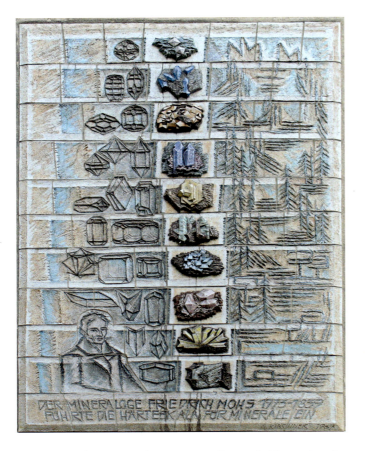

Above: A plaque on Mohsgasse, a small street in Vienna, Austria, memorializes Friedrich Mohs' contribution to science. Doris Antony photo.

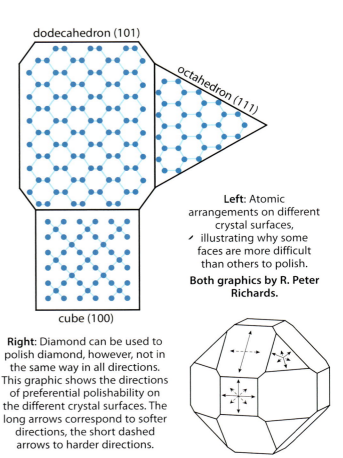

Left: Atomic arrangements on different crystal surfaces, illustrating why some faces are more difficult than others to polish. **Both graphics by R. Peter Richards.**

Right: Diamond can be used to polish diamond, however, not in the same way in all directions. This graphic shows the directions of preferential polishability on the different crystal surfaces. The long arrows correspond to softer directions, the short dashed arrows to harder directions.

HARDNESS

The name *diamond* is said to be have its roots in the Greek word, αδαμαζ (*adámas*), meaning "untamable" or "invincible." George Frederick Kunz (1913, p. 70) wrote in the *Curious Lore of Precious Stones* that "the virtues ascribed to [diamond] are almost all directly traceable to either its unconquerable hardness or to its transparency and purity." Diamond properties such as high luster, refractive index, high dispersion, and extreme hardness all contribute to its value as a gemstone. The combination of its high thermal conductivity, important for carrying away heat generated by friction, and extreme hardness also make both natural and synthetic diamonds extremely important industrial materials for abrasives, drills, and cutting tools.

Hardness, which is a material's resistance to scratching, is actually a much more complicated property than the celebrated Mohs scale of hardness might suggest, as hardness is dependent both on the mineral's surface orientation and the direction of scratching. Quantitative measurements of resistance to abrasion are also very sensitive to the experimental details and methods employed. However, hardness as measured by abrasion is of more interest in mineralogy and diamond polishing and will therefore be the focus of the discussion here.

Diamond-cutters have known for centuries that grinding a diamond on a plane parallel to an octahedral face is next to impossible, and it is no coincidence that the these faces have the highest area density of carbon atoms relative to those at any other orientation. On the other hand, lapidaries have also long known that diamonds also have a "grain" or a "soft" direction that is relatively easy to polish, and these characteristics have now been quantitatively demonstrated (Wilks and Wilks 1965 1992). Hardness measurements on any particular surface are also strongly dependent on any slight misorientation relative to the crystal structure. For example, Wilks and Wilks (1965) showed that "directional hardness" was greatest along the cube-face diagonal of a diamond. Along this diagonal, diamonds are more than 100 times harder than if abraded on a cube face but parallel to the cube axes. Similarly, dodecahedron and most other faces have both hard and soft directions, whereas octahedral faces are very hard in all directions. In consequence, diamond cutters can only polish a diamond's octahedral planes if the facets are slightly misorientated from the octahedral faces.

Despite diamond's extreme hardness, it is actually quite fragile. Diamonds cleave easily and perfectly on {111} planes, the same surfaces that have a maximal number of atoms per area and minimal surface energy. While {111} is the dominant and most familiar cleavage plane, cleavage on the {221} and {110} planes have also been reported as not uncommon (Field 1992b), and that author lists other cleavage planes for diamond. In random directions diamond has a conchoidal fracture that can commonly be observed on broken crystals, as small chips on a crystal's corners or edges, or within the crystal as an internal fracture. Thanks again to its unique structure and bonding, diamond has the highest measured fracture velocity of up to some 7,200 meters per second (Field 1992b).

THERMAL CONDUCTIVITY

One final but particularly notable property of diamond is its extremely high thermal conductivity, which is attributable

A composite image of an ice sculpture and a 22.32-carat diamond from South Africa. The diamond is in the GIA collection, a gift of De Beers. Original photos by Robert Weldon and Marco Gubka.

to diamond's strong bonds together with its extremely high atom density. Thermal conductivity is the rate at which heat travels across a material with a temperature gradient. At room temperature, diamond's thermal conductivity is approximately five times greater than that of copper. Due to their purity, natural Type IIa diamonds are actually even better thermal conductors than Type I diamonds and are said to be the best thermal conductors at room temperature (Berman 1992b). Remarkably, the high thermal conductivity is even greater in diamond made from isotopically purified ^{12}C, which has been found to have up to 50 percent higher thermal conductivity as compared to normal diamonds, which contain a natural abundance of approximately 1.1 percent ^{13}C (Berman 1992, 1992b). Diamonds created by chemical-vapor-deposition (Balmer et. al 2009) have also now become an important material in the electronics industry for removing heat from temperature-sensitive electronic devices.

Because of its high thermal conductivity, sizable diamonds feel cool to the touch, thus explaining the common reference to diamond as *ice*. This extreme property is a convenient diagnostic for gemologists and jewelers, as quick measurements can be made with small thermal-conductivity testers that readily distinguish diamonds from non-diamond imitations.

IN CONCLUSION

Diamonds are among the most studied of all materials, and for good reason. Diamonds possess an internal beauty in their crystal structures and even in their defects and impurities, which also affect their external beauty in their shapes and colors. Of course cut diamonds are revered for their beauty and durability as gemstones, but other properties make diamonds valuable for numerous industrial uses. Furthermore, diamonds' shapes, colors, atomic impurities, isotopic composition and mineral inclusions are providing scientists with valuable clues about geological processes in the mantle and other parts of the deeper Earth and about the history of the Earth itself (Harlow and Davies 2005, Shirey et al. 2013). Learning how to read and interpret these clues is a challenging and fascinating field of study that continues to take place one stone at a time.

ACKNOWLEDGEMENTS: *We are grateful to R. Peter Richards, John Rakovan, and Christopher J. Stefano for reviewing different versions of this manuscript and offering valuable comments. Many thanks to the photographers and illustrators for supplying visuals that greatly enhance this review. We also thank V. N. Kvasnitsa and A. V. Korsakov for supplying unusual specimens for study and photography.*

Dr. John A. Jaszczak is a Professor of Physics at Michigan Technological University and is Adjunct Curator at the A.E. Seaman Mineral Museum. His research specialties include computational solid state physics and nanotechnology education. An avid mineral collector since his youth, his mineralogical interests currently focus on graphite and on the minerals from the tanzanite mines near Merelani, Tanzania.

Katherine Dunnell is a technician in the Department of Natural History, Earth Sciences, Royal Ontario Museum where she has worked since 1997. She holds degrees in Geography and Geology but her passions are in gems, minerals, and museum studies. She feels fortunate to have found a career that allows her to marry those interests.

Top Row:
Left: A rhombic dodecahedron with residual octahedral faces.
Middle: Cubo-octahedron.
Right: Rhombic dodecahedron, again with residual octahedral faces.

2nd Row:
Left: Octahedron.
Middle: Octahedron with embryonic dodecahedral faces.
Right: Octahedron with well-developed dodecahedral faces.

3rd Row:
Left: Stepped octahedron, which creates the cube and dodecahedral faces.
Middle: Slightly asymmetric octahedron.
Right: Rounded tetra-hexahedron with residual cube faces.

4th Row:
Left: Cube with small dodecahedral and octahedral faces.
Middle: Stepped octahedron, which creates the cube faces.
Right: Rounded tetra-hexahedron with dodecahedral type faces.

5th Row:
Left: A re-entrant cube.
Middle: An interpenetrant twinned cube.
Right: A more complete form of an interpenetrant cube.

Bottom Row:
Left: Octahedron with dodecahedral development.
Middle: Octahedron in which stepped growth gives rise to re-entrants rather than striations along the edges.
Right: Octahedron with extreme re-entrant development.

Select drawings from the "Atlas" in *Der Diamant, eine Studie* (1911) by Alexander von Fersman and Victor Goldschmidt. Si and Ann Frazier collection.

DIAMOND STUDIES

by Maximilian Glas

Many collectible mineral species form large, beautifully developed crystals: fluorite, beryl, calcite, quartz, and the tourmalines can have dimensions in the meter range and may weigh many kilograms. Diamond crystals, however, are much more modest in size.

The two largest diamond crystals ever recorded were both found around the turn of the twentieth century, and both weighed just over 3,100 carats. The largest diamond crystal thus far recorded was a 3,150-carat carbonado dubbed *Sergio*, unearthed in 1895 from a mine in Bahia, Brazil. The largest gem-quality diamond ever found is the famous 3,106¾-carat (621.35-gram or 1.37-pound) *Cullinan*, which was recovered in 1905 from the fledgling **Premier No. 2 Mine**, near Pretoria, South Africa. Before it was cut, the Cullinan measured 10.1 by 6.4 by 5.1 centimeters — a mere crumb compared to the average quartz crystal. Like many other large diamond crystals, the Cullinan would not have been considered an aesthetic specimen in the eyes of most collectors, who would have certainly valued the asymmetric Cullinan more for its historical significance than its outward appearance.

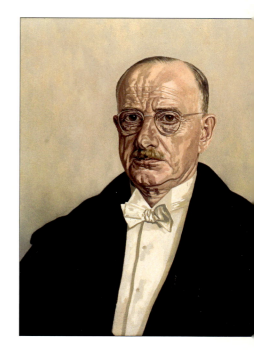

Right: Berend George Escher (1885–1967). The painting is in the Leiden University Library collection.

Below, left: Glass model of the Cullinan diamond with a 1.07-carat, round brilliant diamond for scale. Model, Dave Bunk collection. Diamond courtesy of Morgan Sonsthagen Jewelry. Jesse La Plante photo.

MODEL OF THE CULLINAN DIAMOND; DISCOVERED IN 1905, IT IS THE LARGEST ON RECORD (Wt. 3025¾ CARATS). PRESENTED BY THE TRANSVAAL GOVERNMENT IN 1907 TO KING EDWARD VII, IT WAS SUBSEQUENTLY CUT INTO STONES WEIGHING 516½ & 309 CARATS.

However, the beauty of naturally formed diamonds flourishes in the small scale, which might in part explain why few people collect diamond crystals — they must be content with small formats and disproportionate prices. A diamond crystal in the one-centimeter range is considered quite large and would be easily out of the price ranges of many collectors. The best way to reasonably discover the true beauty of natural uncut diamond crystals is to break out the microscope.

Another place to discover the beautiful and fascinating world of diamond crystals is to review the numerous idealized sketches found in mineralogy textbooks. The best of these is Aleksander Fersman and Victor Goldschmidt's now very scarce *Der Diamant, eine Studie* (Heidelberg, 1911). The two-volume work includes 292 drawings on 43 plates. The remarkable "Atlas" volume contains shaded crystal drawings and other figures rendered from actual stones.

ESCHER'S DIAMOND

Another wonderful source of diamond beauty is Dutch mineralogist Berend George Escher's study (1942) of the intricate surface morphology of a natural diamond crystal; it's a true work of art. The Rijksmuseum van Geologie en Mineralogie (now part of the Nationaal Natuurhistorisch Museum) in Leiden, The Netherlands, acquired the subject stone in June 1937 from the collection of A. S. Dresden of

The Puzzle of Re-Entrant Cube Morphology

by John Rakovan, Alexander G. Schauss, R. Peter Richards

Among the many interesting morphologies seen in diamond crystals is the "re-entrant cube," a form exhibiting cube faces that are highly depressed relative to the edges and corners. This form is relatively rare, although there is a higher than normal abundance in some deposits such as the **Jwaneng Mine** in southwest Botswana (Welbourn et al. 1989).

The overall outlines of these crystals are those of cubes, which appear at first glance to have hoppered growth features. But, unlike typical hoppered crystals whose depressed faces are composed of incomplete layers parallel to the "ideal" face (i.e., incomplete layers of the cube {100} in this case), these diamonds actually show no cube faces. Instead, the re-entrant surfaces approximate other face orientations including the dodecahedron {110} and a tetrahexahedron {hk0}.

The surface microtopography of the crystals is quite rough and appears to be mostly the result of resorption. For example, distinct etch pits are observable with minor magnification. Particularly striking are rows of rectangular etch pits, referred to as *tetragons*, which run along the two diagonals of each cube re-entrant. Scalloped and rounded mounds along the crystal edges and on the re-entrant surfaces are also indicative of dissolution. One exception to this topography is at the intersection of the crystal edges (i.e., at the corners of the cube), where the crystals exhibit flat octahedral {111} surfaces that extend partially along the intersecting edges (forming a 3-pronged star shape).

Although the surface topography suggests etching, the origin of the overall morphology is uncertain. Is it the result of growth as a hoppered cube whose surface has been roughened by slight resorption? Or is the morphology the result of extensive resorption of another preexisting form?

Single crystals of diamond with the cube morphology are far less common than octahedra, and those of sizes greater than a few millimeters are usually composed of a single crystal core, typically of octahedral morphology, with the overgrowth of a fibrous mantle that approximates a cube morphology but with a very rough appearance. Such crystals are commonly referred to as *cuboids* (Howell et al. 2012).

Optical observations and surface topography suggest that the specimen pictured here is a single crystal that does not contain any fibrous components. Furthermore, the highly flat {111} surfaces observed at the crystal corners are inconsistent with the theory that the underlying "fins" of this sample are composed of fibers. On the other hand, the overall cube shape of the crystal may have involved fibrous growth, but if it did the fibrous portions are no longer present or are not optically observable.

One Stone, Two Views
Diamond, re-entrant cube,
1.5 cm wide, 11.45 carats.
Orapa Mine, Central District, Botswana.
Alex Schauss collection,
Jeff Scovil photo

The morphologic origin of re-entrant cube diamonds from the Jwaneng Mine was studied previously and discussed by Welbourn et al. (1989). From an evaluation of surface microphotography, internal morphology, and defect distribution of diamonds with cube-related morphologies, and comparing those to other diamonds from the deposit, those authors concluded that the crystals originally grew with a simultaneous combination of forms: the octahedron {111} and the cuboid (not a true form). Welbourn and colleagues surmised that the octahedral faces grew by a layer growth mechanism, forming "faceted" surfaces, while the cuboidal faces resulted from fibrous growth leading to a prominence of hummocky surfaces. Thus, the original morphology was not that of a hoppered cube. After growth, resorption took place preferentially in the fibrous cuboidal sectors, leaving behind the skeletal or re-entrant cube morphology exemplified by the diamond shown here. Thus, their basic shapes are the result of growth while the re-entrants and surface microtopography are a result of resorption, which is sometimes extensive.

The similarities in morphology, optical properties, and surface topography suggest that the re-entrant cube diamond pictured here formed by the same mechanism of mixed form growth (also referred to as mixed habit growth) followed by preferential resorption of the cuboid sectors.

Right: This 1 cm wide diamond exhibits a habit much like that of the much smaller diamond studied by B. G. Escher. Koivula (1987) refers to this habit as *Mohs Rose*. Locality unknown. Jack Greenspan collection, Harold & Erica van Pelt photo.

Below: Two of 16 drawings from Berend Escher's 1942 study of a complex, composite diamond crystal. The subject diamond weighs just 0.1698 grams. Escher used a microscope to observe the specimen. The specimen is in the collection of the State Museum of Geology and Mineralogy at Leiden; the drawings appear courtesy of Penn State Library.

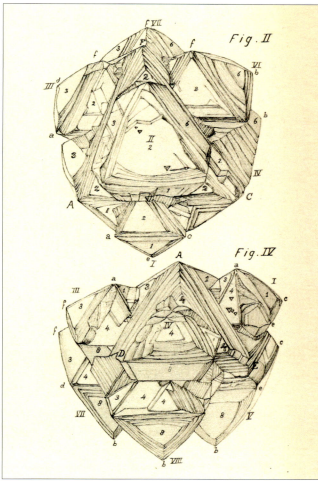

Amsterdam. The colorless, transparent stone weighs just 0.1698 grams (0.849 carats), Escher (1942) characterized the crystal as "a parallel grouping of a central octahedron which carries an octahedron on each of its faces."

To document the diamond crystal, Escher drew realistic portraits of all sides of the crystal. In order to grasp all the fine details, he worked with a microscope. For guidance, he also made an idealized "architectural sketch" and meticulously described all of the crystal faces and their details. He was encouraged by the above-mentioned drawings by Fersman and Goldschmidt, which Escher described as "the best drawings of diamond crystals ever published." The result is an outstanding scientific and artistic feat.

The talent for art and a passion for geometry were apparently plentiful in the Escher family. B. G. Escher was the half-brother of graphic artist Maurits Cornelis Escher, whose paintings and prints are widely known. Geometric forms, including crystals, crystal forms and structures, were major themes in M. C.'s work. Diamond crystals, it would seem, have been a fascinating source of inspiration for scientists, and artists, for some time.

Editor, author, and artist, Maximilian Glas (1948–2005) co-founded, along with Christian Weise, the German magazine Lapis *and the companion* extraLapis *monograph series. He authored, edited and/or designed numerous books, periodicals and catalogues. This article was adapted from Maximilian Glas' "Die Schönheit von Diamantkristallen," originally published in* extraLapis *No. 18: Diamant (2000) and translated into English by Iva Veselinova.*

Fancy-Color Diamonds:
A fancy intense purple red, 3.16-carat round; fancy intense blue, internally flawless, 4.03-carat pear; and fancy intense yellow, 0.66-carat round, courtesy of Fancoldi Diamond Ltd., Tino Hammid photo.

ON THE BEAUTY OF DEFECTS

by Eloïse Gaillou and George R. Rossman

In its pure and perfect form, diamond is colorless. However, in nature or even when made in a laboratory, diamonds are never composed just of perfectly arranged carbon atoms. On the atomic level even colorless and seemingly flawless diamonds contain trace amounts of other elements such as nitrogen or hydrogen, or they may contain structural defects such as missing carbon atoms. When present in specific atomic arrangements and concentrations, most minor components or defects can cause absorption of specific wavelengths that give rise to color.

Diamond of a particular color is not source specific. Virtually every deposit has the potential to produce diamonds of any color. Some mines, however, produce more of certain colors. The **Cullinan** (formerly **Premier**) **Mine** in South Africa, for example, is known for blue diamonds, and the **Argyle Mine** in Australia (page 104) is known for brown and pink diamonds.

Unlike many other minerals and gems, the colors of diamond do not arise from the typical chromophores (chemical elements that give rise to color), such as chromium, which gives the corundum variety ruby its red color and the green in the emerald variety of beryl. For diamonds, it is the presence of minor components such as nitrogen or boron atoms (often referred to as *impurities*) and local defects in the diamond structure, such as missing atoms, that give rise to their color. Collectively, these features are called *color centers*, which introduce a local electron charge imbalance (lack or excess of electrons) in the diamond structure and create new ways for light to be absorbed by diamonds that is often in the range of visible light (390 to 700 nanometers).

DIAMOND CLASSIFICATION

The established type classification of diamonds is based on the presence (Type I) or absence (Type II) of nitrogen atoms, which are bound in the diamond structure and are detectable by infrared (IR) spectroscopy. The presence or absence of nitrogen in a diamond's structure has a significant influence on its color. Other minor components found in diamond can include hydrogen, nickel, silicon, or boron (Field 1992), all of which can also influence color. The table below summarizes the causes of color in diamond. Type classification quantifies a diamond's purity as well as the makeup and form of the nitrogen (and boron) components; it does not necessarily speak to the gemological characteristics of color and clarity, however.

More than 98 percent of natural diamonds contain nitrogen and are classified as Type I (Zaitsev 2001 and references therein, Meyer and Seal 1998). Type I diamonds are subclassified based on the manner in which nitrogen occurs in the crystal structure. In Type Ib diamonds, a single nitrogen atom substitutes for one carbon atom in the structure; the nitrogen content of these diamonds is typically about 100 parts per million (Collins 1980). Nitrogen atoms can also form pairs (Type IaA) or cluster in fours around a vacancy (Type IaB diamonds). Type Ia diamonds commonly contain both A- and B-aggregates and are therefore referred to as *Type IaAB*. The typical nitrogen content in Type Ia diamonds is up to 3,000 parts per million (Collins 1980).

When nitrogen is first incorporated into the diamond structure, it is as single atoms. Most diamonds remain in the earth's mantle for billions of years, and during this time, the

CLASSIFICATION OF DIAMONDS BASED ON IMPURITIES AND COLORS

Type	Subtype	Abundance	Causes of Color		
			Impurities	Plastic Deformation	Irradiation
Type I (nitrogen-bearing, ~5 to 3000 ppm)	Type Ia	~ 98%	Colorless, White, Black, Pale Yellow, Yellow (Cape), Orange, Gray-Blue-Violet suite Chameleon	Brown, Pink, Purple, Red	Body color: Green, Black Surface skin and spots: Green, Blue, Brown
	Type Ib	~ 0.1%	Intense Yellow (Canary)		
Type II (no detectable nitrogen, <5 ppm)	Type IIa	1-2%	Colorless		Body color: Teal Green Surface skin and spots: Green, Blue, Brown
	Type IIb (boron-bearing, ~ 0.1-2 ppm, nitrogen concentration must be lower than boron)	~ 0.1%	Blue	Gray	Surface skin and spots: Green, Blue, Brown

(after Tappert and Tappert 2011).

	SIGNIFICANT CONTRIBUTORS TO DIAMOND COLOR AND FLUORESCENCE			
Name	Description	Main Absorptions / Emissions	Active In	Comments
	Boron defects	2802, 1290, 2456 cm^{-1}	Infrared with tail in the visible	Strong absorptions in the infrared with tailing in the visible
	Hydrogen defects	3107, 1405 cm^{-1}	Infrared, visible	
A-aggregate	2 Nitrogen	1280, 1212 cm^{-1}	Infrared	Often associated with B-aggregates
B-aggregate	4 Nitrogen and 1 Vacancy	1180, 1096, 1010 cm^{-1}	Infrared	Often associated with A-aggregates
C-center	1 isolated Nitrogen	1130, 1344 cm^{-1}	Infrared	Only present in "young" diamonds
Platelets	Extended carbon defects	Between 1375 and 1358 cm^{-1}	Infrared	
Vacancy cluster	Cluster of ~60 vacancies	Absorption continuum	Visible	Present in brown diamonds
N3 center	3 Nitrogen and 1 Vacancy	415 nm	Visible, ultraviolet	
Blue band	Dislocations	Broad 435 nm	Ultraviolet	
H3 center	2 Nitrogen and 1 Vacancy	503 nm	Visible, ultraviolet	
GR1 center	Neutral Vacancy	741 nm	Visible	Due to irradiation
	Unknown	Broad 480 and 800 nm	Visible	Present in chameleon diamonds
	Unknown	Broad 480 nm	Visible	Present in pure orange diamonds.
	Unknown (related to plastic deformation)	Broad 550 nm	Visible	Present in pink, purple and red diamonds.

Right: The nearly flawless *Regent* colorless diamond, 140.64 carats. The Regent was faceted circa 1710 from a 410-carat piece of rough found in the Paritala-Kollur Mine, India in 1698. British Prime Minister William Pitt, acquired the uncut diamond in 1702 and sent it to England to be cut. It acquired its name after Regent Philippe d'Orléans persuaded the Regency Council to purchase the diamond in June 1717. Shortly thereafter, King Louis XV began wearing the Regent, which took its place as a centerpiece of the French Crown jewels. The diamond was assigned to the Louvre in 1887 and is presently on display in the Galerie d'Apollon at the Louvre, Paris. Photo © RMN, Musée du Louvre.

Facing page: Rough diamonds
Hans van Dyk photo
© De Beers

nitrogen atoms tend to aggregate. The A- and then B-aggregates likely form through diffusion processes, which are possible at the high temperature and stabilizing pressure conditions in the Earth's mantle (e.g., Woods 1986). Much rarer, Type Ib diamonds are young. Their formation closely coincided with volcanism that brought the diamonds to the surface before the nitrogen atoms had an opportunity to form aggregates.

Type II diamonds typically contain less than 5 parts per million nitrogen — too little nitrogen to be detectable by Infrared (IR) spectroscopy. The presence or lack of boron defines the two subcategories of Type II diamonds: Type IIa diamonds are effectively boron-free; Type IIb diamonds contain boron detectable by IR spectroscopy (Custers 1952, 1954, and 1955; Collins 1982; Davies 1977), although in quantities that are usually less than 2 parts per million (0.5 parts per million on average) (Gaillou et al. 2012a).

Type IIb diamonds have an interesting and useful electrical property: they are natural "p-type semiconductors." In the diamond structure, boron atoms have only three electrons, while carbon has four; thus when boron replaces carbon in the crystal structure, one electron is missing from one of the bonds normal for the diamond structure. The electron deficiency makes Type IIb diamonds much more conductive than a typical semiconductor. In the diamond structure, boron also has the capacity to "accept" an electron (e.g., Collins and Williams 1971, Field 1992, King et al. 1998) from a neighboring carbon atom, creating an electron "hole" in the structure.

COLORLESS TO NEAR COLORLESS DIAMOND

While all diamonds are on some level imperfect, relatively rare stones contain imperfections in quantities low enough or that are configured such that they do not give rise to absorption of visible light. Such diamonds are termed *colorless*. The most highly valued colorless diamonds are of the Type IIa, which means that the amount of impurities they contain is so low that they cannot be detected by infrared spectroscopy. These stones are sometimes termed *Golconda* diamonds because historic examples of Type IIa colorless diamonds, such as the 105.6-carat *Koh-i-nûr*, the 190-carat *Orlov*, and the 95-carat *Star of the East*, are said to have come from deposits which fell under the jurisdiction of the ancient city of Golconda, in the present-day Hyberabad district of India. Type IIa diamonds usually display weak to no fluorescence; whereas some 37 percent of Type Ia colorless to near colorless diamonds fluoresce (Moses et al. 1997), which is not generally desirable as under certain lighting conditions fluorescence can cause a stone to appear milky or bluish.

Market controls and marketing may make colorless to near colorless diamonds seem rarer than they actually are. These diamonds represent 27 percent of the gem-quality production (Shigley et al. 2001) from the mine near Argyle, Australia.

WHITE / OPALESCENT DIAMOND

Colorless diamonds are distinct from diamonds described as *white*; the latter term implies that the material is opaque.

Left: The 67.5-carat *Black Orlov* or *Eye of Brahma* diamond is among the most famous natural-color black diamonds (studio lighting casts the reflections in blue). The 195-carat rough from which it was cut is thought to have originated in nineteenth century India. The Orlov is set here in a platinum brooch surrounded by round, single-cut and baguette diamonds. Private collection.

Facing Page: The 67.89-carat, VS-2, natural, fancy brown yellow, *Victoria-Transvaal* diamond was cut from a 240-carat crystal found in 1951 in the Premier Mine, Transvaal, South Africa. Smithsonian Institution collection (NMNH G7101-00), Chip Clark photo.

Right: Rough brown diamond, 4 mm long, from Namibia that has been slightly polished on two parallel faces, revealing the color graining.
Smithsonian Institution collection, Eloïse Gaillou photo.

Below: Opalescent diamonds from the *Aurora Butterfly of Peace* collection, 1.94, 1.95, and 1.58 carats.
Curated by Alan Bronstein, Eloïse Gaillou photo.

While opaque white diamonds are found, translucent, "milky" diamonds are more common. The milky aspect is also referred to as *opalescence*. It is caused by a myriad of tiny inclusions in the diamond that scatter the light. The exact nature of the inclusions is unknown. Emmanuel Fritsch (1998), an expert on the causes of color in gemstones, noticed that white diamonds are most often Type IaB (nitrogen mostly in B-aggregates) and contain platelets (extended defects).

Milky diamonds are not particularly rare, but they have not been marketed to any significant extent. Regardless, they will probably never have the gemstone appeal of other less-included diamonds. So far, they are generally only of interest to collectors.

"FANCY COLOR DIAMONDS"

In the 1960s, the Gemological Institute of America (GIA) began introducing nomenclature to describe fancy color diamonds, which exhibit colors that fall outside of the D to Z color scale (see pages 66–67). The system has evolved through the years and today evaluates the "color appearance" of a diamond based on the combined characteristics of "hue (the appearance of red, blue, green, or anything in between), tone (the relative lightness or darkness of a color), and saturation (the relative strength or weakness of a color)." The vast majority of natural, fancy color diamonds are not particularly intense, but those rare diamonds that exhibit strength and purity of almost any hue have proven among the most valuable of gems.

The GIA's colored diamond grading system first describes the diamond's tone and saturation (both of which are, of course, hue dependent) with a grade of "fancy light," "fancy," "fancy intense," "fancy vivid," "fancy dark," or "fancy deep" and then assigns it one of 27 hue names. When they are known, the GIA grades of fancy color diamonds illustrated in this volume will be given in the captions.

BLACK DIAMOND

Surprisingly, there is no such thing as a true black diamond—a diamond with a black body color. In most cases, the black appearance is due to the presence of numerous dark or black inclusions, which are sometimes associated with fractures. The inclusions are commonly graphite although they can consist of other materials, including sulfides. In other cases "black" diamonds simply have a dark body color, usually deep brown. Their true colors become obvious when a fiber optic light is shone through the crystal. Since black diamonds have no variation in tone or saturation, the GIA uses only "fancy black" when grading these stones.

BROWN DIAMOND

Brown is the most common diamond color and is found in a range of intensities from very faint to very dark. With the exception of a few very large stones such as the 545.67-carat *Golden Jubilee* (the largest faceted diamond) and the 407.48-carat *Incomparable* diamond (cut from 890 carats of rough), brown diamonds were traditionally considered low grade and were sold for industrial uses. The opening of the **Argyle Mine** in Australia in the mid-1980s and the Australians' subsequent marketing campaign changed this trend. The public was introduced to terms such as *champagne*, *cognac*, and *chocolate* to glamorize diamond colors from pale to dark brown. The campaign has met with great success, particularly for a mine such as Argyle, for which 72 percent of its diamond output falls in the brown tones (Shigley et al. 2001).

Brown in diamonds is induced during episodes of plastic deformation, which typically take place after the initial crystallization stage, but while the diamonds are still being subjected to high pressures and high temperatures and before they reach the surface of the Earth. The most popular hypothesis is that deformation occurred during periods of kimberlite emplacement, while the diamond was carried to the surface (Robinson 1980, Wilson and Head 2007, Gurney et al. 2004, Howell 2009). However, such late development of color is not necessary, as the brown color is stable under mantle conditions (Smith et al. 2010). During deformation, stress is accumulated in diamond crystals along thin parallel lamellae, which are often referred to as *graining*.

Clusters of as many as 60 carbon atom vacancies produced by the deformation have been demonstrated to be responsible for the brown color, although the detailed mechanism of color formation is not known (Fisher et al. 2009). Other rarer origins for brown colors are also mentioned, such as the presence of defects associated with hydrogen, isolated nitrogen, the presence of "amber centers" or the presence of CO_2 (Fristch 1998, Massi et al. 2005, Hainschwang et al. 2008).

A brown color modifier is frequently displayed by many colored diamonds, for example, brownish-pink or brownish-orange diamonds are found in the market. This brown component significantly decreases the value of a diamond.

The Type IaAB, yellow *Oppenheimer Diamond*, 253.7 carats. Dutoitspan Mine, Kimberley, South Africa, discovered in 1964. Harry Winston presented the stone to the Smithsonian Institution in memory of Sir Ernest Oppenheimer. Smithsonian Institution collection (NMNH 117538), Chip Clark photo.

YELLOW DIAMOND

Yellow is probably the second most common color found in diamond; however, a strongly saturated yellow is rare. Intense yellow diamonds became popular as soon as South African mines began producing them in noticeable numbers. Well-known examples are the 128.53-carat *Tiffany Yellow* diamond mined in 1878 and the 253.7-carat rough *Oppenheimer* diamond mined in 1964. The former was found in the **Kimberley Mine** in Kimberley, South Africa, the *Oppenheimer* in the nearby **Dutoitspan Mine**.

The most common origin of yellow in diamond is the absorption of the N3 color center, a defect composed of 3 nitrogen atoms that are adjacent to a carbon vacancy (e.g., Collins 1982). These Type Ia diamonds are commonly referred to as *Cape* diamonds as they were first found in Cape Province, South Africa. Unless they are quite large, diamonds in this category do not typically present the most intense (vivid) yellow color. Isolated nitrogen atoms, which define the rare Type Ib diamonds, are responsible for the most saturated yellow stones, which are referred to as *Canary* diamonds (Collins 1982, Fritsch 1998, King et al. 2005).

In rare instances, natural yellow diamonds have such a strong green fluorescence that they appear green under direct sunlight or other intense light (Fritsch 1998). They are called *chartreuse* diamonds for the French liquor, or *green transmitter* diamonds, in spite of the fact that they emit rather than transmit green light. The luminescence is due to large numbers of H3 centers (two nitrogen atoms around a vacancy), which emits green light in Type Ia diamonds.

Fritsch (1998) also mentions yellow color centers such as hydrogen-related defects, which impart a brownish-yellow tint, and defects of unknown origin for which neither nitrogen nor hydrogen is seen with infrared spectroscopy.

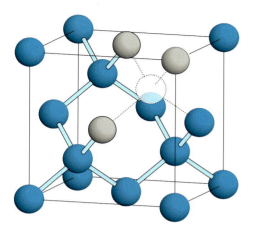

Carbon Vacancies in "Cape" and "Chartreuse" Diamonds

Above: The N3 center defect, responsible for the pale yellow of Type Ia "Cape" diamonds, is composed of 3 nitrogen atoms adjacent to a carbon vacancy.

Below: The H3 center defect, responsible for "chartreuse" yellow diamonds that luminesce green under intense light, is composed of two nitrogen atoms around a vacancy.

R. Peter Richards Graphics.

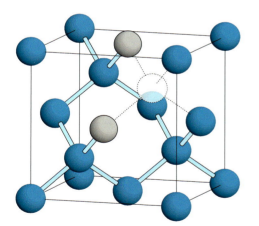

Above: The 132.55-carat *Golden Empress*, a cushion-cut, fancy intense yellow diamond, which was cut from rough found in the Letšeng Mine, Lesotho. The original, 299.35-carat rough diamond yielded the Golden Empress and eight satellite stones. Image courtesy of Graff Diamonds.

 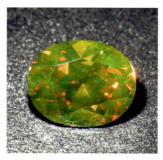 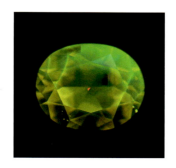 

A single, 2.076-carat "chartreuse" diamond from Brazil is shown under various lighting conditions (**from left to right**): Daylight (flash), spotlight (incandescent), shortwave ultraviolet, and longwave ultraviolet. American Museum of Natural History collection, Robert Weldon photos.

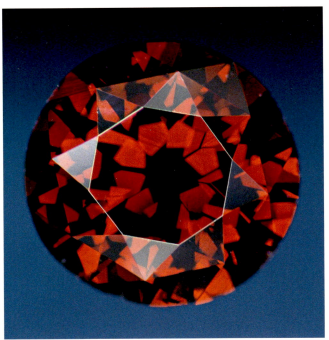

Left: Internally flawless, fancy vivid blue, cushion-shaped *Blue Moon of Josephine* diamond, 12.03 carats. The rough for this stone was recovered in January 2014 from the Cullinan Mine, South Africa.
Joseph Lau collection
Tino Hammid / Cora International photo

Middle left: The VS-2, Type IIa, *DeYoung* red diamond, 5.03 carats.
Locality unknown.
Smithsonian Institution collection (NMNH G9871), Chip Clark photo.

Middle right: Fancy intense pinkish purple, VS2 diamond, 3.37 carats.
South Africa
Leibish & Co. specimen
Ben Yagbes photo

Bottom: A range of pink diamonds that can be seen in Argyle tenders. From left, a 1.02 carat, purplish red (described by HRD); a 1.12 carat fancy vivid purplish pink (described by GIA); a 1.09 carat, fancy intense purplish pink (HRD); and a 0.64 carat fancy brownish red (GIA).
Robert Weldon photo.

PINK, RED AND PURPLE DIAMOND

Intense pink diamonds are as rare as their high value suggests, and the origin of the pink color remains unknown for most of them. There are two categories of natural pink diamonds. The first and most common are either Type Ia or Type IIa diamonds that exhibit heterogeneous color concentrated in the "pink graining," the colored lamellae or bands oriented normal to the (111) face. The color results from a broad absorption band centered around 550 to 560 nm within which most of the visible spectrum, except red, is absorbed (e.g., Collins 1982, Collins 2003, Fisher et al. 2009, Gaillou et al. 2010b).

Thus far, the cause of this absorption feature is unknown, but it has been associated with plastic deformation, which rearranges the diamond's structure, sliding the atoms along glide planes (*slipping*) and creating polysynthetic twinning along 111 (Titkov et al. 2008, 2012; Mineeva et al. 2009; Gaillou et al. 2010b). Even if the exact nature of the defect(s) is not known, various studies converge toward the idea that these defects involve nitrogen atoms, which are associated with vacancies located on or close to the twin planes (Gaillou et al. 2010b, 2012b; Byrne et al. 2012).

Purple and red diamonds are also included in the first group of pink diamonds. In Type Ia diamonds, a purple component is sometimes present when there is no or only a weak absorption at the N3 center. More blue light is thus transmitted, giving rise to the purple tint. Red diamonds are the most intensely saturated of the pink hues (King et al. 2002). They are the rarest members of an already rare color category.

Dissolution of rough diamonds is often marked by the presence of triangular surface features that are referred as *trigons*. They are found on the {111} (octahedral) faces of diamonds. Trigons mirror the image of the face. When trigons are present in rough pink (or even brown) diamonds, they are aligned along the deformation lamellae. They are particularly noticeable on purple and pink diamonds from mines such as the **Mir** and **Udachnaya** in Yakutia, Russia (see pages 96–99).

The second group of pinks consists of exceedingly rare Type IIa diamonds, the color of which originates from absorption by the NV centers, which involve one atom of nitrogen associated with one vacancy. These diamonds have a uniform, light pink color and were the first to be called *Golconda Pink* (Scarratt 1987, Fritsch 1998), a term which has been expanded to include all Type IIa diamonds, whether the color comes from plastic deformation or from the NV centers.

BLUE DIAMOND

Blue diamonds are extremely rare. The largest numbers come from the **Cullinan (Premier) Mine** in South Africa (see page 70–75) and from historical sources in India. Weighing 45.52 carats, the blue *Hope* diamond is the biggest and most famous blue diamond known (see page 6). Other famous blues include the *Wittelsbach-Graff* (31.06 carat) and the *Blue Moon of Josephine* (12.03 carats) diamonds.

The blue color in diamond is caused by boron substituting for carbon (e.g., Collins 1982) in the diamond structure. Boron has an electronic absorption that is strongest in the infrared region and tails into the visible red portion of the spectrum, giving rise to dominant transmission of blue color. A value-dampening gray component is sometimes observed in blue diamonds and is possibly related to defects caused by plastic deformation (Fisher et al. 2009, Gaillou et al. 2012b).

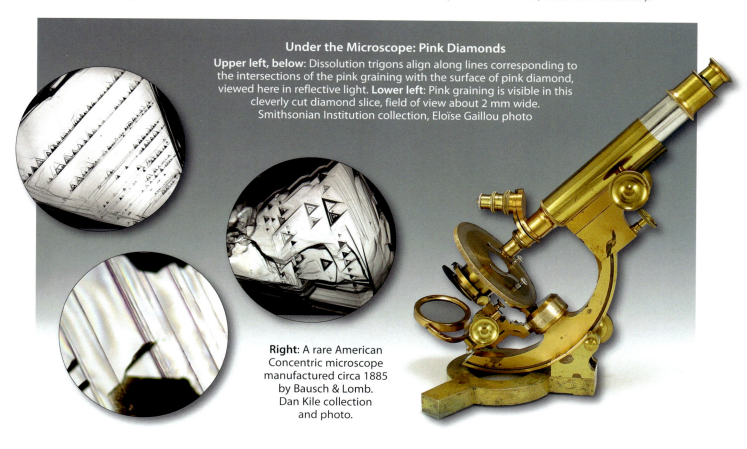

Under the Microscope: Pink Diamonds
Upper left, below: Dissolution trigons align along lines corresponding to the intersections of the pink graining with the surface of pink diamond, viewed here in reflective light. **Lower left:** Pink graining is visible in this cleverly cut diamond slice, field of view about 2 mm wide. Smithsonian Institution collection, Eloïse Gaillou photo

Right: A rare American Concentric microscope manufactured circa 1885 by Bausch & Lomb. Dan Kile collection and photo.

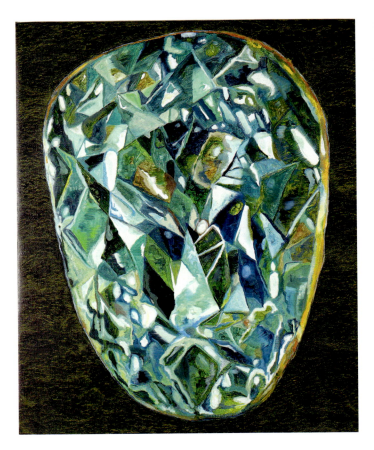

Above: The Dresden Green.
Artist Rasmus Nilausen's 2011 rendition of the famous 41-carat, Type IIa "Dresden Green" diamond, which dates back to 18th century India and is on display in the New Green Vault in Dresden Castle, Germany.
The painting is oil on linen and is in private hands.

Above: Green diamonds, 5.62 carats, total weight. Siberia, Russia.
Marty Zinn collection, Jeff Scovil photo.

Right: Green diamond, 0.85 carats, showing radiation spots produced when the diamond naturally came into contact with a direct source of radiation.
The specimen owner collected the diamond in a river deposit in Lençóis, Chapada Diamantina, Bahia, Brazil, in 2008.
Gerhard Brandstetter collection and photo.

GRAY TO BLUE TO VIOLET DIAMOND

A suite of gray to blue to violet diamonds that come exclusively from the **Argyle Mine** in Australia are rich in both hydrogen and nitrogen (Fritsch and Scarratt 1989, 1992, 1993; Fritsch et al. 1991, 2007a; van der Bogert 2009). These impurities result in the color suite indicated by broad absorption bands of variable intensities centered around 520–565 nm (with a superimposed 551-nm band) and 720–730 nm. Some of these absorptions are related to hydrogen defects (e.g., Fritsch et al. 2007a; Van der Bogert et al. 2009). For the more intensely violet diamonds, nickel-related defects might play an important role in the color (Van der Bogert et al. 2009).

These colors are not as rare as either boron blues or plastically deformed pinks. Well, at least not for as long as the Argyle Mine remains in production.

GREEN DIAMOND

Faceted green diamonds may not be as popular as blue or pink diamonds, but they might be even scarcer. Their rarity is due to the fact that the green color is usually concentrated on the "skin," the outermost layers, of a rough diamond. When that is the case, the faceting process removes the outer, colored crust. The green is due to natural irradiation, which creates vacancies in the diamond structure. The GR1 center is the defect related to a vacancy, which absorbs red and orange while transmitting blue and green. The resulting color can be teal, but most of the time, the blue component is reduced by the presence of the N3 center (frequent in Type Ia diamonds), which absorbs blue light. The 41-carat *Dresden Green* (left) is the most famous example of a green diamond. Housed at the New Green Vault (Neues Grünes Gewölbe) in Dresden, Germany, it was mined in India before 1722. It is of the rare IIa type and displays the teal component, which gives it incomparable appeal.

Radioactive elements such as uranium and thorium, which occur in the geologic environment with the diamonds, are the source of the radiation. The decay of these elements and their daughter products creates alpha-, beta-, and gamma-ray radiation. Only the gamma rays are able to penetrate deep enough into a diamond to give it a green body color. The alpha-rays produce radiation spots on the surface of a diamond (to about 25 μm deep) in the places where the radioactive element came into direct contact with it. Color from alpha-rays is most likely imparted after the emplacement of the diamond-bearing kimberlite at the surface of the Earth. If the diamond is heated to more than 600 degrees Celsius, the blue-green spots turn brown (Vance et al. 1973).

Fritsch (1998) mentions "exceedingly rare" diamonds, in which the green color comes from an absorption band at 720 nm and is related to hydrogen defects.

CHAMELEON DIAMOND

Named after the reptile, diamonds in this category change color from olive-green to yellow (lower right). The gray-yellow to yellow color of these stones is exhibited when they are kept in the dark for a week or more (photochromic phenomenon) or are heated to around 150 degrees Celsius for up to one minute (thermochromic phenomenon, Fritsch et al. 2007b). After being exposed to light for a minute or so, such diamonds turn olivine green. Interestingly, Fritsch et al. (2007b) asserts that yellow is the stable color of these diamonds, as it is their color before being excited by light. Hainschwang et al. (2005) noticed that, in a suite of 39 chameleon diamonds, yellow was metastable and green the stable color in eight of them. They referred to these eight as *reverse chameleon* diamonds.

Both the green and yellow colors are quantified by an absorption band at 480-nm and a broad band centered around 800 nm. When normal (versus reverse) chameleon diamonds are excited by visible light, the 800-nm absorption decreases, giving rise to a greater transmission of light in the yellow part of the spectrum. The exact nature of the defect is not fully understood, but Fritsch et al. (2007b) proposed that the chameleon effect could be related to an interaction between hydrogen atoms and A-aggregates (two nitrogen atoms).

ORANGE DIAMOND

The rarest diamond color of all may be pure orange, with no brown tint (right). The color is indicated by a broad absorption band at 480 nm that, when it is the only/dominant feature present, gives rise to the unusual orange color (Fristch 1998, Wang 2007). No specific defect associated with this color has been identified; however, a few reports suggest a possible correlation between the orange color and the presence of nitrogen, both isolated and in the A-aggregate form (Collins and Mohammed 1982; Fritsch 1998; Wang 2007, 2008). The 5.54-carat, fancy vivid orange, *Pumpkin* is the most famous pure orange diamond. It is privately held but has been part of a number of museum exhibits.

Above: When this fancy vivid orange, Type Ia, 14.82-carat diamond sold at auction in November 12, 2013, it set a record for the highest per carat price — $2,398,151 — paid for any colored diamond at auction. That record has since been broken. Image courtesy of Christie's, Geneva.

Below right: "Chameleon" diamond, 0.72 carats. In this composite image, the same stone is pictured on the **left** in natural light and on the right under intense light. Locality unknown.
Leibish & Co. specimen, Ben Yagbes photo.

Above: A 1.62-carat pink (**left**) with a 1.21-carat bluish-violet diamond (**right**), likely from the Argyle Mine, Australia. Eloïse Gaillou photo

Right: A 9.17-carat rough yielded the fancy deep greyish bluish violet, 2.83-carat *Argyle Violet* diamond. Argyle Mine, East Kimberley region, Western Australia. Photo © 2017 Rio Tinto.

The *Aurora Butterfly of Peace* diamond display under natural light (**above**) and ultraviolet light (**facing page**). Curated by Alan Bronstein, Robert Weldon photos © GIA.

LUMINESCENCE

The term *luminescence* refers to the emission of visible light by a material when the material is exposed to some kind of excitation. Ultraviolet light is a typical source of excitation, one that initiates the emission of light — fluorescence — by most diamonds. A few diamonds will continue to "glow" even after they are not longer being exposed to ultraviolet light. This phenomenon is known as "phosphorescence." Diamonds may also exhibit other kinds of luminescence such as cathodoluminescence, but these require other types of excitation, usually generated by laboratory equipment.

Thirty-seven percent of near-colorless diamonds fluorescence. Out of these, ninety-seven percent display blue fluorescence (Moses et al. 1997). The percentage of fluorescing colored diamonds has not been reported, but a comprehensive study on fluorescence in colored diamonds can be found in Eaton-Magaña et al. (2007). Blue fluorescence is also commonly seen in some colored diamonds, such as pink, white, and Cape-yellow diamonds. In both colorless and colored diamonds, the blue fluorescence is frequently due to the N3 center, which is very often associated with the "Blue-Band" defect. Also known as "Band A," the Blue Band is possibly related to dislocations (crystallographic defect) in the diamond structure and emits light in the blue spectrum (Iakoubovskii and Adriaenssens 1999).

Yellow-green emission is fairly common among brown and yellow-green diamonds. It is often due to the H3 center (two atoms of nitrogen around a vacancy), which is created during plastic deformation. Diamonds presenting an orange tint often display yellow fluorescence (Collins and Mohammed 1982, Eaton-Magaña et al. 2007).

Blue Type IIb diamonds never display fluorescence, but they are sometimes phosphorescent (e.g., Eaton-Magaña and Lu 2011, Gaillou et al. 2012). Most glow a faint blue-green for only a few seconds after exposure to ultraviolet light, especially short-wavelengths. In rare cases, the Hope and the Wittelsbach-Graff diamonds for example, blue diamonds may phosphoresce red and for more than one minute after the light source has been extinguished. While the exact nature of the blue-green and red phosphorescences are not completely understood,

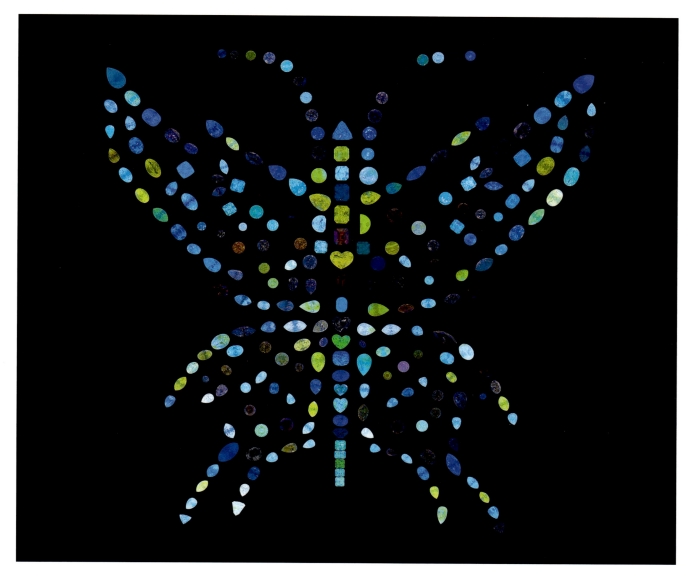

recent research suggests the phenomenon may in some way be brought about by the interaction of boron with other defects or impurities such that they create an acceptor-donor pair recombination.

PERSPECTIVES

Although diamonds are among the most treasured and studied materials on Earth, we do not fully understand the origins of all of their colors. The lack of understanding might be in part due to their rarity and value and thus the fact that samples are not always readily available to scientists. On the other hand, colored diamonds have not always been of interest to scientists or to the gem-buying public. There has long been a comparatively small market for colored diamonds, except among collectors. But that changed in 1987 when the 0.95-carat Hancock Red diamond sold at Christie's for US$880,000. That sale got the attention of both the diamond industry and the public (Alan Bronstein, pers. comm. 2013). The values of colored diamonds increased as did the public's interest and an obsession was sparked. Through further auction sales, museum exhibitions and marketing, public awareness has since grown. The rarity of colored diamonds is in part responsible for the astronomical prices that these special stones sometimes command, but the century-long diamond marketing campaign has no doubt also played a role. In November 2015, the highest per carat price ($48.4 million for a 12.03-carat stone) ever paid for a gem at an auction was fetched by a fancy vivid blue diamond — *the Blue Moon of Josephine* (pictured on page 48). Colored diamonds are decidedly in.

Eloïse Gaillou is the associate curator at the mineralogy museum of MINES ParisTech, formerly l'École des Mines de Paris. She received her PhD in Material Sciences at the University of Nantes (France), which she combined with a Diplôme d'Université de Gemmologie and began her work on natural treated diamonds and continued studying diamonds during her postdoc years. In her position at MINES, Dr. Gaillou oversees the collection of 100,000 mineral specimens and takes care of the permanent and temporary exhibits.

George R. Rossman is Professor of Mineralogy at the California Institute of Technology. After receiving his Ph.D. in chemistry at Caltech he joined their Division of Geological and Planetary Sciences where he now studies the origin of color of minerals and gems, the effects of irradiation on minerals, and analytical methods involving spectroscopy of minerals.

Etch figures of classic terraced trigons on an octahedral diamond crystal face illuminated and imaged by Nomarski differential interference contrast.
Field of view 1.1 mm wide. Kimberley, Northern Cape Province, South Africa.

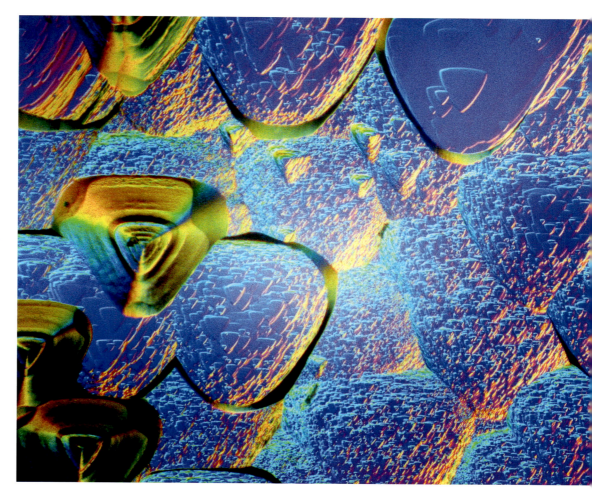

Right: Diamond, field of view 2.2 mm wide. Kelsey Lake, Larimer County, Colorado.

An astounding display of multiple trigon development on an octahedral face of a diamond crystal also using Nomarski differential interference contrast.

Lower right: Diamond, field of view 2.9 mm wide. Kelsey Lake, Larimer County, Colorado.

Polarized light accentuates microdisk patterns on a rounded dodecahedral crystal face, a surface feature resulting from post-resorption dissolution (etching).

All of the images in this article are the work of John Koivula.

DIAMOND: INTIMATE PORTRAITS

by John I. Koivula and Elise A. Skalwold

As one journeys from a diamond's surface into its interior, the crystal's life story unfolds; secrets of its genesis and that of the Earth's depths are revealed, while its enigmas beckon further investigation.

The microscope is arguably the most important instrument in the study of diamonds. Mastery of it combined with expertise in several areas of mineralogy including that of mineral physics, crystallography, and inclusion science, is essential for understanding the nature of diamonds and the geologic processes deep within the Earth. Diamonds are veritable messengers from one of Earth's last frontiers. We invite you to join us for a brief tour through the astounding beauty that is the microworld of diamond.

A FANTASTIC TERRAIN

The surface of a diamond crystal exhibits a variety of features, many of which remain subtle without the aid of lighting and filtering techniques. Surface features reflect the diamond's internal structure and bear witness to the environments in which the crystal grew and/or rode to the surface.

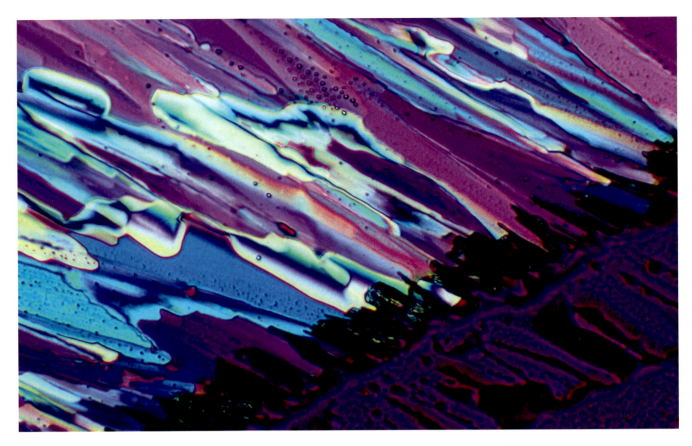

SUBSURFACE SURPRISES

Careful observation is the first step toward identifying inclusions trapped within diamond and in gemology often obviates the need for more advanced and sometimes destructive laboratory tests. Minerals trapped in diamonds can be beautiful and interesting indicators of the environments in which they formed.

Top: Iron compounds in diamond, field of view 2.1 mm wide. Argyle Diamond Mine, Western Australia.

A polarized light image of a surface-reaching cleavage plane, which allowed epigenetic crystallization of birefringent iron compounds in the diamond crystal.

Middle right: Void or "negative crystal" in diamond. Field of view 4.4 mm wide. South Africa.

This inclusion may fool one into thinking it is a solid when it is in fact a void that has assumed the diamond's cubo-octahedral habit. A small, etched dislocation tube extending from the surface to the negative crystal allowed corrosive radioactive fluids to enter the space and color the walls.

Left: Diopside in diamond, 3 mm wide. Locality Unknown.

While the interiors of diamond crystals are often partly obscured by surface features, polished gems may offer a more pristine view within, though as with this image, inclusions in cut stones can be multiplied by refraction and reflection. Framed by small tension cracks, this 0.3-millimeter diopside, the most saturated green inclusion in diamond, identifies its host's peridotitic origin.

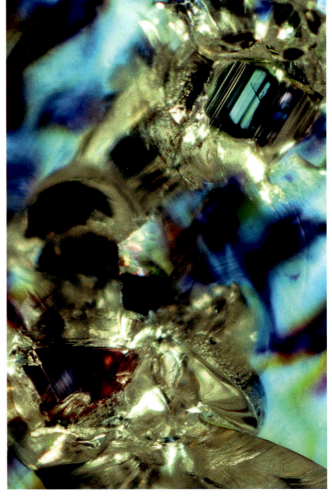

Top: Omphacite in diamond, field of view 1.2 mm wide. Locality unknown.

An elongate pale-green omphacite inclusion. Found only in eclogitic diamonds, omphacite's less than vibrant color helps to distinguish it from the more vibrantly colored peridotitic diopside.

Middle left: Olivine and graphite in diamond, 4 mm wide. Viewed through crossed polarizing filters. Locality unknown.

Hexagonal graphite plates along the inclusion-host interface are examples of carbon spots, which occur when the surface of the interface is parallel to the diamond cleavage plane.

Right: Diopside and pyrope in diamond, field of view approximately 1.5 mm. Yukatia, Sakha Republic, Russia. Dr. Nikolai Sobolev collection.

Surrounded by strain cracks and strain colors, both the diopside and pyrope crystals evidence, through the presence of triangular features on their surfaces, distortion or "xenomorphism" brought about by the pressure under which the diamond formed.

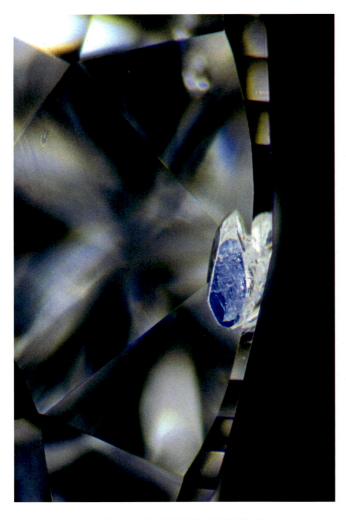

RARE GEMS FROM EARTH'S DEPTHS

The more rough and polished diamonds one examines, the more one realizes that while flaws such as cracks are common, distinctive colorful mineral inclusions are rare and are thus prized by scientists interested in planet formation and in studies of the Earth's interior.

Upper left: Corundum (variety sapphire) in diamond, field of view 4.3 mm wide. Locality unknown.

Exceedingly unusual, this diamond hosts several inclusions of vivid blue sapphire, one of which is seen here. The inclusion was identified using Raman and LA-ICP-MS analysis.

Upper right: Kyanite in diamond, largest crystal 0.4 mm long. Locality unknown.

Kyanite is found only in diamonds of eclogitic origin and is an unusual mineral inclusion in diamond. As is the case with many inclusions, depth of color is dependent on size: very small inclusions of kyanite might appear colorless.

Right, upper and lower: Unidentified inclusion in diamond. Inclusion is 0.4 mm wide. Diamantina, Minas Gerais, Brazil.

The rough, heavily etched surface of this diamond crystal prevents non-destructive identification of its inclusions. Using only a Polaroid analyzer, careful observation under the microscope seems to reveal dichroism as seen in the images. Could it be an extremely rare ruby inclusion? Or is it perhaps just a heavily strained garnet?

Above: Pyrope in diamond, field of view 2.2 mm wide. Yukatia, Sakha Republic, Russia.

As viewed between crossed polarizing filters, this diamond crystal hosts a deep red peridotitic chromium-rich pyrope surrounded by intense strain colors.

Right: Almandine-pyrope in diamond, 9 mm wide. South Africa.

One of the most recognizable inclusions in diamond is orange almandine-pyrope, a solid solution series garnet. This 0.9 mm crystal provides an unusually fine example and signifies its host's ecologitic origin.

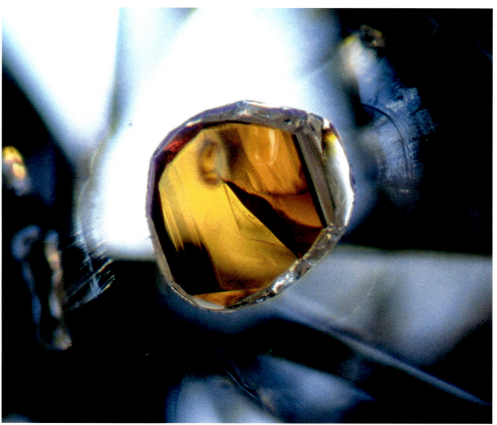

INTIMATE PORTRAITS 59

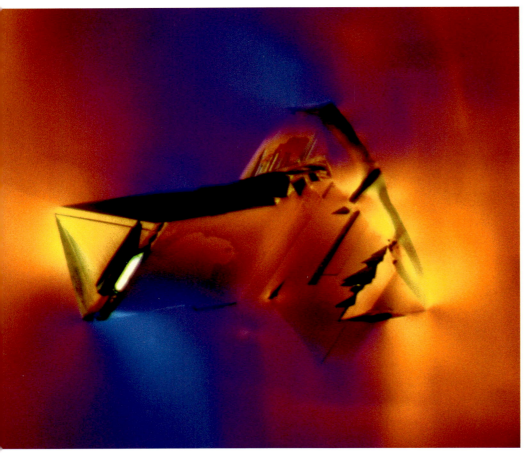

Left: Diamond in diamond. The inclusion is 0.8 mm long. Diamantina, Minas Gerais, Brazil.

Under crossed polarizing filters, the strain surrounding this misaligned, diamond inclusion is revealed. The portions of this inclusion that are virtually invisible are those that are in direct contact with their host. Other areas have a slight interfacial separation that renders them visible here.

Below: Hematite and goethite in diamond, 2.22 carat crystal. Botswana.

All eight octahedral faces of this unusual hematite and goethite phantom are clearly visible in this crystal. The phantom may have resulted from epigenetic alteration of an original iron sulfide inclusion.

Right: Included diamond. The cloud is 0.9 mm wide. Locality unknown.

The edges of a cubo-octahedral phantom in a diamond have been decorated with minute light-scattering inclusions to form a complex looking cloud. Fiber-optic illumination is often needed to clearly see such inclusions.

Lower left: Diamond in diamond, field of view 2.1 mm wide. Locality unknown.

This diamond hosts in its interior an unusual, elongated, low relief roiled-looking stringer of diamond crystals made visible using shadowing techniques.

Lower right: Phantom in diamond, field of view 2.9 mm wide. Locality unknown.

Due to the strain it produces, this stellate phantom in a faceted diamond is only visible microscopically in polarized light. The six distinct lobes or arms of the star are oriented toward the six octahedral points or tips of the host octahedron from which the diamond was cut.

PHANTOMS HAUNT THE MICROWORLD

Just because one doesn't see something, doesn't mean it isn't there: the subtlest micro-features in diamonds can be as intriguing as the boldest inclusions. Keys to examining and studying these subtleties include magnification, illumination, curiosity, and patience.

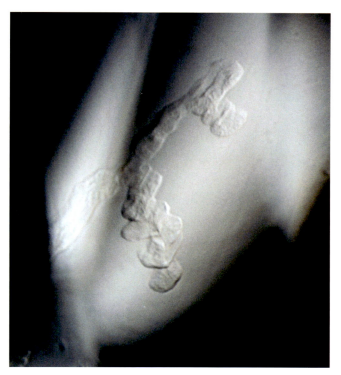

About the authors: John I. Koivula, B.S. is the Analytical Microscopist at the Gemological Institute of America and is a Fellow of the Royal Microscopical Society. A mineralogist, chemist and gemologist for more than 40 years, John is a world-renowned inclusionist and photomicrographer. In addition to hundreds of articles and papers, Mr. Koivula authored The MicroWorld of Diamonds and is co-author of the three-volume Photoatlas of Inclusions in Gemstones.

Elise A. Skalwold, B.Sc. is an Accredited Senior Gemologist involved in curating and research at her alma mater, Cornell University. She is a Fellow of the Gemmological Association of Great Britain (F.G.A.), and a member of the Society of Mineral Museum Professionals.

DIAMONDS AS GEMSTONES

by Dr. James Shigley

Diamond is the premier gemstone, and diamond jewelry is what most people think of first whenever the word is mentioned (Dundek 2009; Cunningham 2011). Although the early history of diamond is shrouded in mystery, this mineral has been recognized as a gem for more than two millennia. Octahedral-shaped diamond crystals, almost certainly of Indian origin, were set in gold rings in Roman times, and even at that time, they possessed both commercial and mystical value. After the decline of the Roman Empire, the use of diamond in jewelry continued on a limited scale in the Islamic world and in India for the next thousand years, and occasional references to this practice can be found in the published literature of that time.

The cutting and polishing of rough diamonds to create faceted gemstones appears to have originated in Europe in the late fourteenth century (Tillander 1995). Initially, primitive equipment and time-consuming polishing methods were used. Although diamonds were still limited in quantity in the marketplace, the development of improved cutting tools and techniques over the next few centuries allowed these gemstones to be shaped and polished in various simple designs. Such experiments with diamond cutting continued, and technical improvements were matched by increased understanding of how physical proportions influenced the optical appearance and beauty of cut diamonds.

The culmination of this process was the development in the late nineteenth century of what we know today as the modern round brilliant cut and other cut shapes that maximize the return of light through the upper facet surfaces toward the observer (Gilbertson 2007). When viewed face-up through the table and other crown facets, a polished diamond is normally described in terms of three major characteristics:

- *Brightness* — the amount of light reflected off the lower pavilion facets and returned through the upper crown facets;
- *Fire* — the appearance or extent of light dispersed into spectral colors;
- *Scintillation* — a combination of the appearance or extent of spots of light that flash as the diamond, the observer, or the light source moves (the "sparkle"), and the relative size, arrangement, and contrast of bright and dark areas that result from facet reflections (the "pattern").

The choice of particular cutting styles can also enhance the face-up appearance of a polished diamond and has a significant affect on its beauty and value.

Upper: A Roman gold and diamond finger ring set with several octahedral diamond crystals.
Courtesy of Benjamin Zucker. Photo by Richard P. Goodbody.

Middle: Gold and diamond finger ring with several table-cut diamonds.
Courtesy of Benjamin Zucker. Photo by Richard P. Goodbody.

Lower: Gold and diamond solitaire ring.
Courtesy of Rose Tozer. Photo by Robert Weldon © GIA.

Facing page: French cutter Atanik Ekyanan facted the 30.62-carat heart-shaped *Blue Heart Diamond* in the early 1900s. Harry Winston purchased the stone in 1959 and set it in a ring, which was purchased by Marjorie Merriweather Post, who in turn donated it to the Smithsonian Institution (Cat. No. G 4873).
Harold and Erica van Pelt photo

MODERN GEM DIAMOND MANUFACTURING

The process of cutting and polishing a diamond crystal or crystal fragment (termed *rough* in the industry) involves a thoughtful and thorough evaluation of the individual piece, since each possesses different attributes such as shape, size, and clarity (Suwa and Coxon 2010). During the manufacturing process, each piece requires decisions that will influence the final outcome of the polished gemstone. The manufacture of a faceted diamond involves inherent challenges:

- As one of the hardest known substances, diamond is a difficult gem material to cut; it only yields to polishing with other diamonds.
- Although optically isotropic, the hardness (or abrasion resistance) of diamond is anisotropic, and it varies with crystallographic plane (difficulty of polishing: {111} > {110} > {100}) (see page 34). Even on each of these three planes, diamond can be polished more easily along certain directions than others (traditionally referred to as the *grain*).
- Diamond has a very high refractive index (2.42) and as a result, a very narrow critical angle (24.41 degrees). The manufacturing process takes advantage of these properties to maximize the brightness of polished diamonds by reflecting as much light as possible from the pavilion up through the crown facets.

- The differences between the various quality grades of faceted diamonds can be subtle, and slight variations in cutting style and/or weight retention can all result in significant differences in a stone's value (see the discussion in Caspi 1997 and in Peters 2010).

Rough diamonds are typically sorted into various size, shape, color, and clarity categories and are then sold by weight. The objective of the cutting process is to obtain the maximum value for the potential faceted stone or stones. Historically this evaluation was made visually, but today it is commonly performed with the aid of optical imaging technology, which creates accurate three-dimensional models of the exterior of the rough as well as a map of internal clarity features. Software then analyzes the information and makes recommendations for manufacturing the finished diamond. The piece is either destined to become a single gemstone, or it is separated into smaller fragments, each of which will yield a cut stone. Historically, rough was separated by physically cleaving it along an octahedral {111} plane. But it could also be mechanically sawed along the cube {100} or dodecahedral {110} directions. Today, lasers may be used to separate the rough along any direction.

Whatever the process, the rough must be marked to show the location of the separation plane. This marking step is complicated, especially when the rough displays an irregular shape, is unevenly colored, or contains flaws or inclusions that may be difficult to see. The step is crucial, however, as more than any other decision, the marking step has the greatest impact on the value of the finished stones. If two cut stones are planned, the decision as to where to split the rough depends on economic factors that are greatly influenced by those shapes and sizes of polished diamonds currently popular in the marketplace.

The next step is termed *bruting* and is the point at which a diamond's basic shape (i.e., round, oval, etc.) is outlined. Today, this process is mainly accomplished using a machine that gradually brings two rotating diamonds into contact such that they are both progressively ground away by mutual abrasion until the desired shape outline is obtained. In some diamonds, the orientation of the cleavage plane of the crystal is not conducive to safely shaping the desired outline; in these cases, a laser is used in the bruting step.

Polishing is the final step in manufacturing a faceted diamond. The diamond is positioned in a *tang,* which is then used to hold it against a rotating metal plate, or *scaife.* This plate is lubricated with oil and is charged with diamond particles, which become embedded in the metal surface. The facets are placed one at a time in a specific order, with the operator regularly checking the quality of the polish of the facet as the process proceeds. As with the cleaving and sawing steps, a facet can only be polished in a certain direction, depending on the orientation of the grain.

High-quality cuts have symmetrically positioned and sized facets, flat polished surfaces, and overall good proportions. Minor variations in proportions such as the table size, crown and pavilion angles, and total depth percentage (ratio of depth to diameter) can have a major influence on the face-up appearance of the diamond and therefore its price.

In larger manufacturing facilities, machines automatically polish all of the facets according to a predetermined plan. Over the past several decades, the diamond industry has been revolutionized by the introduction of sophisticated equipment that performs each of these manufacturing steps. This equipment revolution, in combination with a better understanding of the relationship between diamond proportions and optimum appearance, has standardized the faceting process, making perfectly proportioned diamonds more readily available to consumers.

Above: Using a special holding tool, the diamond can be brought into contact with a spinning metal plate so that each of the flat facet surfaces can be created.
Courtesy of William Goldberg. Photo by Eric Welch © GIA.

Facing page, upper: Beginning with a triangular-shaped diamond "macle" crystal, this image shows the progressive stages of the manufacturing process to create a polished "trillion cut" diamond.
Courtesy J. Kleinhaus & Sons. Photo by Tino Hammid © GIA.

Facing page, middle: The 726.6-carat "Vargas" diamond, found in Brazil in 1938, is marked before cleaving and sawing.
Edmund B. Gerard photo

Facing page, lower: Historically, crystals or other pieces of diamond rough were split or cleaved along certain crystallographic directions using steel wedge and a hammer.
Photo © GIA.

EVALUATING GEM DIAMOND QUALITY

Various qualities of faceted diamonds are available on the market, and this variation is reflected in their market values. The basic framework for evaluating polished diamonds was established as a teaching tool for students by the Gemological Institute of America (GIA) in the 1940s and the early 1950s (Shipley and Liddicoat 1941, Liddicoat 1993). This system, known as the "4 Cs," evaluates polished diamonds in terms of their carat weight, color, clarity, and cut. Since its introduction, the GIA grading system and the associated grade terminology have become the internationally accepted standard for describing diamond quality in a way that can be understood by members of the jewelry trade and even many consumers.

In most instances today, polished diamonds of any value are bought and sold with a grading report from GIA or other gemological laboratories. These reports do not provide a monetary value for a diamond, but the quality grades are closely associated with value in the jewelry trade. Slight differences in any of the four attributes can mean significant differences in commercial value.

The easiest to describe of the 4 Cs is carat weight, which is a direct measurement of the gem's weight on an electronic balance. Color grading is a visual assessment observing the diamond under controlled lighting and viewing conditions and comparing it to the colors of stones in a reference set of *masterstones* (King et al. 2008). For color grading, diamonds are viewed through the bottom pavilion facets, where there are fewer reflections to hinder accurately seeing the body color of the stone (the trained observer is actually judging the relative absence of coloration, or how colorless the diamond appears). The diamond is usually placed on a white plastic tray between pairs of masterstones, which bracket the color of the diamond under investigation. A truly colorless diamond is designated as being a *D color*. Progressively more yellow stones are given grades further down the alphabet to the letter "Z." At the GIA Laboratory, a proprietary instrument is used to measure the color of diamonds below a certain carat weight; this information provides a confirmation of the color grade established by visual observation.

Most diamonds are colorless to pale yellow or pale brown, but on rare occasions they occur in a range of colors (King 2006, Rachminov 2009). These colors are caused by the presence of impurities such as nitrogen, boron, and hydrogen, as well as what scientists refer to as *optical defects*, in the diamond crystal lattice (see pages 40–53).

Diamonds with a stronger coloration, the so-called *fancy color* diamonds, are graded using a similar procedure, but they are viewed through the upper crown facets in order to better assess the intensity of the color (King et al. 1994). The color grade consists of a hue name (yellow, blue, pink, etc.) combined with fancy grade terms, such as *Fancy Vivid* or *Fancy Intense*, which provide a description of both the relative weakness and strength (the saturation) and lightness or darkness (the tone) of the color.

Fancy color diamonds are among the most valuable gemstones; retail prices of colors such as blue, pink, green, orange, and red can in some instances reach $100,000 per carat or more. Prominent auctions in recent years have witnessed sales of individual colorless and colored diamonds for millions of dollars (Rachminov 2009, Shor 2013)

Flaws and inclusions influence clarity, appearance, and in extreme cases, durability. The clarity grade is a way of

E

H-I

K-L

Z

describing where a diamond falls on a flawless-to-imperfect scale (Roskin 1994, Peters 2010). There are eleven clarity grades, each with a particular name and abbreviation. Assignment of an appropriate clarity grade is based on a trained observer's careful examination of the diamond at 10x magnification. The size and number of "clarity features" are noted, along with their position within the stone, nature, color, or relief (the difference in contrast between the feature and the diamond). Taken together, these factors determine the clarity grade. Flawless diamonds are rare and can be quite expensive. Subtle differences in the visibility and nature of clarity features exist among the upper grades on the clarity scale, whereas these features become more obvious at the lower grades.

The final quality attribute is cut, which describes how well the diamond performs in returning a pleasing pattern of light to the observer. In 2006 the Gemological Institute of America launched a cut grading system for standard round brilliant diamonds with color grades on the D-to-Z scale (Moses et al. 2004). The system uses five cut grades from Excellent to Poor. A cut grade for a round brilliant diamond is determined by a combination of measured proportion parameters, in conjunction with visual observations of the symmetry and polish, by trained individuals under controlled lighting and viewing conditions. Each of the five cut grades includes a variety of proportion combinations. A round brilliant diamond can exhibit the best color and clarity grades, but it must also possess an excellent cut grade to display the optimum appearance. A wide variety of diamonds with so-called fancy shapes, such as marquise, oval, and pear, exists in the marketplace, but the trade has not adopted a standard cut grading system for them.

Top, this and facing page: Fancy color diamonds from the Aurora Butterfly of Peace Diamond Collection, ranging from 0.62 to 2.00 carats. Courtesy of Alan Bronstein and Aurora Gems. Photo by Robert Weldon © GIA.

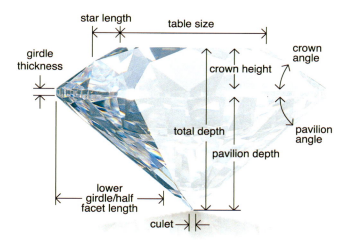

Above: Measurements used to evaluate the cut of a round brilliant diamond. Graphic © GIA.

Facing page, lower: Diamond color is evaluated by examining the diamond under controlled lighting in a special neutral-gray viewing box, and by comparing it to several "masterstones" (such as those shown here) according to the diamond grading procedure developed by GIA in the 1950s. A series of letters starting with "D" (for colorless) is used to designate the color grade. Photo by Tino Hammid © GIA.

Below: Seven of the most common diamond fancy shapes. International Gemological Institute photo

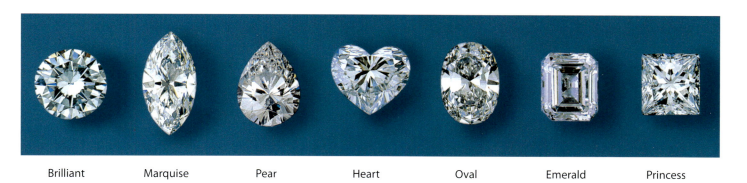

Brilliant Marquise Pear Heart Oval Emerald Princess

DIAMOND IDENTIFICATION

At the time of retail sale, jewelers have legal and ethical responsibilities to disclose information to the consumer about the diamonds and other gemstones that they sell. In the case of diamonds, these disclosures may include whether a diamond's clarity or color has been artificially enhanced or whether the stone is natural or synthetic. Reports issued by the GIA and other major gem-testing laboratories contain this information.

Diamonds that have been treated to improve their clarity or color are regularly encountered in the jewelry trade (Overton and Shigley 2008, Shigley 2008). Those with surface-reaching cleavage fractures are sometimes treated with a special type of glass which fills the opening and makes the fracture much less visible; thus improving the appearance of the diamond. This kind of treatment is not permanent, and if a filled diamond is accidentally heated during jewelry repair, the glass can be damaged and its appearance changed.

Diamonds sometimes contain mineral inclusions that lower the clarity grade. In such instances, a laser can be used to burn a narrow open channel from the surface to the inclusion. Acids are then forced under pressure through the channel and can dissolve or lighten the inclusion. Detection of both these clarity-enhancing treatments can be made visually using a binocular microscope or sometimes only a 10x loupe.

More permanent color treatments, again to give diamonds more saleable colors, have been used commercially since the late 1940s. One of the oldest treatments involves applying a surface coating to a faceted diamond to change its color. Modern variations of this process are currently in use, but because the coating material is softer than diamond, scratches or other damage to the coating can often be seen under magnification.

Other color treatments typically involve exposing diamonds to radiation, followed in some cases, by heating to a moderate temperature. The fact that a colored diamond has been exposed to a source of radiation can be established by advanced gem-testing methods, but it is not always possible to ascertain whether this exposure occurred naturally in the earth or if it was a result of a treatment process. Moreover, the colors of irradiated diamonds can be altered if the stones are subjected to heat during jewelry repair procedures.

ROBERT M. SHIPLEY, SR. (1887–1978)

Both ethics and knowledge are necessary to protect the consumer. A knowledgeable gemologist, without ethics, can cheat the customer by misrepresentation, while the most ethical jeweler can innocently mislead the customer because of a lack of knowledge.
— Robert M. Shipley, Sr.

Born in Missouri in 1887, Robert M. Shipley was a middle-aged man on a mission when, in 1931, he founded the Gemological Institute of America to "professionalize the jewelry trade through education."

Less than a decade before, Shipley had been a successful Wichita (Kansas) jeweler. But in the mid-1920s, he and his wife divorced, Shipley sold the business and moved to Paris. Through his work as a jeweler, Shipley had been confronted with the limits of his knowledge of gemstones, and friend Beatrice Bell prodded him to enroll in a gemology correspondence course given by Britain's National Association of Goldsmiths.

The public did not have a great deal of confidence in jewelers in the early twenty-first century; indeed when Shipley and Bell returned to the United States in 1929, he was one of only a handful of trained gemologists in the world. Shipley and Bell married in 1930. Trying to jumpstart a career, Shipley did some consulting and even wrote a book about gemology, but it was not until the autumn of 1930 when San Diego jeweler Armand Jessop asked Shipley to give a series of 10 gemology lectures that he found his niche.

The success of the lectures and ensuing demand prompted Shipley, in early 1931, to open the Gemological Institute of America in a small office in Los Angeles. The "GIA" offered laboratory testing services as well as on-site and mail order gemology courses. In the decade that followed — the Great Depression, mind you — Robert and Beatrice Shipley established the GIA as the world leader in gemological education and and later with the help of Richard Liddicoat and others, developed the diamond quality grading system. In 1934, the Shipleys also founded the American Gemological Society (AGS), a professional guild with the goal of protecting consumers from fraud.

Further revolutionizing the industry, Shipley's son Robert Jr., invented the optical and later the electronic colorimeters, a universal motion immersion stage, a pocket refractometer, the polariscope, and a gemological polarizing microscope — instruments all specifically designed for jewelers.

With an eye always on the customer, the Shipley family professionalized the jewelry trade, creating lasting standards and an uncommon ethical basis for a market that has for millennia been rife with fraud. As Richard Liddicoat, Shipley's successor at the GIA, remarked on Shipley's retirement in 1952, "His influence will continue to affect the industry for centuries to come."

Above: Zirconium oxide ("cubic zirconia") is a popular diamond substitute. This 22.41-carat stone was cut by Viktor Tuzlukov and photographed by Tino Hammid.

Left: An array of diamond colors can be achieved by exposure to radiation. These diamonds, weighing from 0.12-1.38 carats, were exposed to irradiation and, except for the blue and green stones, subsequent heat treatment. Photo by Robert Weldon © GIA.

Heating under very high pressures and temperatures changes certain brown diamonds to colorless, or it can give them a more attractive color. The colors of these so-called HPHT-treated diamonds are stable, and sophisticated scientific instrumentation is often required to detect them.

Small numbers of synthetic diamonds are being grown today for jewelry use (Shigley 2005). The traditional method involves growing diamond by a metal flux method at very high pressures and temperatures (HPHT growth). A newer method involves growth of thin plates of diamond in a vacuum chamber by a process known as *chemical vapor deposition* (CVD). By these methods, colorless and colored faceted synthetic diamonds have been produced to several carats in size. Lab-created diamonds are discussed in greater detail beginning on page 114. While synthetic diamonds sometimes display distinctive features that a gemologist can look for, positive identification often requires examination by a gemological laboratory (see Shigley, Breeding, and Shen 2004).

Because of diamond's historic importance as a gemstone, a number of less-expensive imitation materials are used as substitutes. However, these imitation materials display different physical and optical properties, such as hardness and refractive index, relative to properties of the real thing. The most widespread imitations in the market today are zirconium oxide ("cubic zirconia") and silicon carbide ("moissanite"). The former can be distinguished from diamond on the basis of thermal conductivity, which can be checked with a hand-held meter. The latter is not optically isotropic (unlike diamond), and the back facet junctions appear to be doubled when a cut stone of moissanite is viewed under magnification.

FINAL COMMENTS

With a celebrated history spanning hundreds of years, diamonds remain the most desired and sought-after gemstone. Gem diamonds, either loose or mounted in jewelry, are the foundation of most retail gemstone sales. While the majority of diamonds sold are in the colorless to near-colorless ranges, diamonds with attractive colors also command very high prices. Within the jewelry trade today, diamonds are bought and sold through a common language of quality grades.

By purchasing a gemstone with a laboratory grading report and examining prices via the Internet, consumers can be assured of the quality of the diamond and that it is both natural (as opposed to synthetic), and not laboratory-treated to change its color or clarity. It is becoming increasingly common for an eye-visible, laser-inscribed identification number, personal message, or company logo to be placed on the girdle surface of the diamond, thereby providing an additional means of identifying an individual stone. Positively identifying certain synthetic and treated diamonds continues to present some challenges, but these difficulties are the focus of much current gemological research.

Dr. James Shigley is a distinguished research fellow at the Gemological Institute of America in Carlsbad, California. Prior to joining GIA in 1982, he studied geology at the University of California Berkeley and at Stanford University. He was the director of research at GIA from 1985-2005 and has been closely involved with the Institute's research program on gem materials.

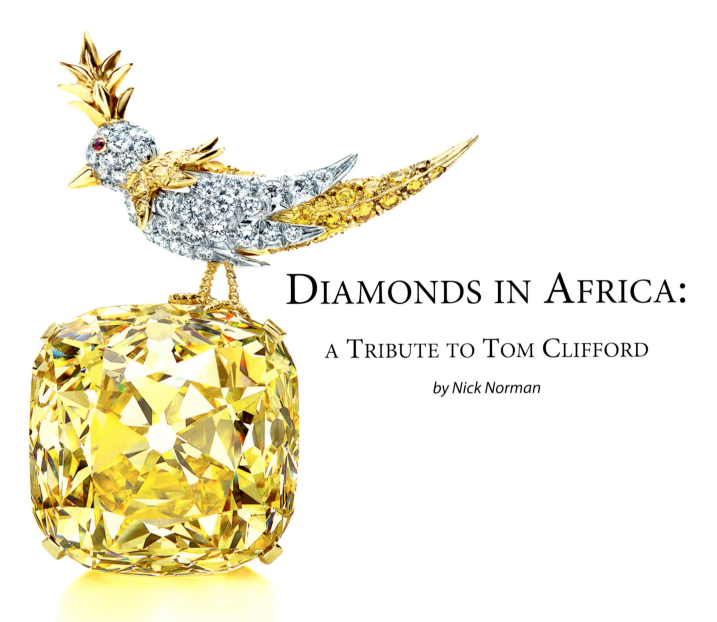

Diamonds in Africa:

a Tribute to Tom Clifford

by Nick Norman

Africa has produced more diamonds than any other continent, and it continues to be the world's most important supplier of both gem-grade and industrial diamond. The continent claims other superlatives as well: the biggest gem diamond ever found, the most "mega-diamonds" (exceeding 300 carats) produced, the biggest productive kimberlite pipe, the most alluvial diamonds mined, and the only substantial coastal and offshore alluvial diamond fields. Africa is the place where kimberlite was first identified as the mother lode of diamonds and where the recognition came to light that, as a general rule, only kimberlite that formed below the deepest continental roots has the potential to carry economically viable grades of diamonds. In any global treatise on diamonds, Africa holds a special place.

Fasten your seatbelts. The next few pages will take you through a dizzying succession of countries and will speed you from the middle of the nineteenth century to today in less time than you have to catch your breath. Before we start though, for those of you not deeply immersed in the diamond business, let me introduce our traveling companion, Tom Clifford. In 1966 — nearly 50 years ago — as a young geologist analyzing the distribution of minerals in Africa, Clifford discovered an association that would change the way geologists and companies prospect for diamonds. He observed that all of the productive primary (kimberlite-hosted) diamond deposits were in those parts underlain by ancient, deep-rooted continental nuclei called *cratons*.

Since that time the first question geologists and savvy company directors ask when a new diamond exploration project is proposed is, "Is it on-craton?" If not, even though there may be kimberlite pipes by the dozen, they will be sterile. Some time after Tom's paper disclosing the association of cratons and fertile kimberlite pipes had been published, a young geologist returned from a conference in Russia and asked him whether he knew that those in the business were now talking of *Clifford's Rule*. Tom was astonished. I count it a real privilege to have known Tom, who was always charming and entertaining company and full of humility.

Above: An 1871 view of the early but rapidly growing Kimberley diggings in South Africa. Image courtesy of the De Beers Group.

Facing page: The 128.54-carat, *Tiffany* diamond set in designer Jean Schlumberger's *Bird on a Rock* brooch. The *King of Diamonds*, Charles Lewis Tiffany reportedly paid $18,000 in 1878 for the 287.42-carat rough, which had been recovered from the Kimberley Mine earlier that year. Gemologist George Frederick Kunz, supervised the stone's cutting. Tiffany & Co. photo.

A BRIEF HISTORY OF DIAMONDS IN AFRICA

If there is a pre-colonial history of African diamonds, which there may well be, it is undocumented. There is a suggestion that early hunter-gatherers along what is known now as the Orange River may have used diamonds to shape stones that were part of their foraging inventories. If this was the case, all that can be said with regard to timing is that they were used hundreds or perhaps thousands of years ago. Folklore elsewhere in Africa might disclose similar employment of diamond, but that part of diamond's history remains open to speculation.

What is beyond doubt is that it is in the dusty plains of southern Africa that the established historical narrative opens. Even here there are shadowy stories of a diamond that was discovered before the *Eureka* diamond was found along the southern bank of the Orange River in the mid-1860s, but we will confine ourselves here to known facts. Retrieved from a collection of children's playthings by a curious adult and displayed on the mantelpiece in the farmhouse where it had been found in late 1866, the stone was spotted by a passing trader, who mentioned his suspicion that might be a diamond and asked if he could take it for identification. In an act of faith that may have characterized the owner of the stone or simply a bygone age, the farmer agreed and after a journey of many weeks and several stops, the stone landed in the metropolis of Grahamstown in the far east of the Cape Colony. When it scratched a friend's ruby ring, local doctor and amateur geologist William Guybon Atherstone confirmed that the stone was indeed a diamond.

Left: By 1903, innumerable wires had been strung across the Kimberley Mine, and aerial trolleys carried men and materials in and out of the rapidly deepening pit. Image courtesy of De Beers.

Below: Africa's first authenticated diamond, the 21.25-carat *Eureka Diamond* was found in 1866 near the Orange River by 15-year-old Erasmus Jacobs; the 10.73 carat brilliant-cut gem shown was cut from the Eureka. Kimberley Mine Museum specimen and photo.

Facing page: The 47.69-carat *Star of South Africa* in a Cartier setting. The historic stone was cut from an 83.5-carat piece of rough that was discovered in 1869 on the banks of the Orange River by a Griqua herdsman.
Private collection. Cartier photo.

Background: Now defunct, the Kimberley Mine, the *Big Hole* is filled with water.
Eureka Hyman photo, 2008.

Compared to the Eureka's 20½ carats and sale price of £500, the next stone acquired by the same farmer two years later in 1869, from a wandering shepherd, was a life-changing 83½ carats with a realized value of £11,200. The *Star of South Africa* can be credited with triggering Africa's first, but by no means its last, diamond rush.

The search moved quickly from the Orange River to its main tributary, the Vaal, where diamonds were found in much greater concentration. The lower reaches of this river, extending just 50 kilometers above the confluence, were to witness one of the great scrambles for nature's shiny treasures in the annals of prospecting.

Five years after the Eureka discovery, the first small stones were found where, clearly, no river had brought them. "What was this?" The bemused diggers asked themselves and each other. Not overly concerned with questions geological, they kept digging in the strange yellow clay, wondering only where the boulders were that they would have to heft out of prospecting pits and mines along the rivers. Soon enough, as yellow clay turned to pale brown, then gray, then blue, they started to encounter solid blocks. These were not the polished rounded pebbles they were used to, though, and there was no sign of the hard bedrock base which lay below the boulder gravels in the river diggings. The rock was getting harder to be sure, but progressively the sharp contact between loose and solid that they were so familiar with was absent. As they continued to dig,

Mining Magnates
Left: Cecil John Rhodes, circa 1900.
Right: Sir Ernest Oppenheimer in 1917.

they started to find solid material with diamonds in it. In the end they had no option but to believe, miracle of miracles, that they had found the mother lode. What had eluded diamond diggers for a thousand years, they had discovered.

One of the early deposits of yellow ground was called "New Rush," which is just what it was: a hitherto unknown kind of stampede, where an Australian twang or Californian drawl was as likely to be heard as the Dutch or English of earlier days. The diamonds were confined to a particular kind of ochre-colored clay, with no boulders to guide diggers to prospective ground, and beyond the perimeters of the roughly circular areas, nothing. There was no water for washing the dirt or themselves, nor riverine scrub to chop down and burn at the end of the day when stomachs grumbled for grilled venison and boiled potatoes. Diamonds there were though, in untold profusion compared to the river diggings. Thus was the town of Kimberley born and with it the name for the mysterious rock — kimberlite — the likes of which had never been seen before.

At about the same time another name came into diamond parlance which would soon be on everyone's lips: "De Beers." The farm on which two of the new mines were situated was called *Vooruitzicht* (meaning "prospect"), a Dutch name too difficult for the quick reference often required. The farm's owner Johannes Nicolaas de Beer, though never more than an incidental player in the story, offered, inadvertently, the solution: one of the mines became the De Beers Mine, the other the Kimberley Mine. With diamonds reaching northern markets like never before, the stability of pricing, critically dependent on the fragile balance between supply and demand, was threatened. It became manifestly obvious that centralized control was essential. In the free-for-all melee that was early Kimberley, that control was effectively up for grabs. After a hard-fought tussle with archrival Barney Barnato, Cecil John Rhodes emerged victorious with all four Kimberley mines under the ownership of the De Beers Consolidated Mines Limited and thus in his control. Rhodes had sown the seed of the most enduring and effective monopoly of all time.

But it was only a beginning. Major producers outside of the Kimberley area, particularly the **Premier Mine** in the former Transvaal (present-day Gauteng) and Jagersfontein in the former Orange Free State (present-day Free State), though complying with marketing arrangements for their own good as well as that of the industry, were nevertheless marginalized. It took the genius and patient dedication of diamond buyer-turned-entrepreneur Ernest Oppenheimer to amalgamate all of the important kimberlite mines in South Africa into a single entity — the De Beers Group.

Ironically it was his acquisition of mining rights beyond the borders of the Union of South Africa that paved the way for Oppenheimer to become chairman of De Beers. Operating through his recently formed Anglo American Corporation which was created to consolidate his gold-mining interests on the Witwatersrand, Ernest Oppenheimer was able in 1920 to purchase, from German owners, the diamond mining rights over a huge swath of the Namib Desert in a corner of South-West Africa (present-day Namibia and formerly German South-West Africa) defined by the Orange River and the Atlantic Ocean in South-West Africa.

But it was only in 1927, after Oppenheimer had acquired practically exclusive rights over a large block of ground in adjacent South Africa, that the value of his purchase started to become evident. Earlier that year an extensive diamond field had been discovered along the coast of Namaqualand, immediately south of the Orange River. Disparate ownership had been consolidated and acquired by aging German geologist and prospector Hans Merensky, who soon saw that realization of his asset would require the energy and drive of a man younger than himself. With iconic vision and perhaps a modicum of good luck, Oppenheimer jumped at the opportunity.

I say that Lady Luck may have had a hand in events because until the Namaqualand discovery, no one had dreamt of what lay beneath the thick dune sand north of the river. Using converted Sherman tanks, Oppenheimer's Consolidated Diamond Mines of South-West Africa started stripping sand. Below it the miners found boulder gravels of fossil beach deposits high above the present shoreline. In the next 80 years, well over 100 million carats of the best quality gem diamonds would be discovered beneath those beguiling dunes. Ernest

Oppenheimer's acquisition of Merensky's rights must surely rank as one of the greatest mining acquisitions of all time.

Apart from its own intrinsic value, though, the discovery brought Ernest Oppenheimer onto the board and soon into the chair of De Beers. Without the acumen of generations of Oppenheimers (after Ernest, son Harry, then grandson Nicky), there can be no doubting that diamonds would never have become the industry we know today, when the brightest, most enduring stone known to man enjoys value and appreciation to match its physical properties.

It is because events in southern Africa over the 60 years straddling the turn of the century have shaped the diamond industry, not only in Africa but worldwide, that this part of the world has been accorded what might seem like disproportionate attention in this short piece. That said, books could be written about the unfolding of the diamond narrative in Namibia, the Congo, Tanzania, Sierra Leone, Angola, Lesotho and Botswana. And all would be filled with colorful stories and outrageous characters. Space does not permit, however, and the following brief résumé allows coverage of only the most salient features of the main diamond-producing countries in Africa. At this juncture it suffices to say that, although the story roams far and wide in Africa, it ends, for our purposes, close to where it started. The last major discovery was Jwaneng, in southern Botswana, only 500 kilometers from Kimberley. Appropriately, De Beers made that discovery.

In concluding this historical sketch, let us revisit two aspects which emphasize dramatically the pivotal role Africa has played in the world of diamonds. First, all exploration by mining companies seeks the source of whatever commodity is sought, and diamonds are no exception. Centuries of diamond mining in India and Brazil had failed in this quest: it took a mere five years in the dawn of the industry in South Africa for the hitherto obscure holy grail — the *blue ground* or kimberlite — to be found. Secondly, it was the geological map of Africa that unlocked the next mystery, one that had perplexed explorers and miners for decades: Why were entire fields of kimberlite pipes sterile?

It was Tom Clifford, working on the geology of the entire continent of Africa, who provided the key. He showed that only those kimberlites that had penetrated the most ancient continental nuclei carried diamonds. It was a revelation that triggered the research that would show that the mantle below the deep-rooted cratons contained the small pockets which came to be known as the *diamond stability field*. Kimberlites form widely, but only those pipes starting below these pockets, where the combined pressure and temperature are such to allow gestation of carbon into gems, were able to sample those coveted wares in their express ascent to the surface. Elsewhere the cupboard was bare.

As to the reasons for the geographic spread of fertile pipes in Africa, the fabulous richness of mines like Jwaneng and the fact that two out of every three mega-diamonds ever found have come from Africa, the jury is still out.

In the following sections, ten major African diamond-producing countries will be briefly reviewed. They are presented in chronological order, based on the date of diamond discovery in each.

SOUTH AFRICA

Although currently ranked as the fourth largest producer in Africa, South Africa opens this discussion because it is here that diamonds were first found on the continent. If ever a company has been linked to a commodity, it is South African-based De Beers' link to diamond. Several of the great gems in the British monarch's regalia were faceted from a single stone — the 3,106-carat *Cullinan* — which dwarfs the next biggest ever found, namely the still huge 995-carat *Excelsior*, which by the way is also from South Africa (Jagersfontein). Indeed, South Africa is home of many of the big mines whose names echo down the corridors of diamond history: Kimberley, De Beers, Jagersfontein, Koffiefontein, Premier, Finsch, Venetia. Three of the mines in Kimberley — Dutoitspan, Bultfontein, and Wesselton — are actively being mined today, deep underground, more than 140 years after they were first opened. Diamond is a proud legacy of South Africa.

---

around them. At the cessation of hostilities we went Oversears. Father's impaired health
 Return we started life at Cullinan Diamond Mine. Only a few white families settling into tents. Heat dust and very few amenities. Premoier Mine life provided me with my earliest memories. We led a life
of freedomon a koppie without even a path. Barefoot we scampereddown to the only stream taking back branches of blue-gum which we packed tightly into buckets Paraffin tins? and arranged t hem next to Mother's beautifyl curtains of blue brocade. Besides being decorative the smell of the blue gums Eucalyptus discouraged flies .The tent was huge and with scarlet linings. I fancy my father had purchase it as war time Army goods. Their huge double bed rested very elegantly on a thick ;layer of sand.I remember one morning seeing my Mother crying bitterly, being comforted by by my father. Poor soul our enjoyment of veld life only meant hardship for he r in the shocking heat which we were bound to end. One daybefore I had started School my Fatter rushed down the hill calling my M. to come at once with the three children. In starched pinafores-- how these were produced under those difficult circumstances I do not know but presently all of the few families working on the Mine were assmebled
 at the washing tables. All empoyees were assembled there and the Manager Mr. Donald McHardy saidthat a large diamond had been found of g reat value. The Mine employees rugged sunburnt men in thin shirts and pants heavy boots. Wide felt hats.
The announcement meant little to me but I was amazed to find my father at my side urging me forward to the long sloping table underzinc roof supported by poles.
M The Manager placed a tiny stone in my left hand and a very large one in the right.
My father supported my hand as I held the Cullinan Diamond in my rather small paw.
the discovery of this gem created g reat
 interest around the world. The biggest
 diamond in the world! Several times I have had the pleasure of visiting the tower
 in London where the Royal Crown and Orbs reflect back to me , reminding me of a very hot day in the Transvaal when it was put into my given me to hold, a little freckled maid of five .

Serendipity, while writing a book on diamonds, the author was introduced to Gladys Snaddon (née Brown) who had just discovered some pages of reminiscences in her mother-in-law's papers which referred to an incident in her youth related to the Cullinan Diamond. She was good enough to arrange for her daughter Jiggs Snaddon-Wood to photocopy the relevant pages. This entry appears courtesy of Gladys and Jiggs.

South African Stunners

Above: A circa 1935 photo of actress Shirley Temple holding the 726-carat *Jonker* diamond rough, which Johannes Jacobus Jonker had discovered on January 17, 1934, in the Elandsfontein Mine, adjacent to the Premier Mine. Harry Winston purchased the Jonker the following year. He publicized the stone by displaying it in venues across the country and inviting celebrities to pose with it. Photo courtesy of Harry Winston Inc.

Upper right: The 2.6-carat *Cullinan Blue* diamond is set in a double-ribbon bow pendant, part of a necklace presented, circa 1910, by Thomas Cullinan to his wife Anne. The diamonds were sourced in Mr. Cullinan's Premier Mine, Gauteng Province. Smithsonian Institution collection (NMNH G10592-00), Chip Clark photo.

Middle right, upper: The 545.67-carat "fancy yellow-brown," *Golden Jubilee* diamond was cut by De Beers' Gabriel Tolkowsky from a 755.5 carat brown crystal found in 1985 in the Premier Mine, Gauteng Province. The diamond was presented to King Bhumibol Adulyadej of Thailand in honor of his 50th coronation anniversary. Photo © Grand Palace, Bangkok.

Middle right, lower: A group of college students, posing with the uncut Cullinan diamond, give a good idea of its size.

Lower right: The 273.85-carat, D-color, flawless, *Centenary* diamond was cut from a 599-carat stone recovered from the Premier Mine, Gauteng Province, in July 1986. De Beers used x-ray imaging to separate the giant diamond, which was faceted by the team of Gabi Tolkowsky, Jim Nash, and Geoff Woolett. Image courtesy of the De Beers Group.

Major African Diamond Deposits

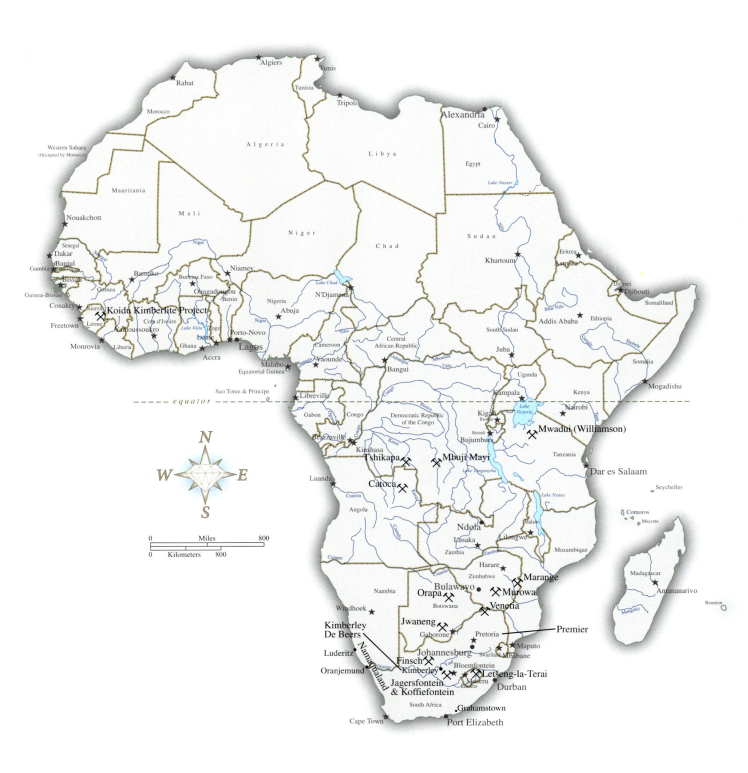

DEMOCRATIC REPUBLIC OF CONGO — DRC

In 1907, forty years after riverbank diamonds in Africa first caught the public imagination, a supposed diamond was turned up in a Belgian prospector's sieve. It was four years before he returned to the spot on the Kasai, a tributary of the Congo River, to confirm the speculative identification and produce more diamonds — lots of them. Back in Antwerp, cutting houses buzzed.

It was soon evident that the river to be following was a tributary of the tributary — the Tshikapa. That and another name, *Mbuji Mayi,* resound through Congolese diamond legend. The latter is a complex of interlinked kimberlite pipes of extraordinary richness that produces of diamonds of extraordinary drabness. For years they were unmarketable. Then came the Second World War, the first substantially "industrialized" global conflict, where precision machining of weaponry on an unprecedented scale was the order of the day. No material could grind to precision better than diamond, and drab is fine — it tools gun barrels as well as the brightest of diamonds. In 1939 the Belgian Congo was producing 67 percent of the world's diamonds, most of them from Mbuji Mayi.

Today the Congo continues to produce more stones than South Africa (an estimated 3.9 million carats in 2012), mainly low-grade material *en masse* from Mbuji Mayi as well as gems from a number of rivers flowing into the country from headwaters in Angola and probably from as-yet-undiscovered kimberlites in the Congo.

Above: The 407.48-carat, internally flawless, "fancy brownish yellow," *Incomparable* diamond. It is alleged that a young girl found the 890-carat rough for Incomparable in 1984 in a pile of rubble outside of her uncle's home in Mbuji Mayi. The stone has traded hands many times and is now owned by Mouawad Jewelers. Tino Hammid photo.

Right: Diamond, 10.45 carats. Democratic Republic of Congo Bill Larson collection, Robert Weldon photo.

Facing page: The distribution of major African diamond deposits reflects closely those parts of the continent underlain by deep-rooted cratons, perfectly illustrating Clifford's Rule. William W Besse cartographer.

Below: Diamond crystals to 12 mm Democratic Republic of Congo Procarat specimens, Jeff Scovil photo

DIAMONDS IN AFRICA 77

Above: The sands of the Namib Desert are reclaiming the buildings in the ghost town of Kolmanskop. Situated 10 km southeast of Lüderitz, Kolmanskop was established in 1908, just after diamonds were discovered there. By 1950 the mine was exhausted and the town site abandoned as the center of Namibian diamond mining moved to Oranjemund.
Paul Bruins photo, April 2015.

Below: Diamond, macle twin, 17.68 carats
Oranjemund Region, Namibia
Max and Jon Sigerman collection. Jeff Scovil photo.

NAMIBIA

From September 1904 to June 1905, four diamonds weighing more than 300 carats (the Cullinan among them) were unearthed from the fledgling Premier Mine in South Africa. But if European *diamantaires* thought the era of the mega-diamond had dawned, they were soon to learn otherwise. Even before the Tshikapa diamonds started to flow into Antwerp, German cutting houses had been seeing a trickle of tiny stones from their west African colony north of the Orange River. It would soon become a thick stream of diamonds, most of which were well under a carat. The first chance discovery, by a worker on the railway line in Lüderitz, came in 1908 and consisted of a stone of a fraction of a carat. In the flurry of activity that followed, small gems were found in breathtaking profusion. Exploration and mining progressed deeper and deeper into the Namib Desert from Lüderitz. But the ever-longer lines of communication into an extremely hostile environment meant that by the outbreak of war in 1914 the bonanza days appeared numbered. When Ernest Oppenheimer's Anglo American acquired the rights in 1919, they hoped that the desert diamonds would reward their purchaser. No one could have dreamt of the scale of that reward, which was realized nearly a decade later when the rich fields immediately north of the Orange River were opened up.

Born from the craton in the heartland of southern Africa via the Orange River umbilicus, the **Oranjemund Mine** produced kilograms of the most perfect stones for decades, including regular prize gems of tens of carats. Delivery by a river loaded in times of flood with pounding boulders and by howling storms along equally punishing boulder beaches ensured that only the best diamonds survived. Even though the scale of production by the desert mines is today a fraction of what it was, at 1.4 million carats per annum (2012), Namibia is still Africa's fifth largest producer.

ANGOLA

The history of diamond mining in Angola is closely connected to events not far to the north in the Congo. The Congolese town of Tshikapa is 60 kilometers north of a border drawn at the 1884 Berlin Conference that separated King Leopold II's Congo from Portuguese Angola. The Chicapa River (or *Tshikapa* as it is called in the Congo) has its source nearly 500 kilometers south of the border in the highlands of central Angola, close to the headwaters of other important African rivers like the Zambezi and the Okavano. The Chicapa-Tshikapa River brings most if not all of its diamonds into the Congo from kimberlite pipes in northeastern Angola and is endowed with alluvial diamonds both north and south of the border. It was only a matter of time then before the infant Congolese interest spread across the border into Angola's Lunda Norte province (1916).

A large part of Angola is underlain by craton, and the distribution of alluvial mining operations — from the Congolese border into the southern half of the country — reflects this. The bulk of the activity, however, is concentrated on the north-flowing rivers from the Cuango in the west to those in Lunda Norte on both sides of the Chicapa.

Although many kimberlites have been identified, there is still only one major kimberlite mine, at **Catoca**. The mine is situated just to the south of the border of Lunda Norte and is thus still in the northeastern quadrant of the country. At 64 hectares, Catoca is among the world's top five kimberlites by size and the fourth biggest producer, contributing 70 percent of Angola's production. Angola is Africa's second most important diamond producer after Botswana and is the fourth largest producer in the world, after Russia and Canada. Ownership of Catoca is split: Angola and the Russian mining company Alrosa each own one third; Brazilian and Chinese interests share the remaining third.

Above: The modern Catoca Mine, near Saurimo in the Lunda Sul province of Angola is responsible for some 70% of the country's diamond production. Artisanal miners, working under very different conditions, account for the other 30%. Paulo Fernandes/Catoca photo, 2010.

Below: Circa 1957 diamond graders in Ghana sort through a batch of tiny stones, the great bulk of which are industrial-quality. Arne Kuilman photo archive.

GHANA

Since the first recorded recovery of diamonds in the Gold Coast (now Ghana) in 1919, the country has produced an estimated 100 million carats. This is a respectable number even though the low quality of that production places Ghanaian diamond value far below that of countries with roughly the same cumulative production by weight, Namibia, for example. At 25 stones per carat, Ghana's stones are no bigger than a pinhead and are too small to cut commercially. And although they are mined and marketed, Ghanaian diamonds are not even favored for industrial use. No wonder you have never heard of them!

Above: Even organized mining operations, such as this one along the Sewa River in Sierra Leone are labor intensive. Here gravel that has been dredged from the river is being sluiced. Leo Klemm photo, 2012.

Below: A beautiful octahedral diamond, 14 carats, 1.6 cm tall. Sierra Leone.
Roz and Gene Meieran collection, Jeff Scovil photo.

SIERRA LEONE

If memory serves, care was taken in the film *Blood Diamond* not to disclose which country was being portrayed. There can be little doubt, however, that the fictional setting for the film was modeled after Sierra Leone. Together with Angola, and to a lesser extent the Congo, Sierra Leone typified the environment where the terms *blood diamonds* and the industry-preferred *conflict diamonds* were coined. At say, US$200 per carat for good stones weighing 1 one carat or more (1 carat = 0.2 grams), 50 grams of diamonds — a tobacco-pouchful — is worth $50,000. With the right contacts in the extensive underworld, a smuggler has no difficulty moving tens of thousands of dollars in diamonds. It is small wonder that diamonds were the chosen currency for financing political conflict in diamond-endowed countries in Africa before the Kimberley Process Certification Scheme was instituted.

Not used lightly, the term *diamond-endowed* applies more legitimately to Sierra Leone than almost any other part of the world. Since mining began there in 1930, the country has produced the bulk of its gems from alluvial diggings. It stands right up there with mega-diamond-producing pipes like Lesotho's Letšeng-la-Terai and the Premier and Jagersfontein pipes in South Africa. Sierra Leone's alluvial deposits have contributed the 969-carat Star of Sierra Leone, the 770-carat Woyie River, and two other stones — each weighing more than 500 carats — that were never named.

The roughly 300,000 carats per annum (seventh largest producer in Africa) — more than either Brazil or Australia — come from alluvial and eluvial deposits in the east of the country and from the **Koidu Mine** on a kimberlite pipe, with one kimberlite dyke currently under evaluation.

Above: Independent miners dig, or in this case dive for, diamond-rich gravel in the Sewa River near Bo in Sierra Leone. The clay and gravel are relayed out of the river, and spread out to dry, and are later brought back down to the river to be screened. Leo Klemm photo, 2012.

Right: An artisanal miner screens diamond-bearing gravel on the banks of the Sewa river near Bo, Sierra Leone.
Leo Klemm photo, 2012.

Below: Diamond trader Mohamed stands outside of his "Diamond Office" in the city of Bo. Shops selling diamonds and catering to potential prospectors can be found all over Bo, Sierra Leone's second largest city.
Christopher Herwig photo, 2006.

Diamonds in Africa

TANZANIA

The story of the discovery in 1940 of diamonds at the **Mwadui** or **Williamson** pipe in northern Tanganyika is as quixotic as the discoverer. Canadian geologist Dr. John Thorburn Williamson was colorful, leaning toward eccentric. The reasons for the particular romance of the story are manifold: the chance entry of Williamson into geology; his decision as a young man to come to the wilds of Africa; his move from the Anglo American Corporation, which had lured him to the Northern Rhodesian Copper Belt, to a junior company in Tanganyika; his resignation from that company to go on his own, determined that they had not tested the area's potential for diamonds; his single-minded persistence with no help other than a couple of local field-hands and no financial backing beyond loans from local traders; and the crowning glory, his discovery of the source of the stones occasionally being turned up in streams, the pipe which still carries his name and is still, at 146 hectares, by far the biggest fertile kimberlite ever found.

Williamson found backers and staff and developed the mine, never marrying, resolutely resisting approaches from would-be partners and mining his pipe with the same steadfast passion that had characterized his discovery of it. He died in 1957 at just over 50 years old. Seventy years since its opening, the Williamson Mine accounts for practically the entire Tanzanian production of around 50,000 carats per annum.

LESOTHO

The highest diamond mine in the world is at a place called *Letšeng-la-Terai* ("turn by the swamp") in the Kingdom of Lesotho (formerly Basutoland); its elevation is 3,100 meters above sea level. The discovery of kimberlite pipes in the Mountain Kingdom is almost as much a story of persistent belief as that of Mwadui except this one is woven around an ex-military man, Basutoland-born Colonel Jack Scott. (Credit for the discovery should actually go to a Sotho, as natives of that country are known, because Scott's arrival followed the discovery of diamonds by local villagers in a valley not far from the border with the South African Free State Province.)

Above: Dr John Williamson, owner of the Williamson Mine in Tanzania presented a 54.5-carat rough pink diamond as a wedding present to Princess Elizabeth, after it was found in 1947. Briefel and Lemer of London faceted the diamond the following year into the 23.6 carat, flawless, round brilliant at the center of the Cartier-designed diamond brooch pictured here. Photo courtesy of Cartier.

Below: Panorama of the Williamson Diamond Mine in Mwadui, Tanzania, as seen on January 28, 2009. Hansueli Krapf photo.

Left: The 603-carat *Lesotho Promise* diamond was recovered from the Letšeng Mine in Lesotho in August 2006. The Promise was carved into the 8 pieces pictured here and eventually yielded 26 individual, D-color, flawless diamonds. Photo courtesy of Graff Diamonds.

Below: A model poses with the 118.78-carat, D-color, heart-shape, flawless *Graff Venus* diamond. The record-breaking gem was cut from a 357-carat rough crystal discovered at the Letšeng Mine in Lesotho in 2015. Photo courtesy of Graff Diamonds.

In 1954 police following up reports of a death in the Kao Valley found as many as one hundred diggers working ground and recovering diamonds. Scott was given permission to conduct a survey of the small country, and before long kimberlite pipes were being found. Gaining permission was more easily accomplished than was the survey, though, as this is terrain of deep precipitous valleys where even today there is minimal access to much of the ground. Logistics were nightmarish, and it took a team of especially dedicated young geologists to negotiate the mountain slopes, collect their samples, and return them to base. Today helicopters would be used; 60 years ago that was not an option for an entrepreneur with minimal backing and little more than a hunch to go on.

At an early stage of the venture, De Beers was persuaded to partner with Scott, but the prospecting provided minimal encouragement. The country's looming independence from Britain, with the inevitable attending uncertainty as to the ownership of mines, further dampened spirits. Consequently, Scott left one of the more promising pipes — Letšeng-la-Terai — open for public digging. Recovery of the occasional large stone of exceptional quality was enough to seduce the South African office of Rio Tinto Zinc into an exploration venture in Lesotho from 1969 to 1972, shortly after the country became independent in 1966. Their pilot work showed the multinational corporation that the pipe was quite small and extremely low-grade. Although Rio Tinto's success in profitably mining low-grade deposits was already being shown at their Palabora copper mine in neighboring South Africa, Letšeng was not only of low grade but was also too small for their voracious appetite. Rio Tinto withdrew. De Beers, via Anglo American, took over, but after 7 years De Beers decided the mine was not a good fit with their corporate strategy, and once again the project lay fallow. It took a combination of the vision,

passion, and dedication of ex-De Beers senior geologist and mining engineer Keith Whitelock, backed ultimately by junior diamond company Gem Diamonds, to reveal Letšeng's true capabilities. Six notably large single crystals were recovered, tipping the scales at 601, 478, 493, 550, and 603 carats. The first of these was found in 1960; the remainder have been recovered since 2006.

Under different ownership, the nearby **Kao** pipe is now in production as well. In all, the estimated yield of operations in Lesotho (mines and prospects) in 2012 was 450,000 carats, making the country Africa's sixth largest producer.

Left: Colorless octahedral crystals (approximately 3 carats each) from the Jwaneng Mine in Botswana. Courtesy of the Diamond Trading Company in Gaborone. Photo by Robert Weldon, © GIA.

Above: The uncut 1,109-carat, Type IIa, *Lesedi La Rona* was found on November 16, 2015, at the Karowe Mine in Botswana, the largest diamond to have been found in over 100 years. Photo courtesy of Lucara Diamond.

BOTSWANA

Many years of laborious, systematic exploration and unshakeable belief in the potential of the bedrock below the Kalahari Desert on the part of De Beers Exploration Manager in Botswana Gavin Lamont and his geologists finally paid off in 1967; they discovered the 118-hectare Orapa pipe. It was bigger than they had dared dream, far bigger than any pipe De Beers had discovered before or since.

Five years later and far to the south, the **Jwaneng** pipe was discovered below 40 meters of Kalahari sand. The jewel in the crown of Botswana diamonds, Jwaneng is by any standard large (54 hectares) and extremely high-grade. At 1.35 carats per tonne, moreover, it is the richest diamond mine in the world.

Other mines in the Orapa "cluster" are also in production under Debswana, (the mine-owning partnership between the Botswana government and De Beers). Also, new, independently owned mines will shortly be adding to the country's delivery of diamonds to world markets. With an estimated 22 million carats output in 2012, Botswana is a substantially larger supplier than even Russia (pages 94–103), the next most important actor in the production stakes.

ZIMBABWE

Extravagant claims are made about the size of the diamond inventory (exploited and yet to be mined) of the much-publicized **Marange** diamond field in the far east of Zimbabwe. In the under-regulated environment of the country under President Robert Mugabe, though, credible figures are hard to come by, and details of the marketing elusive and shadowy. Reminiscent of a time when most diamond production from Sierra Leone reached world markets via completely alternate routes through Lebanon and Liberia, Zimbabwe's gems seem to arrive in merchant windows via Mozambique and India, a route that is almost as informal.

Nonetheless a Kimberley Process Certificate is still better to have than not, and figures attributed to the Kimberley Process Certification Scheme show production of 16.8 million carats in 2013 (13 percent of global production) at an average value of US$33 per carat versus a global average of $93 per carat. Typical rough from Marange shows why its value is roughly a third of what cutters hope to see.

Given the quality of the rough, we can understand De Beers' decision not to move from exploration into mining the large field of alluvial and eluvial diamonds. The fact that the deposit is located in a country with an inclination toward nationalization of foreign-held businesses has presumably taken any remaining luster off the project, and in 2006 De Beers allowed the exploration rights it had acquired in 1980 to lapse. Since then, physical and legislative interference on the part of the government forces with companies owning successor rights have threatened renewal of Zimbabwe's Kimberley Process certification, which remains, to the surprise of many, in place.

The comparison of Marange with Rio Tinto's **Murowa Mine**, located in the center of the country, is stark: the latter operation is, predictably, a model of compliance. It is also small; its total projected reserve of just over 17 million carats of good-quality gems barely exceeds Marange's total yield for 2013.

CONCLUSION

There is little more to say, except to add to the names of distinguished figures. Tom Clifford, three generations of Oppenheimers (Ernest, Harry and Nicky), and Keith Whitelock have already been mentioned. But there are others who have made African diamonds their life-long work.

Just as we South Africans have adopted Tom Clifford as our own; we all but forget that John Gurney is in fact of British origin. If Clifford's Rule gave explorers the short cut they sought, Gurney's geological and geochemical work on the

Leopard.
Kruger National Park, South Africa.
Robert Weldon photo.

lithosphere has turbocharged the exploration machine. Say "G10 garnet" to diamond explorers (or diamond company chairs) and watch their eyes light up. For that we have John Gurney to thank.

Some years ago in London, the mining community honored Chris Jennings as Lifetime Achiever of the Year for his dedicated pioneering work. By honing the theories of geology and geophysics, he led diamond explorers to their targets in areas of crust deeply buried by sand, ice, rainforest, or laterite from the Kalahari to Gabon to Canada. (Speaking of Canada, Rio Tinto, 60 percent shareholder in the famous Diavik Mine, Northwest Territories, can thank Chris for the years of beautiful diamonds produced by that mine, as his involvement in the pipe's discovery and in the Rio Tinto connection were crucial.) We celebrate his life as a South African.

In a non-technical capacity, no-one has played as important a part in the world of diamonds in recent decades as Gary Ralfe, Managing Director of De Beers from 1998 to 2006. During this time he played a pivotal role in guiding the restructuring and privatization of the company. Israeli diamond mining analyst Chaim Even-Zohar, dedicates the second edition of his encyclopedic book, *From Mine to Mistress: Corporate Strategies and Government Policies in the International Diamond Industry* to Gary, saying of him, *inter alia*: "He commenced a journey that turned the manager of the producers' cartel into the leading rough supplier in a new demand-driven, responsible, fiercely competitive industry," and referring to his "great intellect and stubborn intuition" as well as to "a deep sense of loyalty to those he pledged to serve." Hats off to Gary.

Finally, the giant Rio Tinto might not be able to look back on decades as a massive producer of diamonds but for the vision and well-reasoned counsel of South African Baxter Brown. Since hiking the mountains of Lesotho as a member of Colonel Jack Scott's pioneering team in 1959, Baxter has searched for, and found, diamonds from Namaqualand to Venezuela. In the mid-1970s the South African consultant's conviction that the geology of Western Australia was a suitable host for a minable deposit of diamonds was enough to convince Conzinc Rio Tinto Australia to pursue an option many would have thought foolhardy. For years Conzinc Rio Tinto's Argyle deposit in Western Australia (see pages 104–109) produced a third of the world's diamonds — by carats, not by value: the stones are mostly small and not of good color — and is still producing today.

Nick Norman is a South African geologist who has spent most of his 45-year career in mineral exploration. He graduated with an M.Sc. from the University of Natal in 1968 and has worked mostly in Botswana, South Africa, Brazil and Chile, with shorter spells elsewhere in Africa and South America. Recently he has written four books for the popular market, including The Extraordinary World of Diamonds, *published in 2010.*

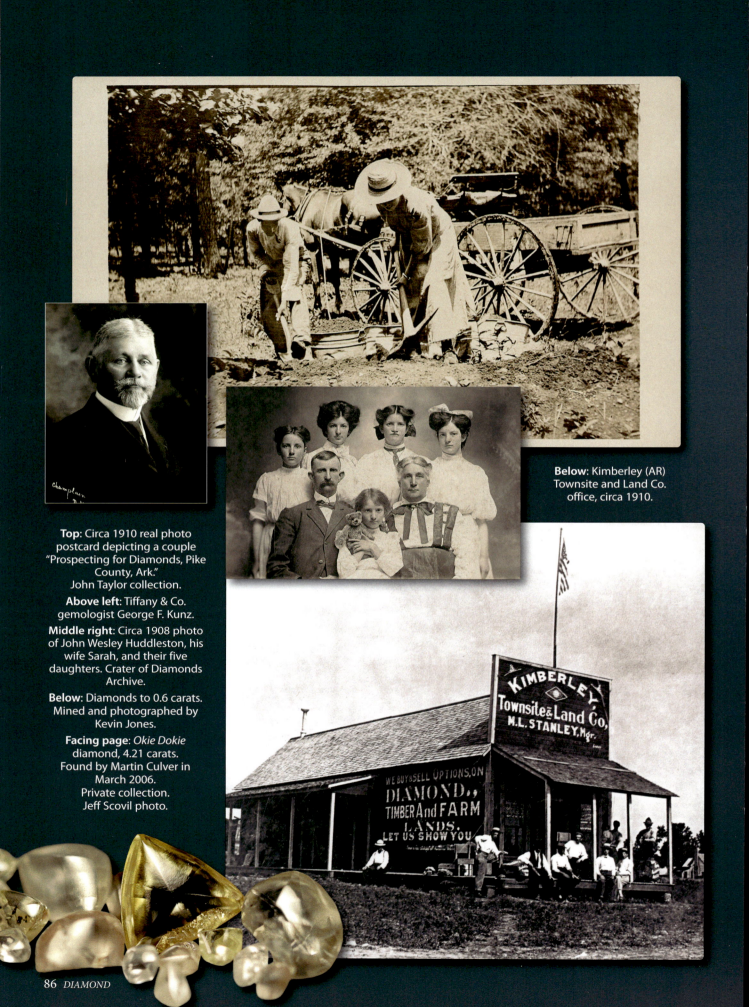

Top: Circa 1910 real photo postcard depicting a couple "Prospecting for Diamonds, Pike County, Ark."
John Taylor collection.

Above left: Tiffany & Co. gemologist George F. Kunz.

Middle right: Circa 1908 photo of John Wesley Huddleston, his wife Sarah, and their five daughters. Crater of Diamonds Archive.

Below: Diamonds to 0.6 carats. Mined and photographed by Kevin Jones.

Facing page: *Okie Dokie* diamond, 4.21 carats. Found by Martin Culver in March 2006. Private collection. Jeff Scovil photo.

Below: Kimberley (AR) Townsite and Land Co. office, circa 1910.

Crater of Diamonds — the Natural State's Gem of a Park

by J. Michael Howard

Although in the 1880s Arkansas State Geologist John Branner suspected that the Prairie Creek pipe might carry diamonds, it remained unrecognized as diamond bearing until pig farmer John Wesley Huddleston discovered two "deemints" (diamonds) on August 8, 1906, on his 160-acre farm. Years after his discovery when recounting his story to Howard Millar, Huddleston recalled that he saw yellow flakes in the soil and, thinking it might be gold, washed some of the material. The yellow flakes were phlogopite, which float, so Huddleston knew that he did not have gold, but when examining the gravel in the bottom of his pan, he noticed two unusual crystals that seemed different from local quartz crystals. One was yellow and the other was white. When Huddleston could not grind a flat spot on either crystal, he suspected they were diamonds.

Huddleston took the stones to Pike County Bank and showed them first to the cashier and then to bank President Joseph C. Pinnix. The latter agreed to send them to Little Rock jeweler Charles Stifft, who in turn forwarded them to George F. Kunz, celebrated American gemologist and Vice-President of Tiffany & Co., in New York. Kunz confirmed that the stones were gem-grade diamonds: a 1.5-carat yellow and a 3.0-carat white. In October 1906 at Kunz's request, geologist Henry Stevens Washington visited Murfreesboro to conduct a geologic and petrographic study of the site. Kunz and Washington visited the site together in January 1907, and by that time some 26 diamonds had been unearthed. But with the Diamond Hoax of 1872 in the not so distant past, Kunz was cautious. Finally in March of 1907, a diamond in a chunk of weathered host rock (lamproite) from the mine was sent to New York, where it was examined by Kunz and Washington, who concluded, "the occurrence of diamonds in the peridotite of Murfreesboro may be regarded as unquestionable" (Kunz and Washington 1907).

On September 19, 1906, Charles Stifft, A. D. Cohen (Stifft's son-in-law), J. C. Pinnix, and Sam W. Reyburn (President of Union Trust Company, a Little Rock bank) purchased an option on the property. The group exercised their option on August 14, 1907, purchasing the Huddleston property for $36,000 (Banks 2008). They organized in December of that year as the Arkansas Diamond Mining Company.

The boundary of Huddleston's property ran through the Murfreesboro pipe, and Millard M. Mauney owned an adjacent 40 acres of potentially diamondiferous land. As it turned out six of those acres constituted the northeast corner of the pipe. Word of the discovery soon got out, and in 1907 a diamond rush overtook the area. So many people converged on Murfreesboro that one local hotel reportedly turned away more than 10,000 prospectors in just one year!

Following the discovery next door, Mauney and his sons made several attempts to mine diamonds, but ultimately decided that land development and tourism were better investments. By October 1908 Mauney was finalizing the sale

Left: Erected in the early 1900s, the original miner's shack was on the site until the 1990s, when it was torn down and a replica built in its place.
Crater of Diamonds State Park photo.

Inset: The Arkansas state quarter was designed by Dortha Scott and issued by the US Mint in 2003.

Facing page, top: Mrs. A. L. Parker found the 15.33-carat *Star of Arkansas* diamond in 1956. She had it cut into a 8.27-carat modified marquise. The set stone, shown here, sold at auction in 1994. Image courtesy of Christie's Auction House.

Facing page, middle: At 40.23 carats, the *Uncle Sam* diamond is the largest diamond ever found in North America. The stone that was cut from it is 12.42 carats. Its present whereabouts are not known.
Crater of Diamonds State Park photo.

Facing page, lower: The 17.85-carat *Roebling* diamond.
National Museum of Natural History. Chip Clark photo.

of a 75 percent stake in his property to the Ozark Company, founded by Horace Bemis. The two — Mauney and the Ozark Company — quickly found themselves at odds. They decided to split the property: 10 acres to Mauney and 30 acres, including 4 acres on the pipe, to Bemis's company, which was renamed the Ozark Diamond Corporation in 1909.

Mauney allowed visitors to collect (for a fee) on his two-acres site, and he and his son Walter developed Kimberley Township (named for the city of Kimberley, then the principal source of diamonds in South Africa) on farmland just south of Murfreesboro. Diamond fever was subsiding and Mauney's real estate venture was faltering in 1911 when an 8.1-carat diamond — the largest to date — was found on the Mauney property. Mauney parlayed the find into renewed mining activity with hopes of bolstering Kimberley Township.

Waiting in the wings were mining engineer Austin Millar and his son Howard, who had abandoned diamond prospecting on a property in Kentucky to join the rush to Arkansas. Although arriving too late to stake a claim on prime property, Austin believed in the deposit, so father and son worked the ground they could, engaged in the affairs of the community, and waited.

Mauney leased his 10 acres to the Millars, taking a 25 percent royalty for all of the diamonds recovered from his land. Then when Horace Bemis died unexpectedly on April 1, 1914, his heirs sold their property to Austin and Howard Millar. The Millars, who at that point controlled the original Mauney property in its entirety, also made an unsuccessful bid to purchase the original Huddleston property from the Arkansas Diamond Mining Company.

In 1919 engineer Stanley Zimmerman arrived to manage the Huddleston property under a newly reorganized Arkansas Diamond Mining Corporation. Unsuccessful in his effort to mine the property commercially, Zimmerman left for three months to tour the diamond mines and operations in South Africa. There he met with Sir Ernest Oppenheimer, head of DeBeers. Reyburn and Zimmerman (1920) published an article in *Engineering and Mining Journal* in which they condemned the Arkansas deposits as uneconomical, but locals claimed that Zimmerman and Reyburn had been paid by DeBeers to "prove" the deposit was not viable. In 1923 after testing Arkansas diamonds for industrial use, the Ford Motor Company attempted to purchase the entire deposit for $1,150,000, but the Arkansas Diamond Mining Company was reluctant, and the deal fell through.

The Arkansas Diamond Mining Company stopped mining in 1932. The Huddleston property was worked sporadically until the early 1940s, when Indiana businessman Charles H. Wilkinson purchased it. When Wilkinson died in 1946, the operation fell to his reclusive widow Ethel. Mrs. Wilkinson leased the property to Martin Aircraft Corporation, which abandoned operations after spending over three quarters of a million dollars and recovering only 246 carats of diamonds over 8 months. Wilkinson, who was an ardent believer in astrology, turned down subsequent significant offers for the property, waiting instead until her astrologer told her to sell.

CRATER OF DIAMONDS

Austin Millar died in November 1951, after which Howard Millar came to an agreement with Ethel Wilkinson to open the property as a tourist attraction. He and his wife would live on the grounds and operate the site, drawing a salary, and Wilkinson and Millar would share expenses and proceeds. They opened the park in April 1952 as *Crater of Diamonds*:

At the Crater of Diamonds, Howard Millar found the perfect outlet for his talents as a writer and promoter, and finally acquired the fame he had sought since those early years in Arkansas. Skillfully, he drew the attention of national magazines, newspapers, and popular new television programs, and brought more fame to the Arkansas diamond field than any person ever had. A barrage of publicity in the '50s and '60s established tourism as a permanent and overriding purpose of the big pipe near Murfreesboro. (Banks 2008)

It didn't hurt when in March 1956 after a heavy rain, Mrs. A. L. Parker found the 15.33-carat *Star of Arkansas*, a white diamond gleaming on the freshly plowed surface. Everything was going along swimmingly until 1963, when Crater of Diamonds employee Roscoe Johnston, helped by Mrs. Wilkinson, opened the Arkansas Diamond Mine or Big Mine on the Huddleston property, and a war of billboards ensued! Cooperation had served everyone better than competition, and soon both mines were struggling.

In 1969 General Earth Minerals of Dallas purchased both the Huddleston and Mauney properties, supposedly aspiring to mine for diamonds. But instead the company principally operated the locality as a tourist attraction and in 1972 offered it to the State of Arkansas for $750,000. The offer was accepted and the Crater of Diamonds State Park has been in operation ever since. The park is open 364 days a year, closing only on Christmas Day.

Since the park's inception, park personnel have systematically recorded the finds; thus reasonable documentation exists as to how many diamonds have been discovered, their weights, colors, and the names of those who recovered them. During 2014, 585 diamonds were recovered. Since 2011, four diamonds weighing more than five carats have been registered.

FAMOUS AND WELL-KNOWN DIAMONDS

To date, *Uncle Sam* is the largest diamond ever found in the deposit, or anywhere in the United States for that matter. It was recovered from a sluice box in 1924 during commercial mining operations. The diamond weighed 40.23 carats and yielded a 12.42-carat, pale rose-colored emerald-cut gem. It was on display for many years at the American Museum of Natural History and is presently in a private collection.

The aforementioned 15.33-carat Star of Arkansas, discovered in the 1950s by Mrs. A. L. Parker was faceted into a brilliant marquise gem weighing 8.27 carats. Before it was cut, Howard Millar and Mrs. Parker visited the Arkansas Geological Commission and laid out the raw diamond in front of State Geologist N.F. Williams. Because of its value, Williams was afraid to touch the stone, but Millar insisted that he examine it, which he finally did. The stone was rarely worn by Mrs. Parker and after her death was sold by Christie's in New York for $145,000 to an undisclosed buyer.

The largest diamond recovered since the state park was founded is the *Amarillo Starlight*. In 1975 W. W. Johnson of Amarillo, Texas discovered the 16.37-carat white stone, which yielded a 7.54-carat marquise gem.

Perhaps the most beautiful of the larger Arkansas diamonds is an unnamed 17.86-carat flawless, yellow hexoctahedral diamond, which was discovered on the grounds by a watchman in 1917. This uncut stone became part of Washington Roebling's (of Brooklyn Bridge fame) collection, which Roebling's son John donated to the Smithsonian Institution, where it presently resides.

Arkansas' Largest Diamonds				
Diamond Name	Year Found	Rough Weight	Color	Finder
Uncle Sam	1924	40.23	white	Wesley Oley Basham
Star of Murfreesboro	1964	34.25	blue	John Pollock
Arkansas Diamond	1926	27.21	yellow	Mrs. Pellie Howell
Roebling	1917	17.86	yellow	Lee Wagner
Amarillo Starlight	1975	16.37	white	W. W. Johnson
Star of Arkansas	1956	15.33	white	Mrs. A. L. Parker
Star of Shreveport	1981	8.82	white	C. Blankenship
Illusion	2011	8.66	white	B. Gilbertson
Lamie	1978	8.61	brown	B. Lamie
Esperanza	2015	8.52	white	Bobbie Oskarson
Connell	1986	7.95	white	K. Connell
Dickinson-Stevens	1998	7.28	yellow	M. Dickinson, C. Stevens
Dunn	1975	6.75	brown	T. Dunn
Cooper	1997	6.72	brown	R. Cooper
Kinney-Walker-Elterman-Higley	2011	6.67	yellow	Kinney III, Walker, Elterman, Higley
Gary Moore	1960	6.43	yellow	Gary Moore
Roden	2006	6.35	brown	Donald Roden
Lee	1988	6.30	white	S. Lee
Newman	1981	6.25	white	C. Newman
Bleeding Heart	1991	6.23	white	Joe Fedzora
Stockton	1981	6.20	white	W. Stockton
Anderson	2014	6.19	white	D. Anderson
Schall	1981	6.07	white	R. Schall
Cooper	1997	6.00	brown	R. Cooper

Another notable yellow stone, the flawless 4.25-carat Kahn Canary Diamond was found at the park by logger George Stepp in 1977. Stan Kahn of Pine Bluff, Arkansas, later purchased the diamond from Stepp. It was set uncut in a ring, which Hillary Clinton wore at her husband President Bill Clinton's Inaugural balls in 1993 and 1997. The diamond is frequently loaned for display at museums and exhibitions around the world.

One stone, the *Arkansas* was recovered in Arkansas and should be mentioned, even though it cannot be directly connected to the Murfreesboro lamproites. It is a perfect hexoctahedral 27.21-carat diamond that was picked up in 1926 by a young girl in a cotton field near Searcy, Arkansas, some 218 kilometers (135 miles) northeast of Murfreesboro. The finder, Mrs. Pellie Howell, sold the stone to Tiffany & Company in 1946 for $8,500. The Arkansas diamond remains uncut and is occasionally placed on display in Tiffany's New York store. Because of its similarity to Pike County diamonds, the stone is thought to have been picked up in Murfreesboro and later dropped near Searcy.

Right: Rough diamonds to 8.82 carats. The largest stone (left) was found in 1981 and was named the *Star of Shreveport*. Private collection. Jeff Scovil photo.

Lower right: Henry Dunay designed this gold and platinum setting for the uncut 4.25-carat *Kahn Canary* diamond. Stanley Kahn collection. Harold and Erica Van Pelt / GIA photo.

Facing page: The 27.21-carat *Arkansas* diamond was found by a child in Searcy, Arkansas, some 218 kilometers from Murfreesboro. Tiffany & Co. collection and photo.

THE NATURE OF ARKANSAS DIAMONDS

Diamonds from Prairie Creek possess several interesting characteristics. On the whole, cutters have noted that gem-grade stones from Arkansas are harder than typical diamonds from Africa. No cube-shaped crystals have been reported and only very rarely have octahedrons been found. Rounded forms including dodecahedrons, trisoctahedrons, and hexoctahedrons are typical. Rounded rice-grain shapes are also known. These rounded habits result from the resorption of diamond by the transport medium during travel from the mantle and during emplacement (Robinson et al. 1989).

Colors are well documented: about 60 percent of the diamonds recovered are white (colorless); 21 percent are brown; and 17 percent are yellow. Howard Millar (1976) reported that rare pinks and blues make up the remaining 2 percent. The average size is around 0.25 carat, but stones from less than 1 point (there are 100 points in a carat) to over 40 carats have been recovered.

Inclusions in Arkansas diamonds vary and can include nickel-iron sulfides, magnetite, diamond, amorphous carbon-iron-nickel-sulfur, pyrope-almandine, graphite, enstatite, forsterite, titanium-iron-zinc-potassium aluminosilicates, chromium-diopside, and pseudobrookite (?). Entrapped major gases include H_2O, H_2, N_2, CO_2, methyl and ethyl alcohol, and argon in highly variable proportions. Magnetite inclusions provide oxidation information concerning the formation of diamond. Magnetite is syngenetic to diamond so, at least in the instance of one diamond, it appears that oxidizing conditions existed at the time that both minerals formed. (Newton et al. 1977, Panteleo et al. 1979).

The percentage of gem-grade to industrial stones in this pipe has not been evaluated, although based on the size, color, and clarity of the stones recovered since 1972, park data suggests that about 10 percent of the Murfreesboro diamonds are gem quality.

GEOLOGISTS AND EVALUATIONS

Arkansas State Geologist John C. Branner and Arkansas Geological Survey Geologist J. Francis Williams (1891) visited the Prairie Creek diatreme in the late 1880s. The pair spent two days searching for diamonds. Both were well educated and had read the reports about kimberlite in South Africa being the host rock of diamonds. Unfortunately, their search was fruitless.

In 1916 Hugh D. Miser, a young geologist with the U.S. Geological Survey, ran a plane table alidade survey of the site, including the Arkansas Diamond Company and Ozark Mining Company's workings. His effort resulted in the first topographic and geologic map of the pipe, which was published along with descriptions of the rocks and mining operations in 1929 in *U.S. Geological Survey Bulletin 808*.

After the discovery of diamond-bearing lamproite in Australia in 1979, the economic potential of such deposits was recognized, and sites such as the Crater of Diamonds were reevaluated. In 1984 Barbara Scott Smith and E. Michael W. Skinner presented data that conclusively proved the Prairie

Creek and associated diatremes were lamproites, not kimberlites as described by previous workers.

The site had already been evaluated by the U.S. Bureau of Mines in the late 1940s and was found to be not commercially viable. Several companies tested the deposit in the early 1990s with the same results: not commercial. However, Howard (1999) pointed out that both tests evaluated only the surficial 12 meters (40 feet) — only some 8 percent of the total known volume of the diamond-bearing facies of the Prairie Creek diatreme, which is highly complex and up to 198 meters (650 feet) deep. The diatreme contains an estimated 78.5 million tons of diamondiferous lamproite breccias and lithic tuffs and 24.1 million tons of non-diamond bearing magmatic lamproite. The evaluations in the 1940s and 1990s both literally just scratched the surface. But the point is moot as shortly after the most recent exploration efforts, the Arkansas Legislature passed a law forever banning future exploration efforts on the park property.

In his dissertation on the geology and xenolith mineralogy of the lamproites in Pike County, Dennis P. Dunn (2002) showed that only about 50 meters of the Prairie Creek diatreme has eroded since its emplacement. Dunn also estimated that erosion released approximately 93,000 carats of diamonds from the host rock and these are now concentrated in the soil.

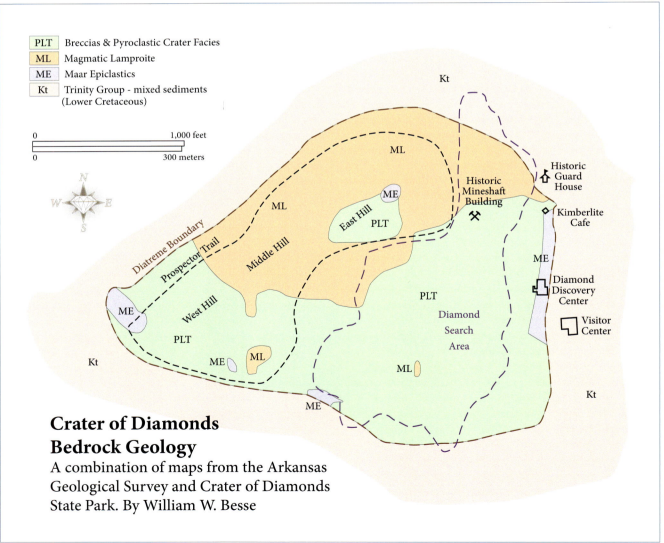

Crater of Diamonds Bedrock Geology

A combination of maps from the Arkansas Geological Survey and Crater of Diamonds State Park. By William W. Besse

Right: A wooden sign welcomes visitors to the Crater of Diamonds State Park.
Amy Ashcraft photo, May 2010.

Below middle: Kids sifting the soil at the Crater of Diamonds State Park, July 2013.
Alisa Abrahamson photo.

Bottom: Since 2004, Air Force Information Officer Rod Stewart has been a regular at Crater of Diamonds and in that time has found more than a dozen diamonds. He is pictured here in April 2010 at the bottom of an 8-foot hole he dug while looking for "pay dirt."
Scott Michelich photo.

Facing page: *Bleeding Heart* diamond, 6.23 carats. Found by Joe Fedzora in 1991. Private collection. Jeff Scovil photo.

DIGGERS

Perhaps the best known and most persistent visitor to the Park was James Archer. Each morning when the doors opened, no matter the weather, Archer was there ready to pay his fee and search for diamonds. He was a hard-working, friendly individual, who had recovered more than 4,000 stones during his 30 years of searching. Archer was known for his willingness to take time with anyone to explain what he was doing and how diamond searching is done. When asked how many diamonds he found, he said he had lost count. He told the author that he had started hunting diamonds to supplement his income, but after years of effort, it was something he just loved doing. In early 2003 at the age of 77, Archer passed away while hunting for diamonds in the park.

SUMMARY

Although those hoping to see a commercial diamond mine established in Arkansas have been disappointed by the various evaluations of the Prairie Creek diatreme, those results have paved the way for the founding of the Crater of Diamonds State Park, the only site in the world where anyone can search for diamonds on diamond-bearing ground. Some 35 acres of the 83-acre, Cretaceous-age diatreme are regularly plowed to expose fresh rock. Since the property became a state park in 1972, over 3 million visitors have recovered more than 30,000 natural diamonds. Park data suggests that it takes about 100 hours of searching for each diamond discovery, but diamonds are discovered at the park every day.

Originally from Hot Springs, Arkansas, author J. Michael Howard twice graduated from the University of Arkansas at Fayettevile: in 1971 BS in Geology and again in 1974 MS in Geology. He worked as economic geologist and staff mineralogist for the Arkansas Geological Survey for 39 years and retired in late 2013.

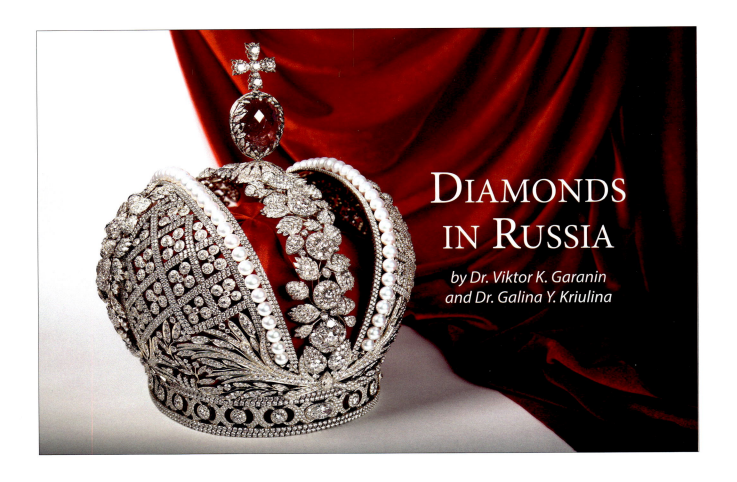

Diamonds in Russia

by Dr. Viktor K. Garanin and Dr. Galina Y. Kriulina

Russia is a country known for luxury and wealth that, when set against a backdrop of solemn skies and faces, seems all the more opulent. In enigmatic Russia, art, furs, and of course precious stones adorn its public institutions, its well to do, and its not so well to do. And in the last half-century, another item has been added to the country's list of riches: Russia has discovered in its borders the world's largest reserves of diamonds — the ultimate symbol of wealth.

Diamonds, though coveted, had not always been a homegrown commodity. In fact, diamonds were not brought onto Russian soil until the eighteenth century. It was via the ancient trade routes that rough and polished diamonds were conveyed to the country's elite from cutting centers in Belgium and Portugal. Those stones had been mined, in turn, from placers in India and later Brazil. Being imported, diamonds have long been a luxury, even for the royal family.

The famed Diamond Fund, Russia's collection of diamonds, precious stones, and metals, has its roots in the House of Romanov, which ruled Russia for three centuries beginning in 1613. The "fund" was started in 1719, when Peter the Great (reigned 1682–1725) bequeathed his magnificent collection to his countrymen and established the Russian Imperial Treasury. He proclaimed the treasury inviolate and ordered that future rulers deposit a portion of their jewels into it.

Russia, its art and architecture, flourished in the Golden Age under Catherine the Great (reigned 1762–1796). Signifying the enormous power and wealth of Catherine's expanding empire and its aristocracy; the royal treasury amassed and flaunted untold fortunes in diamonds and gems. Catherine's coronation crown, crafted by court jewelers George Eckhart and Jeremiah Posier, was famously set with 4,936 diamonds, not to mention a magnificent red spinel that weighs 398.72 carats. Diamonds were set not only in jewelry but also in clothing: they were used as buttons in waistcoats and set in shoe buckles. Diamonds were even wagered in the card and dice games played in Catherine's court.

Iconic diamonds acquired during Catherine's reign include the *Orlov*, which was purportedly stolen from the eye of a deity presiding over the second century Hindu Thiruvarangam Temple in the city of Srirangam, Tamil Nadu, India. The 189.62-carat, rose-cut gem changed hands numerous times before being purchased by one of Catherine's former lovers, Count Grigory Griorievich Orlov. In an attempt to win her back, Orlov presented the Empress with the diamond. The Count was handsomely rewarded, although not with Catherine's affections.

Right: A 1910 photo of miners washing gold-bearing sand in the Ural Mountains of Russia. Diamonds in the Urals were first found when coarse pebbles concentrated by gold mining were searched again for diamonds. Library of Congress collection (10335-A, no. 191), Prokudin-Gorskiĭ, Sergeĭ Mikhaĭlovich photo.

Facing page, upper: Created in 1762, the Great Imperial Crown is set with 4,936 diamonds, 74 pearls, and a 398.72-carat red spinel. Moscow Kremlin Diamond Fund collection and photo.

Facing page, lower: The 189.62-carat Orlov diamond was found in India and is set in the Imperial Sceptre. Moscow Kremlin Diamond Fund collection and photo.

URAL MOUNTAIN DIAMONDS

Eighteenth century Russia was seized with a passion for diamonds, and the possibility of discovering great concentrations of domestic diamonds fired the minds of many public figures and scientists of the time. But luck did not smile on Russia until July 4, 1829, when Pavel Popov, a 14-year-old serf, picked the first diamond found in Russian territory out of his gold pan. Popov, who was granted his freedom for the discovery, found the 0.52-carat diamond in a gold placer, one of the **Krestvozdvizhenskaya** ("Holy Cross") group of mines on the Koyva River Basin near Gornozavodsk, on the western slope of the Ural Mountains in Perm Krai.

Similarities between the alluvial deposits in the Urals and diamondiferous sands in Brazil led Otto Moritz Ludwig von Engelhardt (1778–1842), mineralogy professor at Tartu University in Estonia, to predict that the Russian deposits would likewise prove to be rich in diamonds, but it is German geographer and naturalist Alexander von Humboldt who is associated with the earliest discoveries of diamonds in Russia. In the month before that initial discovery, Humboldt visited with Adolf Polje, whose wife Varvara Petrovna had inherited the properties. Humboldt suggested that the coarse pebbles concentrated after washing the gold-bearing sands be reworked. Young Popov found that first diamond while doing just that.

Two days later, the mine's safe held two more diamonds. The second and third crystals, weighing 0.66 and 1.27 carats respectively, were found by another teen: Ivan Sokolov. In all, four diamonds were found in 1829, and in 1830, twenty-six diamonds were recovered from the Krestvozdvizhenskaya placers. In the ensuing half century, about one hundred diamonds were recovered from the deposit; the largest of these weighed just under 2 carats. While washing of gold-bearing sands across the Urals during this period yielded relatively few diamonds, most of those recovered were true gems, which exhibit uncommon beauty and transparency. The largest diamond ever found in the Ural Mountains tipped the scales at 25 carats.

In 1937 an extensive search of the western slope of the Middle Urals was initiated, and large diamond placers were eventually located. However, the newly discovered placers proved to contain only small quantities of the precious stone. The Urals' most significant alluvial deposits are concentrated north of the city of Perm in the **Krasnovishersky** district and east of Perm in the **Krestvozdvizhenskaya** region. In the early 2000s, JSC Uralalmaz, a privately held company controlled by Israeli businessman Lev Leviev, efficiently mined the Krasnovishersky placers concentrated by the Kolcha, Rassolninskoe, and Volynka rivers. By 2013, however, those placers were all but exhausted.

The primary deposits for the Ural diamonds have not been found, but a recent paper by Liaginhas et.al (2009) suggests, on the basis of the genesis and eruption ages of these diamonds, that the kimberlite-lamproite pipes lie on the eastern part of the East European Craton, but they are deeply buried under sediment. In other parts of Russia, however, geologists have been profoundly successful in sourcing diamonds.

SIBERIAN DIAMONDS

In November 1897 the first diamond found in Siberia was recovered from the **Mel'nichnaya River**, near the town of Yeniseysk But being that the diamond weighed only 3.2 carats, the government was unwilling to fund further exploration, and thus more than 50 years passed before Siberia produced a second diamond.

Three major Siberian river systems flow into the Arctic Ocean: the Ob' is the westernmost system, the Yenisey is in the middle, with the Lena in the east side. The Mel'nichnaya River, where the first diamond was found, is a tributary of the Yenisey (Jenisej); indeed, the alluvial deposits located between the Yenisey and Lena rivers held great promise, but it would take many years of intensive research before Yakutia, the world's largest diamondiferous province, would be opened.

Mineralogist and geochemist Vladimir Vernadsky (1908) published the first of a multi-volume monograph entitled *Essays in Descriptive Mineralogy* in which he wrote (Native Elements), "The minerals occurring with diamond include zircon, magnesium-rich olivine [forsterite], an unusual brown mica (phlogopite), chromium-pyrope, chrome diopside, magnesian titaniferous iron ore (picroilmenite), perovskite, and so on." How, after only one diamond had been found in Siberia, Vernadsky was able to accurately identify the major mineral species, including the specific enrichments that would be associated with Siberian diamonds remains a mystery. He nevertheless confidently and correctly mused, "It is very likely that significant diamond deposits exist in Russia, although until now they remain undiscovered."

Nikolay M. Fedorovsky (1936, p. 85) made further strides toward the discovery of diamond-bearing kimberlites in Siberia, pointing out that "In the USSR, systematic search of diamonds has not yet been carried out, but according to the South African model, diamonds must be sought in the areas of distribution of heavy magnesian magmas that are rich in olivine. In South Africa, diamonds are usually found with ilmenite; garnet, specifically pyrope; chrome diopside, etc. Brazilian diamonds are found in association with amethyst, topaz, and euclase. Of all the regions of the USSR, the one that most resembles Brazil is on the eastern slope of the southern Urals, south of the city of Miass. South African-type deposits have not yet been discovered, but it is possible that they will be found in the many volcanic regions of Siberia and the northern Urals."

In the 1930s, Alexander P. Burov was leading the search for diamonds in the newly formed USSR. The cause was aided by petrographer and mineralogist Vladimir S. Sobolev who, in his paper *Petrology of the Traprocks of the Siberian Platform* (1936), pointed out the similarities between the geologies of the Siberian and South African Karoo plateaus. One year later, Sobolev analyzed petrographic samples from the Taimyr Peninsula and discovered a unique basic rock, which he thought might be an analog of the South African ultrabasic formations that typically accompany diamond-bearing kimberlites (Turkevich 1963).

Burov and Sobolev compiled a survey of the geologies of foreign diamond deposits that, along with the discovery of extensive areas of basic volcanic rocks in Russia's Khatanga district, advanced Sobolev's hypothesis. G. G. Moor tested rock samples collected by the Arctic Institute Expedition and in 1940 published an article reaffirming the likelihood that diamonds were present in north-central Siberia. Saint Petersburg State University professor Alexander Kukharenko was likewise convinced that diamonds were also waiting to be found in eastern Siberia. With industrial diamonds a critical strategic import and war imminent, these voices were heard and the Kremlin authorized a team to begin systematic exploration of eastern Siberia for diamonds. Interrupted by World War II, researchers resumed their work with renewed vigor in 1946, and on Aug 7, 1949, they found 22 diamonds in the rich gravels of the **Sokolinaya Sandbar** in the Vilyuy River, not far from the village of Krestyakh in east-central Siberia.

In the early 1950s, intensive prospecting for primary (*in situ*) sources of diamond was focused on this area. Geologists Larisa Popugaeva and Natalya Sarsadskikh pioneered the use of indicator minerals in diamond prospecting. The team

Above: At its peak the 525-meter-deep, 1.2-kilometer-wide Mir Pit produced some 2 million carats of rough diamonds per year. The town of Mirny sits at the mine's edge.
Stepanov Aleksandrovich photo.

Facing page, upper: Diamond in kimberlite, the crystal is 1.5 cm wide.
The specimen was found circa 1960 in the Mir Pipe, Malo-Botuobinsky district, Sakha (Yakutia) Republic.
Houston Museum of Natural Science collection,
Erica and Harold van Pelt photo.

Facing page, lower: A plaque commemorates Yakutia's first diamond find made on the Sokolinaya Sandbar on Aug. 7, 1949.
United Russia photo.

---

systematically sampled the Daldyn River sediments looking for pyrope and found success on August 21, 1954. Situated on the Daldyn River in the Sakha (Yakutia) Republic, eastern Siberia, the first primary diamond source found in the Soviet Union was dubbed *Zarnitsa*, meaning "Summer Lightning."

One year later and some 600 kilometers south, Yuri I. Khabardin found the *Mir* ("Peace") pipe and sent a now famous telegram to Moscow: "Lit the pipe of peace. Tobacco is great." Vladimir Shchukin discovered a third pipe *Udachnaya* ("Lucky"), on June 15, 1955, just two days after Mir was found. Udachnaya is just 17.5 kilometers west of the Zarnitsa Pipe. In 1957 the state-owned Yakutalmaz group of companies was established to manage development and mine the properties. They recovered their first diamonds a few months later. Within 5 short years, the Yakutsk Diamond Province became the fifth largest diamond producer in the world.

It was not until 1975 that researchers found *Yubileynaya* ("Jubilee"), one of Russia's largest diamond-bearing kimberlites. Yubileynaya is situated in the Alakit-Markhinskoe Kimberlite Field of the Yakutian Kimberlite Province, 15 kilometers northwest of the settlement of Aykhal. The giant crater was filled with stratified sedimentary and volcanic rocks and thus was not uncovered by direct sampling, but the alluvial diamond deposits north of the buried pipe were a clear indication that the pipe was nearby.

Yubileynaya was ultimately located by means of a magnetotelluric survey, a geophysical method that detects a disruption in the magnetic fabric that is created by a kimberlite pipe, which has punched through and disturbed the surrounding geology. A low flying aircraft dragging a magnetometer can detect a circular anomaly in the magnetic field that is associated with a pipe. Because the earth's magnetic field is strongest near the poles, magnetotelluric methods are most effective at latitudes greater than about 45 degrees. Some modern diamond deposits have been found exclusively through magnetic prospecting, but most often the method is used in combination with mineralogical sampling.

Amakinskaya Expedition geologists discovered the **Krasnopresnenskaya Pipe** during detailed prospecting, including a magnetotelluric survey, of the upper Alakit-Markhinskoe Kimberlite Field in 1984. The pipe, located in the Alakit-Markha Kimberlite Field in the Daldyno-Alakitsky region of Yakutia, was overlain by sediments and dolerite sills up to 115 meters thick. Interestingly, a 100-plus-meter thick intruding traprock bisected and altered Krasnopresnenskaya, the upper part of which was found first. The mineralogical trail

that had been left behind as the kimberlite moved ultimately led geologists to the root of the pipe.

In February 1992, a few months after the dissolution of the Soviet Union, ALROSA formed as a closed, joint-stock company to develop and operate Russia's diamond mines. In October 2013 ALROSA went public, and the following month the Russian Federation owned 44 percent; the Sakha (Yakutia) Republic owned 25 percent; various Sakha municipalities held 8 percent; and the remaining 23 percent was in the hands of private and institutional international investors. The company is traded on the Moscow Stock Exchange.

Exploration and development continued under ALROSA.

The Nakynskoe Kimberlite Field and the **Botuobinskaya Pipe** within it were both discovered in 1994. Two years later, researchers located the **Nyurbinskaya Pipe** in the same field, which is situated 205 kilometers northwest of Nyurba and 350 kilometers northeast of Mirny. Data gathered in the 1970s had suggested that the Nakyn area held promise, but exploratory drilling to depths of 40 meters revealed nothing, and prospecting efforts in the area were abandoned until 1994, when an in-depth and systematic geological and geophysical field survey was carried out. The rich kimberlites were finally discovered buried beneath some 70 meters of sediment.

Siberian diamond discoveries and development continue,

as is demonstrated by the evaluation in 2011 of the kimberlites in the Verkhne-Munskoe (Upper Muna) Field (Oleneksky district). The Verkhne-Munskoe deposit in this field consists of four kimberlite pipes: **Zapolyarnaya**, **Deimos**, **Novinka**, and **Komsomolskaya-Magnitnaya**. According to ALROSA, Verkhne-Munskoe is sizable, with more than 38 million carats in reserve, the diamonds tend to be high-quality, but a lot of rock has to be moved in order to recover them. Industrial mining of these deposits is scheduled to begin in 2018.

Over the last 60 years, more than 1,200 kimberlite bodies and related structures have been discovered in the Sakha (Yakutia) Republic; about 10 percent of these are diamond-bearing. Of those roughly 120 kimberlites, 24 produce mostly industrial-grade diamonds, and just 9 — the **Mir**, **Aykhal**, **Internatsional'naya**, and **Udachnaya** underground mines and the **Yubileynaya**, **Komsomol'skaya**, **Zarnitsa**, **Nyurbinskaya**, and **Botuobinskaya** open pits — are currently being worked.

ALROSA has four processing plants in Yakutia that enable the company to profitably mine a number of low-grade deposits. Kimberlites with lower diamond content such as Yubileynaya and Komsomolskaya are exploited for industrial diamonds and are profitable because of their close proximity to richer pipes and thus have access to the processing operations associated with the latter.

Above: The V. Grib deposit was discovered in 1996, and the mine went into production in 2011.
Photo courtesy of Otkritie Holding.

Left: Rough diamonds from the mines of Arkhangelsk
Photo courtesy of ALROSA.

ARKHANGELSK DIAMONDS

With an area of some 6 million kilometers, the flat, sediment-covered East European or Russian Platform provides the geological framework for much of eastern and northern Europe, from Scandinavia to the Ural Mountains and from the Barents Sea to the Black and Caspian seas to the south.

The Northern Dvina River drains most of northwest Russia into the Arctic Ocean and was an important trade route until the seventeenth century. Diamonds, along with pearls, are said to have long been found since the Middle Ages on the banks of the Northern Dvina. The stones were commonly used as soldier's amulets, as the alluvial diamonds had a tumbled appearance and did not particularly look like gems.

As the pipes in Siberia began to open, prospecting for diamond-bearing kimberlites in the remote north gained momentum, but direct sampling suggested that the area was devoid of kimberlites, which as it turned out, were overlain with thick sediments and in some places further obscured by ancient glacial moraines. Geophysical and magnetotelluric methods were thus more useful than mineralogical sampling in ultimately locating the primary kimberlites.

Unlike in Yakutia, where geologists from across the country worked to locate the kimberlites, credit for the discovery of the Arkhangelsk fields sits squarely with local geologist and archaeologist Alexander M. Stankovsky, who was convinced that the Arkhangelsk region was geologically similar to the Yakutsk diamondiferous province. As Louis Pasteur famously quipped, "Fortune favors the prepared mind." Given the extensive experience and success in Yakutia, teams quickly located the Arkhangelsk pipes.

The first kimberlite pipe (**Pomorskaya**) was uncovered in February 1980. And a period of rapid discovery ensued. Numerous kimberlite bodies, including industrial occurrences **Lomonosova**, **Arkhangelskaya**, **Karpinskogo-1**, **Karpinskogo-2**, and **Pionerskaya,** were all found between 1981 and 1982. The discovery in 1996 of the rich **V. Grib Pipe** was significant in that it established the region as an important source for industrial diamonds. V. Grib went into production in 2014.

Technically speaking, the "Arkhangelsk Diamondiferous Province" is an historical designation. From a geological and tectonic point of view, the area of alkaline-ultrabasic volcanism is located in the southeastern coast of the White Sea, and the province is often referred to as the *Winter Coast* or *Zimnii Bereg*. The kimberlites are integral to the White Sea-Baltic subprovince which is part of the East European province of kimberlites and carbonatites (Frolov et al. 2005).

In total more than 100 kimberlites in a 20,000 square kilometer area in Europe's far north have been identified. The diamond province extends from the southeastern coast of the White Sea to the northwestern edge of the Russian Plate.

With an average diamond content of 1 carat per tonne of ore, the Arkhangelsk deposits are not as rich as the Yakutsk pipes, but the Arkhangelsk mines produce a high proportion of coveted fancy-color diamonds, especially yellows, greens, pinks, and blues.

Six of Arkhangelsk's most important diamond-bearing pipes, including **Lomonosov**, are concentrated in the 14-square-kilometer Zolotitskoe Field. The **Vladimir Grib** ("V. Grib") Mine (named for its geologist discoverer) is located in the Chernoozerskoe Field. Additional Arkhangelsk kimberlite fields that have been mapped, include **Kepinskoe**, **Verkhotinskoe**, **Megorskoe**, and **Mel'skoe**, but the pipes in these fields have either low diamond contents or are barren.

The ALROSA subsidiary PJSC Severalmaz runs the industrial diamond mining operations in the Zolotitskoe Field, where the Arkhangelskaya and Karpinskogo-1 pipes are presently in production. Lukoil, Russia's second largest oil company, owns and operates the V. Grib Pipe, which is situated northeast of the Zolotitskoe deposits.

Many authors have noted that Arkhangelsk pipes exhibit a diverse range of geochemical characteristics. The Zolotitskoe Field on the Winter Coast, for example, hosts micaceous, aluminum-magnesium rich kimberlites (Kononova et al. 2007), while the Chernoozerskoe Field hosts iron-titanium-rich kimberlites (Kargin et al. 2015).

Arkhangelsk pipes vary in size from the gigantic Pionerskaya (36.9 hectares) to the large Lomonosova, Karpinskogo-1, Karpinskogo-2, and Arkhangelskaya (between 10.2 to 20.2 hectares) to the modest Pomorskaya (5.6 hectares). The width of the crater facies is proportional to the size of the pipe: the crater facies in the large Arkhangelskaya Pipe is 140 meters wide, but is 160 to 170 meters wide in the much larger Pionerskaya Pipe (Bogatikov et al. 1999).

Arkhangelsk kimberlites intrude alkaline-ultrabasic rocks of the Belomorsky Complex in the Middle Paleozoic (410–362 million years) (Arzamastsev et al. 2005) and in most cases, also intrude carboniferous sediments which are Permian (290–250 million years). In addition, some pipes are only covered by recent loose Quaternary sediments (Bogatikov et al. 1999).

The broad craters of the pipes are composed of tuffaceous sedimentary formations. The diatremes or vents are first filled with columnar bodies of xeno- and tuffaceous-breccia and later with autolithic porphyry kimberlite magma. In some cases, however, the pipes only contain xeno- and tuffaceous-breccia (Bogatikov et al. 1999, Verzhak 2001).

Arkhangelsk diamonds are unique in the world because of their sculptural quality, resulting from dissolution and resorption caused by their extensive contact with aggressively corrosive fluids. Up to 30 percent of the crystals from the Grib and up to 70 percent from the Lomonosov Pipe are rounded or deformed and are commonly lower in quality and more prone to break than are diamonds from other localities. Less diamondiferous or near barren bodies in the Kepinskoe and Verkhotinsko fields appear to have been subjected to prolonged and even more intense corrosive fluids, which have effectively minimized their diamond populations.

Above: Diamond "macle," 7.9 carats. While the specific source of this specimen is noted only as "Russia," the rounded edges and distortion suggest that it may have come from the Arkhangelsk region. Bill Larson collection, Mia Dixon photo.

In depth research by Kriulina et al. (2012) has shown that visually homogeneous, cubic, orange-brown crystals from the Arkhangelskaya Pipe can be divided into three groups based on the aggregation states of nitrogen impurities and internal growth structures they contain. In addition plastically deformed, sharply zoned, cubic crystals are unique to the M. V. Lomonosov deposit.

These authors also show that detailed studies of gray, dodecahedral crystals from the Arkhangelskaya Pipe have high contents both of nitrogen and hydrogen, with nitrogen concentrated on specific crystal planes. Furthermore, the various zones of the crystals are made up of carbon with different isotopic compositions. The only analogous crystals are found in the *Snegurochka* ("Snow Maiden") Pipe.

Of the mineral inclusions identified within the diamonds, a distinctive feature is that they are either devoid of or contain only negligible sulfide inclusions (Rubanova et al. 2009). This absence may be due to the early segregation of sulfide melts, which lasted until the kimberlites formed. There may be a similar explanation for the absence of paramagnetic nickel centers within the diamonds, another unique characteristic of Arkhangelsk diamonds, (see Rubanova et al. 2009). These authors also showed that mineral inclusions and the isotopic composition of the carbon making up the diamond crystals indicated that V. Grib diamonds primarily formed in peridotite whilst the diamonds from M. V. Lomonosov have their origins in both deep-seated peridotites and eclogites.

SINGULAR STONES

Through the decades, Russia's rich deposits have produced some extraordinary diamonds. On October 21, 2012, an 888.15-carat diamond was pulled from the depths of the Yubileynaya Pipe. The colossal diamond is the fourth largest recovered from a Russian mine but being industrial-grade, it was not given a name.

Historically, names have been assigned to gem-quality diamonds weighing over 50 carats or with unusually bright colors. The largest named diamond found on Russian soil is the 342.57-carat *XXVI S'ezd KPSS* ("Congress of CPSU"). About the size of a chicken egg, the lemon-yellow stone's name commemorates the Twenty-Sixth Congress of the Communist Party, which opened by Leonid Brezhnev on February 23, 1981. The diamond was recovered from the Mir Pipe on December 23, 1980, and is part of the Kremlin's Diamond Fund.

Also acquired by the Diamond Fund, Russia's second largest named diamond *Alexander Pushkin*, weighed in at 320.65 carats and was mined Dec. 22, 1989, from the Udachnaya pipe. Udachnaya has produced a number of large stones, including a 700-carat black, industrial-grade diamond found in 2003. To date ALROSA has recovered 31 diamonds weighing more than 100 carats from its Russian operations.

In advance of its 2013 initial public offering of shares, ALROSA began selling fancy colored stones through Sotheby's auction house. This decision involved some political trauma as the diamonds or other objects that GOKHRAN Russia, the official state precious metal and gems repository, categorizes as "unique" are not supposed to leave Russia, and the agency blocked a planned sale of a 47.48 carat stone, cut from a 128-carat crystal, in the spring of 2013. But in September 2013, Sotheby's auctioned a Russian 40.45-carat, pear-shaped faceted gem that the GIA graded as a natural "Fancy dark brown" with a clarity of "VVS2." The stone sold for US$401,000 (Lot 493).

In the same auction, ALROSA put up a diamond and platinum necklace (Lot 492), consisting of three cushion modified brilliant-cut, fancy colored diamonds: a 1.02-carat Fancy vivid purple-pink; a 0.5-carat Fancy intense pinkish purple; and a 0.36-carat Fancy vivid purplish pink diamond. All three stones were recovered from the Arkhangelskaya Pipe in the Zolotitskoe Kimberlite Field in Arkhangelsk. The necklace commanded US$293,000.

PROSPECTS AND CONCLUDING REMARKS

The diamond contents of the pipes in Yakutia and Arkhangelsk vary widely and are dependent upon factors including the depths at which the diamonds formed and the distances they traveled to the surface (the longer the trip, the greater the dissolution). Indeed, most of Russia's kimberlite pipes are barren.

Right: Tabular, hexagonal diamond, 1 cm tall, ~2 carats. Sakha (Yakutia) Republic. Rich Olsen collection, Jeff Scovil photo.

Facing Page: Russian Diamonds

Upper left: Faceted diamonds set in platinum, the largest stone is 1.02 carats and was given a color grade of fancy vivid purple-pink. Photo courtesy of Sotheby's.

Upper middle: Diamond, 241.21 carats. Nyurbinskaya Pipe, Nakyn Field, Sakha (Yakutia) Republic. Photo courtesy of ALROSA.

Upper right: Diamond crystal, 1 cm long, on matrix. Sakha (Yakutia) Republic. Canadian Museum of Nature collection (ex Bill Pinch), Michael Bainbridge photo.

Lower left: Faceted, pear-shaped, fancy dark brown diamond, 40.45 carats. Sakha (Yakutia) Republic. Photo courtesy of Sotheby's.

Lower middle: Faceted diamond, 54.09 carats. Photo courtesy of ALROSA.

Lower right: Diamond, 78.3 carats. Nyurbinskaya Pipe, Nakyn Field, Sakha (Yakutia) Republic. Photo courtesy of ALROSA.

Modern mineralogical techniques enable present-day prospectors to assess deposits, predicting their productivity and estimating the quality of the diamonds. Researchers at M. V. Lomonosov Moscow State University are constantly developing and improving methods for predicting and evaluating diamondiferous kimberlites.

Analysis of the compositions and morphological features of certain minerals can aide researchers in reconstructing the history of mantle material beginning with the formation of the pipe. Chromite, for example, is an indicator of the depth of the magma chamber. If the kimberlite has a high (greater than 60 weight percent) chromite content (as at Mir and Udachnaya, for example), then the source is deep, and the pipe has excellent potential for diamonds.

Because diamonds are altered as they develop in the mantle and as they are transported to the surface, the pipe must have formed rapidly if the quality of the diamonds is to be preserved. The **Internatsionalnaya Pipe** is an example of a diamond source that formed and transported diamonds to the surface rapidly. As a result, the pipe is diamond-rich (8 carats per tonne), and some 85 percent of the crystals are octahedral, having retained their original form. In contrast, only about 1 carat of diamonds is recovered for each tonne of rock removed from the V. Grib Pipe. The production is modest in spite of the fact that the composition of the primary mantle material would indicate that the host rocks were at one time diamond-rich. The crystals from V. Grib have been subjected to dissolution and resorption and the resulting forms are modified octahedra and dodecahedra. And probably many of the crystals have dissolved completely. A great deal of attention is paid to the mineralogy of the kimberlites and related rocks, which are important survey and assessment tools. An early focus was the study of microcrystalline (less than 100 microns) oxides found in massive kimberlites and the rocks they have intruded.

The search for new fields expands across the world, as does the demand for diamonds from both the industrial and jewelry markets. Despite advances in diamond synthesis, natural stones remain in high demand. Prospects for the discovery of new deposits on Russian territory are favorable, and the search continues unabated.

ACKNOWLEDGEMENTS: *The authors wish to thank Iva Veselinova and Dr. Maria Alferova for their invaluable assistance in translating this text and Dr. Jeff Harris for his thorough review and helpful suggestions. We are further grateful to Dmitriy Belakovskiy for facilitating the submission, Dr. Andrei Prokopiev and Dr. Konstantin Garanin for their editorial skills, and to Andrey Ryabinnikov at ALROSA, for supply photographs to illustrate this and other texts in this volume.*

ARGYLE DIAMONDS

by John Chapman

In the mid-90s more than 30 percent of the world's diamond production by volume was being extracted from a single source: the Argyle Mine in remote northwestern Australia. Output of the mine, owned by Rio Tinto, has since dwindled to a quarter of its peak production as the operation has moved deeper and ore extracted from a narrowing body of diamond-bearing rock. Decisions to tunnel under and tap a deep orebody have prolonged the life of the mine and promise to extend the supply of Argyle diamonds, which changed the industry the moment they appeared on the world stage in 1983.

The diamond production profile is unlike that of any other commercial diamond deposit. The volume of diamonds is prodigious, reaching a peak of 43 million carats in 1994 (Janse 2007). A large proportion of the production is comprised of brown diamonds and diamonds that are heavily included with black graphite *piques* and cracks (Chapman et al. 1996). The average diamond size is small — less than 0.1 carat, making the average value per carat relatively low by world standards (Shigley et al. 2001). The ore, on the other hand, is relatively high grade, averaging six carats per tonne — more than ten times higher than that of most other mines. The high-grade ore compensates for the low per carat value and ensures the economic viability of the project. Despite the abundance of low quality diamonds, however, 5 percent of the mine's output comes in the form of colorless gems and a particular curiosity that has become the hallmark of the mine — pink diamonds (Shigley et al. 2001).

During the early years, Argyle Diamonds entered into a sales agreement with the De Beers' Central Selling Organization, but retained a percentage of the production for independent sale. Argyle's unconventional diamonds were not a good fit for the Central Selling Organization's sales model, and it worked to figure out how to market this vast new quantity of low value diamonds, as three-quarters of the production was deemed "industrial," as opposed to the categories of "gem" and "near-gem." Without a ready market, De Beers began stockpiling much of this classification.

Astute Indian *diamantaires*, however, realized that skilled laborers in India could economically produce an attractive faceted gem from a low value diamond even if it meant

---

Above: During the Argyle Mine's open pit phase, more than 1 billion tonnes of rock were shifted or processed to deliver only enough diamonds to fill a domestic swimming pool.
Rio Tinto photo, circa 2010.
Facing page: Rough diamonds showcasing the flagship colors of Argyle diamonds.
Argyle Mine, Kimberley Division, Western Australia, Australia.
Image © 2017 Rio Tinto.

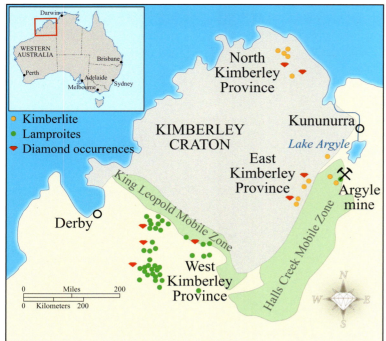

Left: Kimberlite, lamproites and diamond deposits in the Kimberley area, Western Australia.
William W. Besse map.
Center left: A selection of Argyle diamonds, each weighing about 0.5 carats.
John Chapman photo.
Lower left: Diamond rough can look a lot like gravel.
Background: Rough diamonds.
John Chapman photo.
Facing page, top left: At 41.7-carats, this is the largest diamond from the AK1 deposit.
John Chapman photo.
Facing page, middle left: A 2-carat, light brown diamond octahedron with surface etching.
John Chapman photo.
Facing page, middle right: Diamond crystal with deep surface pits, 13.16 carats.
Museum Victoria collection, Arkenstone photo.
Facing page, lower left: A circa 2010 view of the portal to the Argyle underground diamond mine.
Facing page, upper right: Assorted rough.
All photos on this spread, unless otherwise noted, are © 2017 Rio Tinto.

discarding large portions of the stones. Argyle Diamonds embarked on an aggressive marketing campaign to stimulate demand for brown diamonds, branding them with appealing terms such as *champagne* and *cognac*. In 1996 Argyle Diamonds determined that its interests would be better served by operating outside the Central Selling Organization. Its departure from the cartel signaled to other producers that selling rough diamonds independently was a viable option.

At present, Argyle diamonds continue to be polished almost exclusively in India, where more than 250,000 workers saw, shape, and facet the millions of gems that are sold each year through the Rio Tinto sales office in Antwerp, Belgium. The vast majority of the finished stones weigh just a few points (1 point = 0.01 carats) and are 1 to 2 millimeters in diameter. Once considered industrial, champagne and cognac diamonds now enjoy a healthy segment of the jewelry market, satisfying the demand for affordable, low-cost diamond jewelry and extending the palette for designers.

GEOLOGY

Argyle diamonds are believed to have been formed 1.58 billion years ago (Richardson 1986) at a depth of 180 to 205 kilometers and at a temperature of near 1250 +/- 50 degrees Celsius (Stachel et al. in press). Four-hundred million years after they formed, a plume of rising molten magma tapped into the reservoir of diamonds and shot them to the Earth's surface in a volcanic burst (Pidgeon et al. 1989). This magma cooled to form a carrot-shaped orebody known as *AK1*, which is divided into a north and south component, each of which represent different volcanic events, though since its emplacement geological forces have tilted the body steeply.

The composition of the igneous magma corresponds to a lamproite that differs subtly in its mineral composition from kimberlite, which is traditionally associated with diamond (Shirey & Shigley 2013). While the Prairie Creek lamproite in Arkansas (pages 86–93) had long been known to be diamondiferous, AK1 was the first lamproitic deposit found to

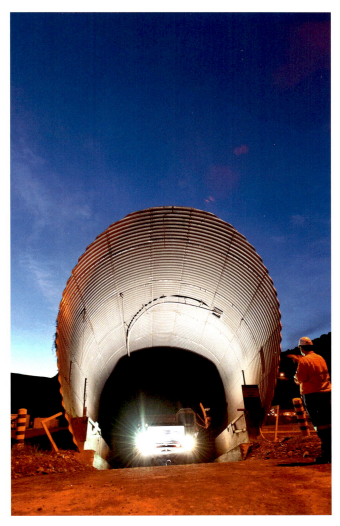

be commercially viable. That discovery led geologists to expand their prospecting canvas to include lamproites around the world as potential diamond sources, and in fact a lamproite in the **Bundelkhand** region of Madhya Pradesh, India, had been of interest to Rio Tinto. Hopes of development are fading however, as the project would require clearing a forested area that is important habitat for tigers and other wildlife.

UNIQUELY ARGYLE

The bulk of Argyle diamonds (50 to 70 percent) are irregular in shape, about 25 percent are *macles*, and 15 to 5 percent (fewer as size decreases) are aggregates. Octahedra and dodecahedra are minor constituents, totaling only about 5 percent of diamonds (Hall & Smith 1984). Breakage brought about both by geologic forces and by recovery and processing operations affects more than 80 percent of diamonds. The large number of broken crystals and irregular shapes combined with the dark inclusions crystals typically contain make a typical parcel of unsorted rough look a lot like aquarium gravel — stark contrast to their dazzle after faceting.

The surface textures of Argyle diamonds vary from smooth and glossy to severely etched. Both extremes can be the result of chemical attack after the diamond has formed, with the more aggressive attack producing large shallow hexagonal pits. Such pits are commonly etched into the crystal surfaces of Argyle octahedral diamonds and distinguish them from diamonds from other localities, the surfaces of which typically exhibit triangular etch pits. In some instances the etching is severe, forming deep channels and cavities within a stone.

Distortions of Argyle lattices also make them challenging to polish. The rate at which diamond can be polished depends on the orientation of the crystal, which can present "easy" and "hard" directions (see page 34). In a textbook diamond crystal, those directions are easily identified from the crystal axes, but twin crystals and irregularities known as *naats*, mix soft and hard directions thus making the faceting process significantly more challenging.

COLOR

Nitrogen is the most common impurity found in diamond. The nitrogen content affects many properties including color, thermal conductivity, and even the crystal's resistance to plastic deformation (Clackson & Moore 1992, Nailer et al. 2007). Argyle diamonds generally have low concentrations of nitrogen, typically less than 500 parts per million, and there are virtually no Type II diamonds (see page 41–43) (Chapman et al. 1996). Nitrogen, however, is responsible for the color of yellow diamonds at Argyle and while also present in colorless and brown diamonds, the nitrogen configurations are not color centers. Plastic deformation of the diamond lattice, on the other hand, is responsible for the brown, pink, and red tones that dominate Argyle's output.

Blue-gray and violet diamonds are also prized from the mine. These colors are rarer than the famous pinks; the best command prices on par with the best of the pinks in the annual tenders of polished gems. These sales typically showcase 50 to 80 stones, chosen for their size or depth of color. The tendered stones are scrutinized by select buyers, who are invited to view and bid on the gems. A spin-off of these showcase diamonds is the lavish, limited edition catalogues promoting the stones. With print runs of just a few hundred, the catalogues are themselves quite collectable.

The fancy pink, blue-gray, and red diamonds are cut and polished in Perth by a few skilled artisans with decades of experience in handling these precious crystals. Those pink diamonds that are too small to warrant tender status are processed by contract polishers in India and are sold to specially appointed *Select Atelier* jewelers, who are located in several countries.

Prices in excess of one million dollars per carat have been achieved for the better pink diamonds, and prices continue to rise as discerning buyers and investors seek to acquire these rare and spectacular gems the supply of which will cease when the Argyle Mine closes.

CERTIFICATION

While the Argyle pinks command high prices, they face growing competition from artificial diamonds and treatments that achieve increasingly comparable colors at a fraction of the price. However as with pearls and semi-precious gems, such competition also has the potential to elevate the demand for the natural material, subject of course to the public's trust in certificates.

Retailers and wholesalers contract gemological laboratories to evaluate diamonds and colored stones. These reports describe a stone's color, inclusions (clarity), carat weight, and cut. In addition, laboratories will identify any treatments or enhancements that a stone has undergone and will determine whether a diamond is natural or synthetic. Certification is key to consumer confidence.

Both the Gemological Institute of America (GIA) and Argyle Pink Diamonds grade and certify pink diamonds. Gemological laboratories exploit phenomena of fluorescence and optical absorption of specific wavelengths of visible or infra-red light to distinguish the origin of color. As it turns out, Argyle "pinks" feature an almost unique phenomenon in that they are *photo-chromatic*: their color is bleached under ultraviolet light and is almost entirely removed when exposed to a high-intensity, short-wavelength light source. But alarm at this color loss is short-lived — the color is restored with a few minutes of exposure to daylight, or more specifically blue light.

The GIA describes colors from "light fancy pink" to "intense vivid pink," "fancy deep pink" and in extreme cases "fancy red." The Argyle grading scale assigns three hues: "purple-pink" (PP), "pink" (P), and "pink-rosé" (PR). The Argyle system couples the hue with a numeric prefix, ranging from 1 to 9, which corresponds to color saturation. Conventionally the color grade of a diamond is determined by comparison with select *masterstones*, which have been carefully selected from a broad selection of diamonds of various hues and saturations. Clarity is not nearly as critical with fancy

Left: Fancy brown rough diamond, 8.72 carats from the Argyle diamond mine. Image © 2017 Rio Tinto.

Right: The Argyle diamondiferous lamproite was discovered when geologists followed alluvial deposits from Argyle, such as those in the pictured Smoke Creek area, where native boab trees have been replanted. Bill Bachman photo.

Facing page: Four of the fancy colored, faceted diamonds offered at the 2013 Argyle Tender. The largest in this suite is the 2.02 "fancy intense purple pink," princess-cut gem (**third from the left**) named the *Argyle Seraphina*. All were sourced from the Argyle Mine, Western Australia. Image © 2017 Rio Tinto.

colored diamonds as it is with the colorless variety, and the majority of Argyle pinks contain visible inclusions, often consisting of small, fluid-filled cavities.

PRESENT AND FUTURE

The current underground operation only started delivering ore in 2013. The expansion is the result of almost 8 years of excavating, tunneling, and engineering that cost in excess of $2 billion US dollars. Ore is extracted from the underground mine through a process known as *block caving*, whereby rock is caused to drop from the ceiling of an enlarging cavern. The rocks break as they fall, and the broken rock is extracted from 273 draw points and conveyed from an average depth of 280 meters by belts (some up to 2 kilometers long) to the processing plant at the surface.

The fruits of this investment will be reaped as the annual volume of diamonds leaving the recovery plant rises over the next few years to an expected annual output of 15 to 20 million carats. While well shy of the mine's peak, the output will double that of recent years, (about 8 million carats in 2011) when the ore was trucked from the depths of an open pit.

Argyle diamonds have not only been mined from the AK1 primary source. Over the past billion years the lamproite has been eroded by sub-tropical rains lashing the volcanic hill. The diamonds were washed into Smoke Creek, a drainage river that has snaked different courses over time. Stretches of old river bed have been excavated to extract the diamonds, which were liberated by the more gentle forces of nature rather than the blasting and crushing methods employed by primary deposit processing. These alluvial diamonds formed Argyle's production in 1983. With an eye on the environment, the company replanted the trees and vegetation it had removed to access the alluvial diamonds, and a similar reclamation program is planned for the main pit.

Three-hundred full-time workers fulfill the day-to-day demands of the Argyle mining operation with many contractors engaged on short-term assignments for specific engineering projects. These workers mostly live in nearby Kununurra or the state's capital Perth, some 2,000 kilometers distant. A growing proportion of the workforce comprises aborigines who are trained as mine operators and maintenance personnel. The remoteness of the operation means chartered aircraft are relied upon to ferry the workers to and from the mine for stints that vary from one to a few weeks.

The underground operation will extend the mine's life until at least 2020. The legacy of the Argyle Mine will be almost a billion carats of rough diamonds. Until then, the output will continue to be a source of income for thousands of miners, polishers, and traders and provide joy to millions of consumers from village brides to Hollywood celebrities.

John Chapman has a degree in Physics and has been active in the diamond industry for over 30 years, with roles spanning industrial diamond testing, diamond property research, diamond population modeling, and developing machines and instruments to sort and grade both rough and polished diamonds. John has worked for Rio Tinto Diamonds for much of his career. He is currently Director of Gemetrix Pty Ltd, a diamond consulting company and manufacturer of the PL Inspector fluorescence viewer.

COLORADO DIAMONDS

by Dr. Terry C. Wallace, Jr.

In the late 1860s the discovery of diamonds in South Africa (see page 70–75) captured the world's attention. In 1869, for example, an 83.5 carat rough diamond, christened the *Star of South Africa* (pictured on page 73), was sold for £11,200 (Balfour 1987) — the present day equivalent of more than one million US dollars — and a major diamond rush was on.

In 1872 John Slack and Philip Arnold, a couple of slick con men posing as lucky prospectors, decided to take advantage of the interest in diamonds and staked a series of claims in the northwestern corner of Colorado, at a site that today is known as *Diamond Peak*. They showed up in San Francisco with a bag full of diamonds and rubies and seeking investors for their great diamond strike. The shady duo secured financing from West Coast elites hoping to cash in on another "49ers Rush". Flush with cash, Slack and Arnold brought a couple of mining experts to Colorado to confirm their amazing claim.

The story of the diamond strike spread like a wildfire, spurring a brief hope that diamonds would be the next big rush in the west. The *San Francisco Chronicle* (Oct. 7, 1872) ran a series of exuberant proclamations, the Wild West equivalent of the modern tweet: "LARGE QUANTITIES OF DIAMONDS AND RUBIES OBTAINED. Ant Hills Built of Precious Stones. The Tales of Arabian Nights Surpassed."

The story raised eyebrows and was debunked within a year when Clarence King, the distinguished geologist leading the Fortieth Parallel Survey, visited the area. King and his party quickly realized that the gems had been imported. Alas, the Diamond Peak claims turned out to be a hoax; the sandstone clandestinely salted with all sorts of gemstones, enough to convince some gullible "experts" (who had actually never seen a diamond deposit), but not enough to carry the ruse particularly far. This would have been only one of many mining swindles in Colorado if not for the remarkable irony that *real* diamonds would be discovered a century later, due east of Diamond Peak along the Front Range of the Rocky Mountains!

In the mid-1960s geologists became focused on a series of unusual rock deposits along the Front Range of the Rockies and its topographic extension into Wyoming. These rocks turned out to be kimberlites, typically filled with crustal xenoliths. The xenoliths were truly puzzling: they were dominantly blocks of Paleozoic sediments, completely out of place in surrounding Precambrian granites. Finally, a close examination of the surrounding geology showed that these xenoliths were contained within circular features consistent with a *diatreme* — an explosively emplaced plug or pipe.

The diatreme looked like those associated with kimberlite pipes in Africa, but there was great skepticism that these deposits could actually be "belches from the deep." Careful examination of the petrology of the rocks, however, confirmed that it was kimberlite. The realization that kimberlites were fairly common along the Front Range began to dawn on geologists, and within a decade more than 90 kimberlite pipes and dikes had been identified from just north of the Wyoming-

Above: A September 2002 field trip to the Kelsey Lake Mine, Larimer County, Colorado. Photo courtesy of GIA.

Facing page: Diamond crystals to 4 mm wide and faceted stones to 0.177 carats from the Kelsey Lake Mine, Larimer County, Colorado. Dave Bunk Minerals specimens, Jesse La Plante photo.

Colorado border 200 kilometers south to Boulder, Colorado. Most of the kimberlites and associated rocks are located within the State Line Kimberlite District, Larimer County, Colorado.

Despite the presence of kimberlites, the pipes were not known to be diamondiferous until 1972, 11 years after the initial discovery. And that first diamond discovery was serendipitous. While working on a thin section of a garnet nodule collected from one of the kimberlites, a couple of United States Geological Survey technicians saw deep scratches etched in a grinding wheel. Looking at the nodule with a microscope, they found a colorless crystal — a diamond! Other diamonds were quickly found, and a mini-diamond rush was on. A number of the kimberlite pipes in the State Line district were found to contain 0.5 to 1.5 carats of diamond per 100 tonnes of kimberlite. If the diamonds are of good gem quality, this is an economic grade, although the small sizes of the kimberlite pipes make these deposits only marginally economic.

For a brief period in the 1990s diamonds were extracted from two of the pipes, and 21,000 carats in diamonds were recovered. The largest diamond mined was a 28.3-carat yellow crystal, which was christened the *Colorado Diamond*. Most of the diamonds found are clear and weigh less than one carat. The value of the stones mined probably did not exceed a quarter of a million dollars. Although considerable reserves of ore remain, it is unlikely that any further mining will be pursued as diamonds are just too common worldwide!

GEOLOGY

Colorado's diamonds are found in their host kimberlite. In the mid-1960s geologist began to recognize that a series of strange blue-green breccias that had been mapped along the Front Range from just north of Denver to the Wyoming State Line were kimberlites. Geologists had noticed that the "breccias" contained some fascinating xenoliths such as eclogites, peridotites and dunites, only found in the upper mantle. These rocks also had minerals such as garnets and olivines with distinctive chemistries. These "breccias" also carried blocks of Paleozoic rock sediments and Precambrian granites. When the kimberlite was analyzed from a sample collected at a quarry near the Colorado-Wyoming border in Colorado's Larimer County, (Chronic et al. 1965), it was determined that the exotic (originating some distance from their present position) boulders, cobbles, and upper mantle minerals and rocks had in fact been ripped from the surrounding environment as the kimberlite rapidly ascended from depths of 150 kilometers to the surface and erupted. Today more than 100 distinct kimberlite pipes that range in size from 1 to 500 meters in diameter have been identified along the Front Range.

The origin of kimberlites has been a subject of study for 50 years. In general, kimberlites are found in the interiors of old cratons (see pages 11–12), well away from present day tectonic activity or lithospheric deformation. Most theories of kimberlite genesis assume a formation in the sub-continental lithospheric mantle, or even deeper in the transition zone. Volatiles mobilized by the melting create a kimberlite magma between 150 and 450 kilometers below the surface. Upward explosive movement of the magma is driven by the release of volatiles (mostly CO_2 and water) that entrains mantle and crustal material as it moves to the surface. Occasionally, the mantle material contains diamonds, which are formed at

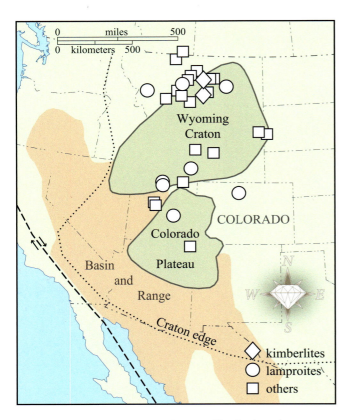

Above: Map showing the distribution of kimberlites, lamproites and related volcanics. Red symbols indicate Cretaceous emplacement ages; open symbols are Cenozoic ages. William W. Besse map, after Curie & Beaumont 2011.

Below: Kimberlite containing large xenocrysts from the Kelsey Lake Mine. Robert Weldon photo © GIA.

depths of 250 to 150 kilometers, and those diamonds are released into the kimberlite. The map above shows the Kimberlite Corridor in the interior of the North American Plate (Currie & Beaumont 2011). The kimberlites are located far from the leading edges of the continent, well away from present day tectonic activity or lithospheric deformation.

The Colorado kimberlites are all situated in a belt within granitic core rocks of the Rocky Mountains. This core is Precambrian in age and represents crust that was formed some 1.7 to 1.9 billion years before the present. This ancient continental block is usually referred to as the *Wyoming Craton*. Based on fission track radioactive isotope decays within various minerals, the kimberlites are thought to have intruded into the Wyoming craton between 350 and 380 million years before the present. This finding suggests that this region was far from a plate boundary at that time, although the Antler Orogeny was taking place to the west (most of the evidence of this mountain-building phase is in present day Nevada, especially the Battle Mountains). The kimberlite pipes along the Front Range appear to be concentrated along ancient faults or sutures which recorded collisions and rifting in the ancient cratons, suggesting that the kimberlites followed opportunistic pathways through the crust before erupting at the surface.

KELSEY LAKE MINE

The most successful of the diamond prospects was centered around Kelsey Lake, which is located just south of the Wyoming-Colorado border, 4 kilometers west of US Route 287. Nine kimberlite pipes are spread over a one-thousand-acre area. The pipes are modest in size; the surface exposure for each is about 10 acres. Three of these pipes are known to contain diamonds, and two were mined. The most studied of the Colorado kimberlites are a cluster of 9 pipes located just south of the Wyoming border that were mined from 1996 to 1998. The **Kelsey Lake Mine** open pit excavated two of these pipes. The cores of the two mined kimberlite pipes are dominated by what is known as *tuffistic kimberlite breccia*, a complex welded facies of angular rock fragments that includes xenocrysts of pyropic garnet, diopside, picroilmenite, phlogopite with a fine-grained crystalline matrix that includes serpentine, olivine, perovskite, spinel, apatite and zircon (Rogers 1985). These kimberlites produced the largest diamonds ever found in Colorado.

Open pit mining started in 1996 after an Australian firm, Redaurum, acquired the mining rights to the two pipes in 1995. Success was modest, but like many Colorado mining adventures, the political drama outsized the ore. After only 200 carats had been recovered, Redaurum was sued by Union Pacific, the original owner of the property. In a rich irony, Union Pacific had been deeded the property in the Pacific Railway Act of 1862 (i.e., public lands were given to a private corporation), which called for a railway to be built from Council Bluffs, Iowa, to Sacramento, California. Union Pacific sold the Kelsey Lake lands in 1896 but claimed that the sale did not pertain to the mineral rights. The suit was settled, but Redaurum decided that diamond mining in Colorado was not all it had been cut out to be. Eventually the property was sold to the Canadian firm McKenzie Bay. The Canadian company had done their homework: they estimated a recovery rate of 3.5 carats per ton of ore and a total reserve of nearly 700,000 carats. Further, the mines had an exclusive contract with a consortium of Denver diamond dealers that called for a price of US$115 dollars per carat. Alas, the mining operations never got off the ground, and the mines remained idle until 2007 when remediation activities began. Surface expression of the mines has since disappeared.

Although the mine only operated for two years, it produced diamonds totaling some 21,000 carats; thus potential for an

Top right: Diamond crystals weighing 1.09, 7.18, 0.99 carats, respectively.
Sloan diatreme, Larimer County.
Private collection,
Jeff Scovil photo.

Middle: This 5.39-carat "fancy deep brownish yellow" (GIA) gem, the *Colorado Diamond*, was cut from a 28.3-carat piece of rough recovered from the Kelsey Lake Mine.
Photo courtesy of GIA.

Lower: Under reflected light differential interference contrast illumination, the trigons on the surface of a diamond from Sloan Ranch are highlighted in color.
Field of view 2 mm wide.
Dan Kile collection and photo.

economic mining venture remains. The diamond reserves of the Kelsey Lake Mine are estimated at several hundred thousand carats — perhaps the story of Colorado diamonds has another chapter.

NOTABLE FINDS

In 1994 the Kelsey Lake operation yielded a 14.2-carat colorless diamond. And in 1996, Redaurum unearthed a 28.3-carat stone, dubbed the *Colorado Diamond*. New York diamond cutter Bill Goldberg faceted the highly etched crystal into a 5.39 carat, pear-shaped diamond graded by the Gemological Institute of America (GIA) as "Fancy Deep Brownish Yellow." Though the GIA lab was not asked to assess the finished stone's clarity, lab notes (Fryer 1997) reveal an etched feather in the pavilion and indicate that it would have been given a clarity grade of *Slightly Included* (SI). Viewed at low-temperature and using a desk-model spectroscope, the GIA lab also reported that the absorption spectrum "showed a strong 'Cape series' and weak sharp bands at about 545 and 563 nm," properties consistent with hydrogen-rich diamonds. *BizWest* (September 22, 2000) reported that the Colorado Diamond sold to an anonymous buyer for $87,500.

On July 14, 1997, the mine's Number 2 kimberlite pipe produced a slightly smaller 28.18-carat diamond "fairly octahedral" crystal, which cut a 16.87-carat gem. The GIA graded the finished stone as a U to V color, "I2" diamond. The diamond was displayed in venues across the state, and the *Rocky Mountain News* (Williamson, September 25, 1997) fanned pie-in-the-sky flames, touting that "the largest finished diamond ever recorded in North American will probably fetch as much as $500,000 at auction." Grand Junction jeweler Thomas Hunn, who handled much of the mine's gem production, purchased the diamond, which Heritage Auctions sold in its May 4, 2015 Fine Jewelry Auction for a whopping $185,000 (including buyer's premium). The Redaurum operation also recovered a 12.42-carat rough diamond that same month.

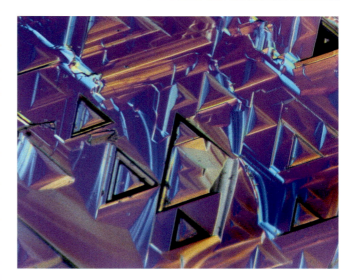

Terry C. Wallace is the Principal Associate Director for Global Security at Los Alamos National Laboratory. He received his undergraduate degree in Mathematics and Geophysics at New Mexico Tech and his PhD in Geophysics at Caltech. He was a professor at the University of Arizona for 20 years where he was also the Curator of the University of Arizona Mineral Museum. He has written widely on popular mineralogy topics, and his collecting specialty is silver.

Laboratory-Grown Diamonds

by Dr. James E. Butler and Dr. Boris N. Feigelson

Laboratory-grown diamonds have been appearing lately on the gemstone market and are also important to a diverse array of advanced technologies. The chemical composition of diamond is the simplest of all gemstones. It is composed of a single element — carbon. Given that the synthesis only requires one element, one would expect the process to be relatively straightforward, but for reasons we shall explain, diamond has proven one of the most difficult gemstones to grow.

Carbon is an unusual element in that it can form multiple types of bonding between atoms (sp^3, sp^2, and sp orbital hybridization), which in turn lead to many crystalline and non-crystalline structures. Graphite and diamond are the two most common crystalline forms of carbon, while carbon nanotubes, fullerenes, and graphene are examples of other structures of carbon (see pages 25–26). These materials differ primarily in the type of chemical bonding between the atoms. This complexity, paired with the metastability of diamond at ambient conditions, makes diamond difficult to grow.

In the early 1950s, two general methods for the growth of diamond in the laboratory were demonstrated: High-Pressure and High-Temperature (HPHT) growth in ultra-high-pressure devices and Chemical Vapor Deposition (CVD) from low-pressure gas reactants. The former method developed into an industry, while the latter only progressed after further research, which lasted through the 1990s.

In addition to satisfying scientific curiosity, the motivation for growing diamonds in the laboratory was to synthesize diamond materials whose properties and morphology were controllable and could thus be reproduced specifically for a variety of technological applications. Diamonds formed in nature contain an array of defects and impurities such that mined diamonds are unique in many of their properties (like snowflakes) and are thus less desirable for many applications that require uniform and consistent physical properties. This paper will briefly describe both the HPHT and CVD growth methods and give examples of the diamonds grown and some of their applications.

HISTORY

With the advent of the first crystals grown by man, diamond became the Holy Grail for crystal growers. Scientists made numerous unsuccessful attempts between 1879 and 1954 to convert graphite to diamond. Only in 1939 did Soviet physicist Ovsei I. Leipunskii (1939) clearly show why all previous endeavors to make diamonds had failed. Leipunskii accurately calculated the pressure/temperature phase diagram for carbon and demonstrated that previous attempts were conducted at pressures and temperatures in which graphite is thermodynamically stable and diamond is not.

Even with all its unique and fascinating properties, diamond is not thermodynamically stable at ambient conditions, while graphite is. Interestingly, the equilibrium line between graphite and diamond on Leipunskii's phase diagram, confirmed by the Berman-Simon calculations from 1955 (Field 1992), is almost exactly the same as that used today. The definition of the equilibrium line between graphite and diamond was essential for future high-pressure diamond synthesis because in order to transform graphite to diamond, it is necessary to be in the diamond stability region.

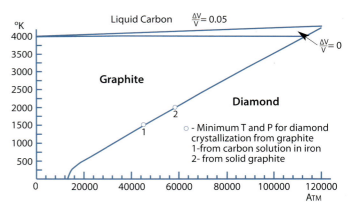

Phase diagram for carbon, as calculated by Leipunskii in 1939, that predicts the pressure and temperature regions in which diamond and graphite are stable. The diamond/graphite equilibrium line is the line between diamond and graphite with the circles marked *1* and *2*.

Leipunskii accurately predicted the physical-chemical conditions for diamond synthesis from graphite. Importantly, diamond synthesis requires very high pressures. The most remarkable of Leipunskii's ideas was to convert graphite to diamond by dissolving graphite in molten iron thus lowering the pressure required for diamond synthesis. He estimated the lowest pressure and temperature conditions for diamond crystallization from carbon dissolved in the molten iron to be about 45 kilobar (~45000 Atm or 4.5 GPa) and about 1230 degrees Celsius, very close to those actually used in industrial diamond production today. Interestingly, they are also fairly close to the conditions under which natural diamonds are thought to form (1250 degrees Celsius and 5.0 GPa).

Facing page: HPHT-grown synthetic yellow diamond crystals and gems faceted from synthetic diamond, all of which were manufactured in Russia.
Tino Hammid photo

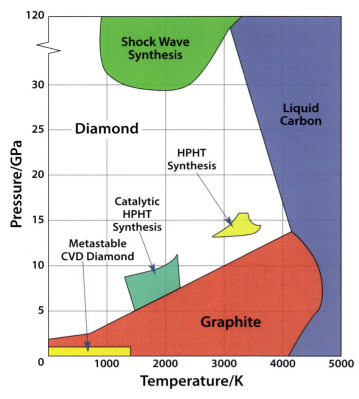

Above: Modern phase diagram of carbon. The equilibrium line between diamond and graphite is defined by Berman-Simon calculations published in 1950.
Paul May graphic, after Bundy (1979).

Below: Synthetic diamond crystals grown at the General Electric labs in Schenectady, New York, on December 16, 1954. The crystals in the photo on the **left** were burned in O_2 and formed CO_2. Photos courtesy of the H Tracy Hall Foundation.

If diamond is not a thermodynamically stable phase of carbon at ambient conditions, why doesn't it convert back to graphite? And why can we hold diamonds in our hands once they form at very high pressures? Remarkably, diamond remains a diamond even at temperatures up to 800 degrees Celsius in air and up to 1600 degrees Celsius in inert atmospheres such as argon and hydrogen. This stability of diamond at ambient conditions is possible because of the high activation barrier of the transformation between diamond and graphite. In the phase diagram of carbon, there are pressures and temperatures within the graphite stable region where diamond does not have enough energy to convert to graphite (above). In this area diamond is said to be *thermodynamically metastable* or, in other words, *kinetically stable*.

HIGH-PRESSURE HIGH-TEMPERATURE (HPHT)

In 1953 the Swedish company ASEA (Allmanna Svenska Elektriska Aktiebolaget) produced the first man-made diamonds. In order to create sufficient pressures and temperatures in a volume reasonable for the diamond synthesis, the company developed a unique high-pressure (HP), multi-anvil, split-sphere apparatus. ASEA did not publish their results, opting to keep them secret.

One year later in 1954, General Electric announced that it had successfully synthesized diamonds using their newly designed high-pressure "belt" apparatus. General Electric developed a high-pressure-high-temperature (HPHT) process of diamond synthesis by dissolving graphite in a molten transition metal (solvent-catalyst) at pressures where diamond is thermodynamically stable. This process became the basis for the mass production of synthetic industrial diamonds, which are produced in the form of powders, grits, polycrystals, and composites with different metals. Since its introduction, HPHT synthetic diamond production has increased annually and currently exceeds 300 tons per year.

The key to the success of making diamonds in the lab was the development of the equipment necessary for creating pressures and temperatures sufficient for the transformation of graphite to diamond. HPHT diamond synthesis requires extreme pressures, far beyond those used by any other technology. Generation of these pressures is *per se* a daunting problem, which is exacerbated by the very high temperatures needed to melt the metal solvent-catalyst and overcome the activation energies of diamond formation.

The development of HP devices for diamond manufacturing combines unique design, intensive engineering, and the development of special materials. All HP diamond-making machines include three main components:

1. The device to generate the pressure (the HP apparatus);
2. The device to apply force to HP apparatus to generate pressure (usually it is a few-thousand-ton press);
3. The device that is inserted into the HP apparatus chamber where diamond synthesis will occur.

This last component is used for synthesis only once and is usually called a *furnace* or *HP cell*.

Each HP cell consists of a few key parts: the HP container, special gaskets, a heater, and the charge for diamond synthesis. The HP container is a solid medium, which transmits pressure from the HP apparatus to the charge and provides thermal insulation between the heater and HP apparatus. The gaskets seal the high-pressure chamber and simultaneously support the most loaded parts of the HP apparatus, preventing them from fracturing. Depending on the setup, these gaskets can be specifically made or self-formed (self-extruded) by consuming some of the container material when pressure is generated. No single material can routinely withstand the high pressures for diamond synthesis without eventual mechanical failure. Only the right combinations of tungsten carbide/cobalt alloys with a properly designed HP apparatus and additional optimal support from the gaskets allow a HP apparatus to withstand the required pressures.

There are two families of HP apparatuses producing diamonds: uniaxial and multiaxial or multianvil devices.

Right: The cylinder (middle) and the anvils from the high pressure belt apparatus in which General Electric's first diamonds were successfully synthesized. Photos courtesy of the H Tracy Hall Foundation.

Below left: Coins cast from iron (**top**), copper, and nickel, three of the metals which may be used in the solvent-catalysts. Images © Theodore Gray.

Below right: Diagram of the belt apparatus. Boris Feigelson / Lithographie graphic.

Examples of uniaxial devices include the *Belt* and *Torroid* type apparatuses. Examples of multianvil type apparatuses include the cube press and the pressless modification of the split-sphere apparatus (BARS).

Regardless of the type of ultra HP apparatus used, the techniques of diamond synthesis are generally similar. Transforming graphite directly into diamond requires pressures exceeding 120 kilobar (12.0 GPa) and temperatures higher than 2700 degrees Celsius. To decrease the activation barrier of the graphite to diamond transformation, metal solvent-catalysts are used. Dissolving graphite in molten metal (solvent-catalysts) destroys the graphite lattice and uses the molten metal-carbon solution to decrease the activation barrier, which then allows diamond to form at lower pressures and temperatures. The most commonly used and most effective solvent-catalysts are alloys of metals from the iron group (iron, nickel, cobalt), manganese, and chromium.

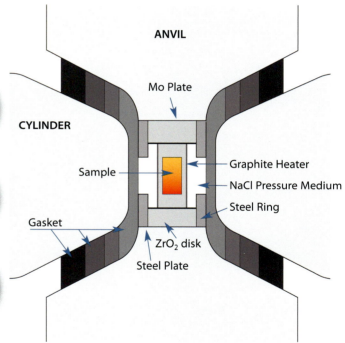

The prepared HP cell is placed inside the HP apparatus and high pressure is generated. When the required pressure is achieved, the charge, consisting of graphite and the solvent-catalyst, is heated by a current passing through the heater inside of the HP cell. It is first necessary to reach a temperature sufficient to melt the solvent-catalyst; this occurs somewhere between 1200 and 1500 degrees Celsius, depending on the metal solvent-catalyst and pressure.

HPHT film growth (FG)

In practice, the typical charge for diamond synthesis consists of multiple metal solvent-catalyst and graphite disks in a "sandwich" arrangement. When metal melts at the conditions where diamond is stable, it dissolves graphite, and diamond spontaneously nucleates from the solution as soon as the solution is supersaturated enough with carbon. The nucleated diamond crystals continue to grow, surrounded by a molten metal film. Carbon is supplied to the growing diamond from the dissolving graphite by diffusion through this molten metal film. This process, known as the *HPHT film growth* (FG) method, is used to produce diamond powder and grit in sizes ranging from microns to 1 millimeter. Various grit and powder sizes can be made by adjusting the supersaturation and the time of the synthesis. A lower supersaturation during the diamond synthesis produces fewer nuclei, and because of greater available space in the reaction volume, larger crystals can be grown over a longer period of time.

The number of growing crystals can only be controlled by eliminating spontaneous nucleation and by introducing seeds for the growth initiation. In this way it becomes possible to

Thermodynamics Refresher

Thermodynamics looks at the relationship between heat energy and mechanical work.

Definitions

Temperature (T) measures the movement of molecules

Entropy (S) = disorder / randomness

Enthalpy (H) = total heat in a system

Gibbs Free Energy (G) = thermodynamic equivalent of potential energy

Absolute Zero (|0|) = theoretically the lowest possible temperature

4 Laws of Thermodynamics

0th LAW: When two systems are put in contact with one another, they will exchange energy unless or until they are at equal temperatures.

1st LAW: Energy can neither be created nor destroyed. It can only change forms.

2nd LAW: An energy system tends to increase rather than decrease in entropy.

3rd LAW: As the temperature of a system approaches absolute zero, the entropy of the system also approaches zero. (i.e., no movement, no disorder).

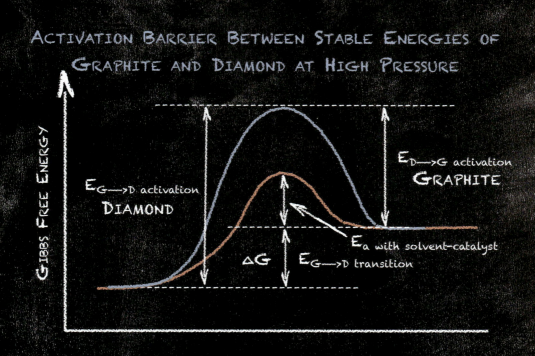

Driving Force — Supersaturation

The driving force for any transformation in a system is defined by the difference between the Gibbs free energy in the final (G_f) and initial (G_i) stages of the system. If that difference ($\Delta G = G_f - G_i$) is negative, there is a driving force for the transformation.

To synthesize diamond from graphite, a solvent-catalyst is melted in contact with the graphite. When the solvent-catalyst is melted at pressures at which graphite is stable; graphite will dissolve into the liquid metal until carbon saturates the solution. At that moment the system will reach equilibrium (its lowest Gibbs free energy). The concentration of carbon in the liquid metal (molten solution) will reach a maximum, and the chemical potential (μ) of carbon in the system will achieve its lowest value. No more graphite will dissolve in the metal and no more changes in the system will occur.

When, on the other hand, the solvent-catalyst in contact with graphite is melted at pressures at which diamond is thermodynamically stable, the graphite will dissolve in the liquid metal and carbon will crystallize from the solution as diamond because this will lower the free energy of the system. At that point, carbon has a lower chemical potential in the form of diamond $\mu(D)$ than in the form of graphite $\mu(G)$, and the driving force for diamond crystallization is proportional to that difference: $\Delta \mu = \mu(D) - \mu(G)$. This difference in chemical potentials defines supersaturation.

In solution, the threshold concentration of solutes that can be dissolved into the liquid (in this case, carbon into a liquid metal) is used as the criterion for the supersaturation of the solution and to measure the equilibrium solubility of the solute. The solution is supersaturated when the actual solute concentration (C) is higher than the solute solubility (C_{sat}). The level of supersaturation (σ), which is the driving force behind crystallization can be calculated from C_{sat} and the actual solute concentration C: $\sigma = (C - C_{sat})/C_{sat}$. Thus diamond will crystallize from the solution at pressures at which diamond is stable and when its solubility in the solvent-catalyst is lower than the solubility of graphite. The higher the pressure for a given temperature, the larger the difference between the solubilities of diamond and graphite and thus, the greater the driving force for the formation of diamond.

The crystallization of any new solid phase starts with the creation of small nuclei. To continue growth, a nucleus needs to exceed a critical size (the critical nucleus) or it will dissolve back to liquid. The nucleation rate and size of the critical nucleus depend on supersaturation: greater supersaturation leads to higher nucleation rates; smaller critical nuclei leads to higher nucleation densities.

There is a narrow area near the equilibrium line in which diamond is the stable phase but no spontaneous diamond crystallization is observed. The chemical potential of diamond in this area is a little lower than that of graphite, but not enough to create sufficient driving force ($\Delta \mu$) to surpass the activation barrier for the diamond to crystallize. In other words, the solution is not supersaturated enough to initiate spontaneous diamond nucleation; thus any forming nuclei will dissolve back to solution. To start spontaneous diamond nucleation, the supersaturation must be increased by applying higher pressure for the given temperature.

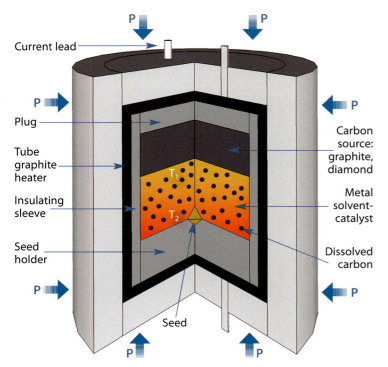

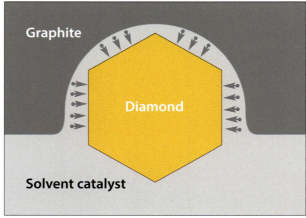

 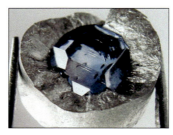

Upper left: Schematic diagram of the BARS HP cell and temperature Gradient Growth (TGG) method. Under this method 50 to 60 kbars of pressure is applied; the cell is heated on a gradient from 1350°C to 1550°C ($T_1 < T_2$); the metal solvent-catalyst melts, the carbon source dissolves, saturating the solution, and growth starts. It takes 3 to 5 days to grow a high-quality, 1 carat diamond crystal. Boris Feigelson / Lithographie graphic.

Upper right: Diagram of the HPHT film growth (FG) method in which the growing diamond is surrounded by a film of molten metal. Carbon from the dissolving graphite diffuses through the film, supplying the diamond. Boris Feigelson / Lithographie graphic.

Lower left: Diamonds grown in a BARS HP cell are shown here still embedded in the metal solvent-catalyst. Metal diameter is 1.2 cm wide. Boris Feigelson photos.

grow larger crystals in the limited space of the growth volume. Small, spontaneously grown diamond crystals can be used as seeds. The activation energy for the crystallization on a seed is much lower than that required for spontaneous nucleation. As mentioned earlier, there is an area near the equilibrium line where the supersaturation in the solution is not enough for spontaneous diamond nucleation, but this supersaturation is adequate to grow diamonds on seeds.

By using diamond seeds and the HPHT FG method, diamonds reaching sizes of 3 to 4 millimeters may be grown. It is very important to keep stable supersaturation during the entire run to grow high-quality, single crystal diamonds. The supersaturation controls growth rates and diamond crystalline quality. Higher supersaturation results in higher growth rates, but if growth is too fast, the quality of the resulting crystals will deteriorate. As a rule, slower growth provides higher-quality crystals, but a balance needs to be struck as growth rates that are too low do not make economic sense.

HPHT Temperature Gradient Growth (TGG)

The value of supersaturation in the film growth method depends on the complicated task of maintaining precise and stable pressure and temperature conditions during long growth runs. A small shift in either pressure or temperature changes the supersaturation and compromises diamond crystal quality. To overcome the problem of complex growth control and high degrees of the supersaturation uncertainty in the FG method, General Electric introduced an HPHT Temperature Gradient Growth (TGG) method for diamond synthesis in the 1960s.

HPHT TGG is based on a well-known technique for growing crystals from solution. The solubility of solutes depends on temperature, and this phenomenon is exploited to create and regulate the supersaturation by controlling a temperature gradient in the solution. Carbon solubility in liquid metals increases with temperature. To create and use a temperature gradient for diamond growth, a new type of HP cell is used. A carbon source is placed in the hotter region of the growth volume while the diamond crystal seed, separated from the source by the thick layer of a solvent-catalyst, is located in a region with a lower temperature. Diamond growth is conducted at a pressure and temperature where the solvent-catalyst is melted and diamond is thermodynamically stable.

The carbon source can be graphite, compacted diamond powder, or a polycrystalline diamond. When graphite is used, the first stage of the TGG is similar to a standard FG diamond synthesis from graphite. The entire graphite disk quickly converts to the diamond polycrystalline agglomerate replacing the graphite. At this first stage of the TGG, diamond agglomerate formation is driven by the difference of graphite and diamond solubility at given pressure and temperature. After this transformation, the newly formed diamond agglomerate dissolves in the solvent-catalyst and dissolved carbon is transported from carbon source to the seed area along the temperature gradient (to cooler temperatures) in the layer of molten metal. Carbon transport by diffusion is driven by the difference in carbon concentration near the source and near the seed. In addition, temperature gradients in the molten metal combined with gravity induce liquid-convection, an important part of the total carbon transport from the carbon source to the seed. Lower carbon solubility at the lower temperature in the area near the seed creates the required supersaturation, and diamond crystallizes in this area. Thus, TG diamond crystal growth is driven by the difference of diamond solubility in the liquid metal at different temperatures. It is important to keep the supersaturation below a critical level, so that growth occurs only on the seed without spontaneous nucleation of diamonds within the solvent or on other surfaces around the seed.

The main parameter controlling the supersaturation in the TGG method is the temperature difference between the source and the seed. Control by only one growth parameter — temperature gradient — is the key difference between the HPHT TGG and HPHT FG methods. The HPHT TGG method is preferred for growing large single crystal diamonds for the gem market and for high-tech applications.

HPHT Colored Diamonds

Different types of diamond can be grown using HPHT techniques. Type Ib diamonds (see pages 41–43) with *C-centers* — single nitrogen substituting for carbon atoms — have colors ranging from yellow-brown to fancy yellow and yellow-orange. The hue strongly depends on nitrogen concentration, the type of metal solvent-catalyst, growth temperatures, and growth rates. Depending on growth temperatures, C-centers can transform to different degrees during the growth into A-centers, and mixed Type Ia-Ib diamonds can be grown.

Type IIa colorless diamonds with very low nitrogen concentration are also grown using special procedures. When nitrogen concentration in grown diamonds is 1 part per million or less, the diamonds are colorless. The addition of elements such as titanium, zirconium, and aluminum to the solvent-catalyst allows nitrogen to "bind" in solution by forming nitrides. These elemental additions are called *nitrogen getters*. To make Type IIb blue diamonds, the same procedures used for diamonds with reduced nitrogen growth are employed, but some amount of boron is added to the growth environment. Growing diamonds with reduced nitrogen concentrations requires more advanced technology for solvent-catalyst preparation and growth environment control, more precise control of pressure and temperature parameters, and lower growth rates to maintain crystal quality.

It is also possible to grow HPHT diamonds with different hues of green by exploiting nickel-based solvent-catalysts or by combining the yellow with blue hues in the diamond crystal by balancing the nitrogen and boron content. Pink or red diamonds cannot be grown by the HPHT method; however, pink or red colors can be produced by irradiating diamonds containing the right concentrations of C-centers with high-energy electrons to create carbon vacancies, then subsequently annealing them at temperatures of about 800 degrees Celsius to create the nitrogen-vacancy (N-V) centers.

CHEMICAL VAPOR DEPOSITION (CVD)

As we have discussed, diamond is metastable at low pressures and over a wide range of temperatures, but can diamond be synthesized at conditions at which it is metastable? Where graphite is a stable and diamond is metastable, carbon in both phases is more stable than carbon in gaseous

Above: Colored diamonds faceted from synthetic HPHT rough produced in Russia.
Tino Hammid photo.

hydrocarbon forms; carbon in the form of methane (CH_4), for example. As a result, graphite and diamond can be formed from gaseous phases by the chemical reaction of hydrocarbon decomposition.

While at low pressures graphite is thermodynamically more stable than diamond and has a greater chance of being formed from hydrocarbons, the kinetics of diamond or graphite nuclei formation, as well as the kinetics of the phase growth and phase removal of the two, determine whether diamond or graphite will form. Given specific temperatures and chemistries, diamond may prevail over graphite and can be grown by Chemical Vapor Deposition (CVD), even at low pressures where diamond is the metastable phase.

Chemical vapor deposition (CVD) is the growth of a material by decomposing gaseous reactants, usually at less than atmospheric pressure, and growing a solid film or crystal. In the case of growing diamond by CVD, the reactant gases always contain hydrogen and carbon as both elements are critical to the growth process (Butler & Woodin 1993, Celii & Butler 1991, Goodwin & Butler 1997). The reactant gases are "activated" above or near the growing surface of the diamond seed crystals by either a plasma, combustion flame, or contact with a hot metal or filament surface greater than 2000 degrees Celsius. The role of the activation process is to create atomic hydrogen and hydrocarbon radicals, such as the methyl radical CH_3, in the gas. The radicals impinge on the growing surface, which is usually a seed crystal of diamond. The surface temperature of the seed is usually between 600 and 1300 degrees Celsius.

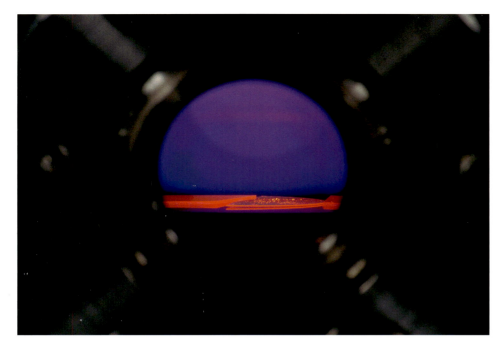

Left: Diamond seed crystals growing in a Seki CVD reactor at Macquarie University in New South Wales, Australia. Andrew Edmonds photo.

Below: Schematic of the generic CVD process for growing diamond. In this process, the reactant gases, typically CH_4 (0.1 to 8 percent), a rare gas (helium or argon, 0 to 30 percent) and H_2 (balance) flow through the reaction vessel at pressures of between 0.01 and 1 atmosphere (7 and 760 torr), but generally in the 30 to 300 torr range. James Butler graphic.

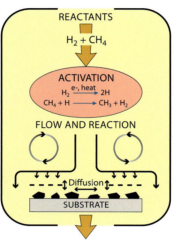

The plasma or hot filament dissociates the molecular hydrogen and hydrocarbon into atomic hydrogen and a complex mix of hydrocarbon species and transports them to the growing diamond surface by a combination of diffusion and convection. The surface atoms of diamond seed crystals are terminated with C-H bonds, which stabilize the surfaces as diamond as opposed to graphite. The gaseous atomic hydrogen reacts with the surface C-H bonds to remove (abstract) the surface hydrogen (as H_2 going back to the gas) and leave a broken bond on the diamond surface. Subsequently, another gas hydrogen atom or a gaseous hydrocarbon radical (CH_3) collides and reacts (adds to) with the surface carbon to generate the original surface or add a carbon atom to it. Typically, a carbon atom is added to the surface for every 10^5 to 10^7 collisions of gaseous hydrogen atoms at a surface carbon atom site. The newly added carbon on the surface is incorporated into the diamond lattice by a complex series of further hydrogen abstraction and carbon addition reactions (Butler & Woodin 1993, Goodwin & Butler 1997).

In some cases the reactant gases may also contain other elements such as oxygen, nitrogen, boron, or silicon. Nitrogen, boron, and silicon atoms often incorporate into the diamond lattice to create defects (*dopants*), which modify the color and/or the electronic properties of the material. In many cases where the impurity atom is larger than carbon, a missing carbon atom(s) in an adjacent lattice position(s) (*carbon vacancy*) will be next to the impurity atom, creating defects such as nitrogen-vacancy and silicon-vacancy complexes. The incorporation or formation of these defects depends on the local atomic arrangement on the growing surface. These defects often incorporate in the grown diamond inhomogeneously.

As described earlier, bulk diamond formed by growth on a particular crystal face (crystal plane) is referred to as a *growth sector*. Observations of the pattern of defect concentrations in such growth sectors using optical spectroscopy, cathodoluminescence, or photoluminescence is helpful in determining the origin or mechanism of the diamond growth (Martineau et al. 2004). Growth sectors are distinct features of natural and HPHT synthetic diamonds, although each type exhibits different characteristic patterns.

Oxygen or oxygen-containing reactants are also often used in the CVD growth process. In the complex gas-phase chemistry above the growing diamond surface, most of the oxygen is consumed to form the very stable molecule carbon monoxide (CO), which seems to play no role in the growth chemistry other than making some carbon unavailable for incorporation into the growing crystal. However, a small fraction of the oxygen will arrive at the growing surface as oxygen atoms, hydroxyl radicals (OH), peroxy radicals (HO_2), etc. These can react with any non-diamond carbon on the surface to either etch it back to the gas phase or assist in diamond formation. During combustion growth of diamond with oxygen and acetylene, the oxygen is critical to creating the high-temperature flame that generates the hydrogen atoms and carbon radicals for the growing surface (Goodwin & Butler 1997, Carrington et al. 1989).

All growth of diamond begins with a diamond nucleus or seed. The formation and stability of diamond nuclei are beyond the scope of this discussion and are generally irrelevant for most CVD diamond growth. Most growers start the CVD process from seed diamonds in one form or another, which they place on a non-diamond material such as silicon, tungsten, molybdenum, etc. When multiple seed crystals are used, the growing diamonds will collide with each other and overlap to form a polycrystalline aggregate, a coating on a non-diamond substrate, or a plate of polycrystalline diamonds.

Right: Microwave CVD diamond components have a transmission spectrum from 220 nm to > 50 µm. They also conduct heat better than any other material. Image courtesy of Element Six.

Upper middle: Single crystal CVD diamond plates find many high-tech applications including radiation and X-ray dosimeters and detectors. Image courtesy of IIa Technologies.

Lower middle: Ultra sharp, wear-resistant diamond knife. Fraunhofer IAF photo.

Bottom right: Flexible CVD diamond heat spreaders. Fraunhofer IAF photo.

Inset: SEM image of a 30 nm thick, nanocrystalline CVD diamond MEMS resonator structure. Lidija Sekaric photo.

CVD Diamond Applications

CVD diamond materials are a continuum of materials with physical, optical, and electronic properties, which can be both engineered to fit an application and reproducibly controlled to form a reliable product. One such continuum is in the grain size of the material, ranging from a few nanometers, through hundreds of micrometers, to single crystals, and even mosaic tiles of single crystals, which form large plates of quasi, single crystal diamonds. Examples of this range of materials, each with different crystalline grain sizes are shown on this page.

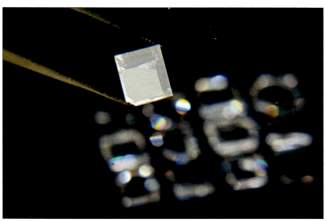

Properties including optical transparency, color, thermal conductivity, and electrical conductivity can be similarly engineered in the CVD growth process.

The growth of CVD diamond materials has been extensively developed since the mid-1980s for industrial and technological applications exploiting the extraordinary physical and chemical properties of diamond. These applications include cutting tools, substrates for heat-spreading under high-power electronic chips and diode lasers, optical windows for industrial high power lasers and megawatt microwave transmission, electrochemical cells for wastewater remediation, radiation dosimeters, windows and coatings for corrosive chemical environments, micro-electromechanical systems (MEMS) resonators and sensors, wear-resistant pump-seal coatings, atomic force microscope tips, high-pressure diamond anvil cells, biosensors and biocompatible coatings, and many others.

The growth of high-quality single crystal layers and bulk for both technological and gem applications began in the late 1990s (Linares & Doering 1999, Wang et al. 2003). Among the important technological applications of single crystal diamond materials are high-energy particle detectors (Isberg 2002, Kania 1993), high-voltage electronic devices (Butler et al. 2003), quantum computing and photonics (Kennedy et al. 2002,

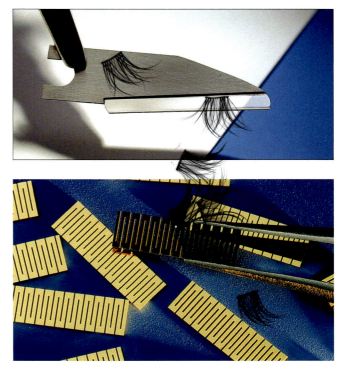

LABORATORY-GROWN DIAMONDS 123

Left: Synthetic diamond grit.
Image courtesy of Element Six.

Middle left: Single crystal CVD diamond engineered for ultra-low absorption and birefringence along with long optical path lengths are used in monolithic diamond Raman lasers.
Image courtesy of Element Six.

Below: The *Apollo Rose,* a single crystal CVD faceted gem, approximately 4 mm wide, with negatively charged nitrogen-vacancy centers used to demonstrate quantum qbit in diamond.
Apollo Diamond specimen,
James Butler photo.

Lower left: Cutting tools create significant demand for manufactured diamonds.
Vic Rzonca photo.

Bevertos et al. 2002), and high-power Raman lasers (Mildren et al. 2008). Polished polycrystalline CVD diamond windows several millimeters thick and up to 125 millimeters in diameter are brazed into vacuum mounting rings and because of their high optical transparency and high thermal conductivity find uses in high-power lasers and microwave devices.

An early (circa 2001) faceted single crystal CVD diamond gem known as the *Apollo Rose*, pictured above, is colored by a moderate concentration of negatively charged nitrogen vacancy centers. This diamond was the first used to demonstrate the extraordinarily long coherence time of the electron spins of the nitrogen-vacancy centers and the first quantum *qbit* in diamond as a matrix (Kennedy et al. 2002). Further, high-quality single crystal CVD diamond is being used to generate diamond Raman lasers. Such lasers exploit both the high yield of Raman scattering in diamond and the high thermal conductivity of diamond. The latter property minimizes the thermally-induced lensing, which degrades the optical quality of the laser beam (Mildren et al. 2008).

Recently, CVD single crystal diamond growth has become an active field. Multiple factories with more than 100 growth reactors were being developed at the time of this publication. CVD gem materials have appeared in the gem trade in small quantities with all reputable sources identifying and declaring the gems as *CVD* or *Lab grown*.

Right: Metallic inclusions, remnants of the solvent-catalyst, are frequently present in HPHT diamonds. They appear black in transmitted and metallic in reflected light.
Field of view 4 mm wide.
John Koivula collection and photo.

Below: A magnet picks up a colorless HPHT grown diamond with metal inclusions. Kirk Feral photo.

Middle right: Irregular-shaped black inclusions in a CVD grown, faceted diamond. Field of view ~4 mm wide. Ping Yu Poon photo © GIA.

Lower right: Diagrams of a diamond crystal (**upper**) with only octahedral growth sectors grown by HPHT TGG on a (100) face of a seed and a CVD grown cubic crystal grown on the flat face of a single crystal.
R. Peter Richards / Lithographie graphics.

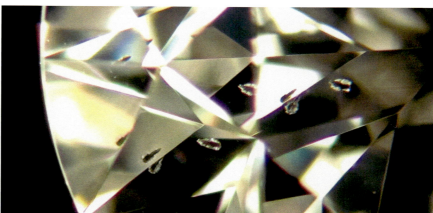

HPHT VERSUS CVD DIAMONDS

HPHT and CVD methods effectively complement each other. Currently, HPHT grown diamonds are used to make substrates (seeds) for CVD single crystal diamond growth, and high purity CVD single crystal films grown on HPHT substrates open the door to new electronic and optical applications of synthetic diamonds.

There are distinct differences between HPHT and CVD gem diamonds, the most significant being that HPHT diamonds mainly contain metal inclusions of the growth solution, while CVD diamonds often contain non-diamond carbon inclusions. Another difference is the presence of multiple growth sectors in HPHT diamonds that are similar but not identical to those seen in natural diamonds. A *growth sector* is a "crystal volume" which is grown under a particular crystal face during the growth and advance of this crystal face.

As discussed, HPHT diamonds start from very small seeds. For the HPHT FG method, growth occurs on all of the crystal faces and surrounds the seed, while in the HPHT TGG method, only one face of the seed is exposed to the growth solution. CVD single crystal diamonds also exhibit growth sectors, but on a much different scale because they are grown on large substrates with one face dominating the exposed surface area. The rate at which impurities are incorporated into the diamond is dependent on the growth sector. Also the

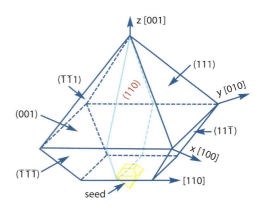

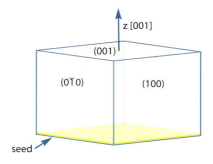

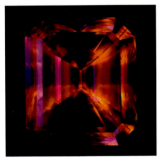
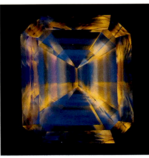

Gemstone images, left: This HPHT-grown, 10.08-carat, Fancy deep blue, faceted diamond was brought into the GIA laboratory in Hong Kong for evaluation in September 2016. It is the largest HPHT-grown diamond that the GIA has examined to date. Weak color zoning with a banded structure were observed under magnification. The diamond contained a few tiny metallic inclusions and fractures. Gemologists Terry "Ping Yu" Poon and Wuyi Wang (2016) evaluated the diamond, which had been declared "synthetic." Microscopic examination under crossed polars revealed "no detectable strain, indicating a very low density of dislocations." Under ultraviolet radiation, the sample exhibited a distinctive hourglass growth pattern (**lower photos**) and strong blue phosphorescence, both indicative of HPHT growth. The diamond exhibited strong red-orange fluorescence under long-wave ultraviolet radiation (**left**) and yellow fluorescence under short-wave ultraviolet (**right**). Such fluorescence is uncommon in natural diamonds. The pattern of fluorescence indicated that the octahedral form {111} was the dominant growth sector as it exhibited a "much stronger blue fluorescence" than that exhibited by the far less developed cube {100} growth sectors.
New Diamond Technology (Russia) specimen,
Johnny Leung photos © GIA.

Cross sections, left: Slices cut from an HPHT TGG grown crystal. The zoning patterns record the growth history of the crystal. Both slices were cut along the (110) plane; inhomogeneous nitrogen (yellow) and nickel (brownish) distributions are apparent in them. Nitrogen in the center (colorless) part of the crystal transformed from C-form to A-form as the crystal was growing. Boris Feigelson photos.

Bottom right: A single crystal CVD diamond layer grown on the (100) face of a substrate (seed) made from HPHT grown diamond. Boris Feigelson photo.

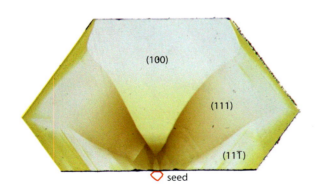

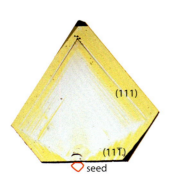
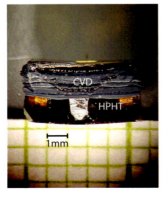

boundaries between growth sectors more readily accumulate impurities, dislocations, and other defects during growth.

The diamond pictured on the middle left is particularly instructive. The original crystal from which this slab was cut was grown using an iron-nickel solvent-catalyst. The growth rate of this crystal was changed during the run: from fast in the beginning to slower and finally to very slow. The incorporation of impurities into the crystal depends on both growth sectors and growth rates. The pictured crystal is a good example of both dependencies. In the (001) growth sector, the yellow part has a medium concentration (~50 to 100 parts per million) of nitrogen in the form of C-centers and close to 0 parts per million of nickel impurities. No transformation of the C- to A-centers occurred in this area because the kinetics of this transformation depends on the presence and concentration of nickel impurities. Above the yellow area in the (001) sector, the growth rates were very low; as a result, the nitrogen incorporation was low, and the nitrogen concentration in the C form is about 1 part per million, which is why this area looks colorless. Incorporation of nitrogen and nickel impurities in the {111} growth sectors is substantially higher than in {100}. The total nitrogen concentration in {111} sectors of this crystal is about 300 parts per million. The nickel concentration is higher in the ($1\bar{1}1$) and (111) growth sectors than it is in the ($\bar{1}\bar{1}\bar{1}$) and ($11\bar{1}$), and it is even higher in the beginning of the growth: the brownish area contains Ni related N^+ centers of about 20 to 25 parts per million. Except in the yellow areas at

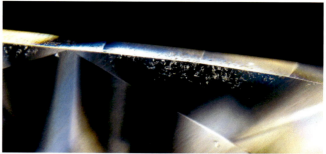

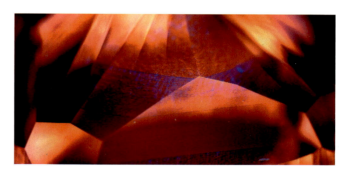

Above: This 5.19 carat, CVD grown diamond with J-equivalent color and VS2-equivalent clarity is the largest GIA had identified by the end of 2016.
Johnny Leung and Tony Leung photo.

Top right: A detail view of the above CVD diamond reveals internal features consisting of needles and pinpoints. The common black non-diamond carbon inclusions usually observed in CVD diamonds, did not appear to be present.

Middle right: Microscopic examination between crossed polarizers of the above CVD diamond revealed high-order interference colors, attributed to strong lattice dislocation.

Lower right: Fluorescence imaging of the above CVD diamond showed strong red fluorescence with bundles of violet-blue. Up to six growth layers basically parallel to the table were revealed.

The three photos on the right are by Billie "Pui Lai" Law © GIA.

the end of the growth, almost all of the nitrogen in the {111} sectors transformed from C to A form. Thus the typical impurities, their forms, and their spatial distributions are distinct for HPHT versus CVD diamonds.

GOING FORWARD

In spite of great technological strides, global production of man-made diamonds for the gem market is negligible compared to the production of natural diamonds. Two major world players, Element Six, a subsidiary of DeBeers, and Sumitomo Electric Industries, employed the TGG method using belt technology and CVD growth to produce Type Ib and IIa diamonds up to 10 millimeters, but these are exclusively for industrial applications. The first man-made diamonds introduced to the gem market in the beginning of 1990s were grown by BARS technology, which was developed in the former USSR. Today, this technique can routinely produce any type of diamond crystal weighing up to 6 carats. The small size of this device makes it economically efficient to grow only one crystal per run, which can be beneficial for the production of custom diamonds. A few small HPHT facilities in Russia, Ukraine, Europe, and Japan likewise produce limited quantities of gem diamonds by means of the BARS, Torroid and Belt technologies, and increasingly CVD diamonds for the gem market are being produced around the world.

Recently Chinese cubic presses were successfully adapted in Russia to grow diamonds using the TGG technique. The large sample volume of this machine allows the growth of high quality Type IIa diamonds up to 60 carats and this crystal weight can be readily increased. This development in HPHT diamond growth should have serious implications not only for the gem market, but combined with the CVD diamond growth also for the development of high-tech diamond applications.

Dr. James E. Butler retired from the Naval Research Laboratory in 2010 after 35 years of research. He currently is a consultant on Diamond Materials, Leading Scientist of the Diamond Electronics Laboratory of the Institute of Applied Physics RAS Nizhny Novgorod and St. Petersburg Electrotechnical University (2012-2017), co-founder of Diamond Foundry, Vice President for Diamond Technology at Euclid Techlabs, Research Associate at the Natural History Museum of the Smithsonian Institution, and Visiting Scientist in the Department of Physics at Vanderbilt University.

Dr. Boris Feigelson is a research scientist at the U.S. Naval Research Laboratory (NRL) in Washington DC, having begun his career in 1981 at the Institute of Monocrystals, Siberian Branch of the Soviet Academy of Science, Novosibirsk. There he developed the high-pressure multi-anvil split sphere technology (BARS technology) for single crystal diamond growth. His group was the first in the Soviet Union to produced large gem-quality, single crystal diamonds. Dr. Feigelson went on to found Adamas, a diamond synthesis lab in Minsk, Belarus, and then the Moscow Research Center Basis, where he was a director. He has continued to develop crystal growth and HP technologies at NRL, where he has been employed since 2001.

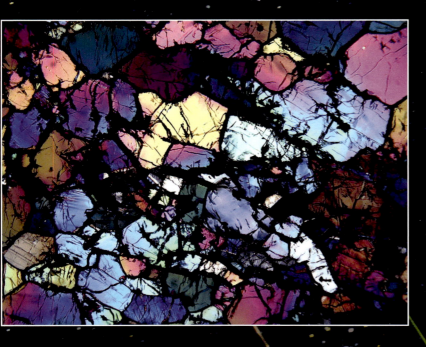

Left: Cross-polarized microscope image of a ureilite. The minerals olivine and pyroxene appear as large colored grains, and the black bands running between these grains contain both graphite and nanodiamonds. Field of view about 5 mm wide. Smithsonian Institution photo

Lower left: A piece of the Novo Urei meteorite — the first meteorite in which extraterrestrial diamonds were found. The interior of the meteorite is visible on the right; the smooth surface on the left is the "fusion crust," which melted as it passed through the Earth's atmosphere. 5 cm long. Adam Mansur / Smithsonian Institution photo (Catalogue number USNM 307).

Lower right: Spanish chocolatier Enric Rovira has made edible versions of meteorites, such as these chocolate truffles known as *Bescuit*.

Background: Composite photo of the Leonids meteor shower, photographed in Monument Valley, Arizona. Sean M. Sabatini photo, 2001.

DIAMONDS IN THE SKY

by Emma Bullock

Meteorites — rocks that come from the moon, Mars, or the asteroid belt and survive passage through the Earth's atmosphere to land on the surface of our planet — are host to an array of materials. Some of this material is primitive and includes the first solids that formed in our solar system, some of which have remained essentially unaltered to this day. Other meteorites record processes such as fluid flow, temperature changes, and impacts that occurred on their parent body and show us how our solar system evolved. One of the most interesting and perhaps unexpected materials that we find in meteorites is diamond.

Diamond was first identified by Jerofejev and Lacbinov (1888) in the **Novo Urei** (Новый Урей) meteorite, which fell in the Russian village of Karamzinka, Ardatovsky district of Mordovia in September 1886. Meteorites of this type, known as *ureilites*, come from asteroids that are large and differentiated. Ureilites are carbon-rich (up to 6 weight percent; Le Guillou et al. 2010), with the carbon occurring as graphite and diamond. While the majority of asteroids are in a stable orbit between Mars and Jupiter, occasionally their orbit is disturbed and they collide with one another. These impacts can generate tremendous heat and pressure — enough to produce diamond. Such diamonds are certainly not gem quality, and even those that are a couple of millimeters in diameter are heavily fractured.

An interesting aside is that the Novo Urei meteorite had broken into several pieces upon landing, and fragments from one of the stones were eaten (McSween 1999)! No one knows quite what inspired the peasants who found the rock to eat it, although meteorites have been thought by some cultures to have magical properties. Eating it was nevertheless no mean feat, considering how tough it must have been! Even cutting and polishing a ureilite can be quite a challenge!

Subsequently, large diamonds have been found in other types of meteorites such as the **Canyon Diablo** iron meteorite, which fell in Coconino County, Arizona, some 50,000 years ago and formed the Barringer or Meteor Crater. Iron meteorites come from the cores of large asteroids, and have experienced high temperatures and pressures. Whether the black diamonds, known as *carbonado*s, found in Canyon Diablo formed in space (e.g., Haggerty 2014) or as a result of the heat and pressure produced when the meteorite struck the earth (e.g., Smith and Dawson 1985), is unclear.

Composite image of the Tycho supernova remnant combines x-ray and infrared observations obtained with NASA's Chandra x-ray Observatory and Spitzer Space Telescope, respectively, and the Calar Alto observatory, Spain. It shows the scene over 41 hours in April 2003, more than four centuries after the brilliant star explosion witnessed by Tycho Brahe and other sixteenth century astronomers. Tycho is 15.5 arcmin across.

Diamonds can also be found in impact craters, especially those where the meteorite impacts a carbon-rich rock. The presence of diamonds has helped to identify prehistoric impact sites such as the Popigay Crater, Krasnoyarskiy Kray, Russia (Masaitis 1995), and the Nördlinger Ries or Ries Crater in the German state of Bavaria (Hough et al. 1995).

Not all diamonds found within meteorites formed through shock: a special variety of microscopic material can be captured from within the most "primitive" types of meteorite. Collectively known as "presolar grains," these tiny bits of matter are highly resilient and survived interstellar travel and processing when our own solar system formed. Many of these grains are thought to have formed in another star long before our sun was born and to have been ejected by a supernova.

Diamonds are the most abundant type of presolar grains. They were first identified by Lewis et al. (1987) in the primitive **Allende** meteorite. Presolar diamonds truly are tiny, averaging only a few nanometers in diameter. They are thus referred to as *nanodiamonds*. To give an idea of their scale, Ed Anders, one of the discoverers of nanodiamonds, described them as follows: "If bacteria had engagement rings, these diamonds would be about the right size."

Nanodiamonds have been found in several other primitive meteorites as well; notably the carbon-rich meteorites **Orgueil** (Tarn-et-Garonne, southern France; Hill et al. 1997), and **Murchison** (Victoria, Australia; Zinner et al. 2003), and the **Abee** enstatite chondrite (Alberta, Canada). Nanodiamonds in the latter meteorite are unusually large, up to 100 nanometers, and have a curious lath-like habit (Russell et al. 1992).

Nanodiamonds in meteorites are far too small to be seen in a microscope image — the average size of a nanodiamond is

The meteorite that formed the Nördlinger Ries Crater in Bavaria, Germany, is thought to have been some 1.5 kilometers in diameter, striking the Earth at an estimated 20 kilometers per second. The tremendous energy generated by the impact turned the graphite in a nearby deposit to some 72,000 tonnes of tiny (less than 0.2 millimeters) diamonds, which are strewn throughout the suevite (impact breccia) that has been used in the construction of area buildings (Emsley 2001) including the above pictured "Daniel," the celebrated 90-meter tall steeple of Saint Georg's Church. Corey Neumeier photo.

Left: Jupiter as seen through the Hubble Space Telescope on April 16, 2006. Conditions on the gas giant may be suitable for hosting diamonds. Jupiter's "red spot" seen here in the lower right hand portion of the planet has apparently been joined by another, smaller swirling storm (lower middle) that has a diameter similar to that of Earth.
NASA, ESA, A. Simon-Miller (Goddard Space Flight Center), I. de Pater, M. Wong (UC Berkeley) image.

Middle right: Cross-polarized microscope image of the primitive Allende meteorite. The rounded features are *chondrules* — melt droplets of olivine and pyroxene that formed very early in our solar system. The black regions between the chondrules are a fine-grained matrix that contains nanodiamonds, which likely pre-date our solar system; field of view is ~8 mm wide.
J. M. Derochette photo

Lower: A secondary electron image of two large diamond crystals in the matrix of the Sutter's Mill meteorite, as prepared by a focused ion beam scanning electron microscope (FIB SEM). NASA Johnson / M. Zolensky photo.

Background: On a clear night, a zillion stars are in view from timberline on Mt. Antero, Chafee County, Colorado, USA
Craig Hazelton photo, July 10, 2015

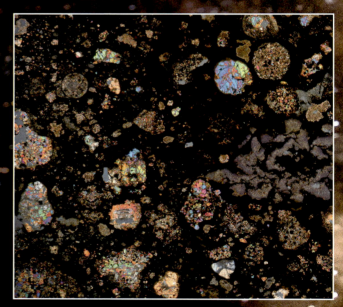

2-3 nanometers, and since both diamonds and graphite are carbon, both appear black in polarized light.

We use a variety of analytical techniques to study meteorites. In order to separate nanodiamonds from the rest of the meteoritic material, pieces of meteorite are dissolved in acid. The nanodiamonds, being resilient, survive as a residue, which can then be analyzed by techniques such as stepped combustion (heating samples in stepwise increments and analyzing the gases given off), transmission electron microscopy, and x-ray diffraction. However, the minute size of a single nanodiamond makes them, at present, difficult to analyze, as an average nanodiamond contains only a few thousand carbon atoms. Thus, much of our knowledge of nanodiamonds comes from analyzing multiple grains at the same time. The results indicate that nanodiamonds are the carriers of some isotopically unusual xenon, hydrogen, and carbon. This has led to the suggestion, noted above, that they formed in stars other than our own sun. Nanodiamonds remain enigmatic though; we await advances in analytical instrumentation in order to fully understand their story.

Further out in our own solar system, the giant planets of Jupiter, Saturn, Uranus, and Neptune may have regions with suitable conditions for hosting diamonds. Research teams (Delitsky and Baines 2013) theorize that methane present in the atmosphere of the gas giants Jupiter and Saturn may dissociate into hydrogen and carbon, possibly as the result of lightning storms. At the less extreme temperature and pressure conditions in the upper atmosphere, this carbon combines to form graphite, but as it sinks toward the hotter, denser lower atmosphere it is transformed into diamond. These ideas are controversial and are based solely on modeling — we do not yet have any direct spacecraft observations of diamonds in the atmospheres of these planets. The upcoming Juno mission to Jupiter and the Cassini mission to Saturn will provide further information and help to verify whether the conditions needed

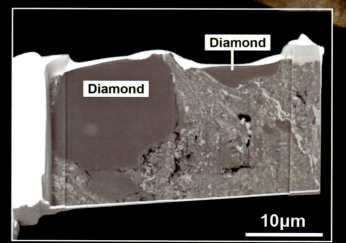

Right: Fragments of the "Sutter's Mill" meteorite which fell Sunday April 22, 2012 in California's gold country. The carbonaceous chondrite contains diamonds as large as 10 microns in diameter. NASA / Eric James photo.

Middle left: A 1.27 cm wide vial of nanodiamonds from the Allende meteorite, as seen through a magnifying glass. Chip Clark / Smithsonian Institution photo (Cat. No. 97-36209).

Lower: A persistent electrical storm was seen for months in Saturn's cloud tops. Such storms may separate carbon from methane in the planet's atmosphere, allowing it to precipitate as graphite and ultimately diamond. The colors in this image are exaggerated to make visible colors outside of the visible spectrum. Photo Cassini Imaging Team / SSI / JPL / ESA / NASA.

to form and preserve diamonds are found there. Similarly, diamond oceans have been suggested to be present on the ice giants Neptune and Uranus (e.g. Eggert et al. 2010), but this idea is highly controversial, and needs further investigation (Ghiringhelli et al. 2007).

Finally, recent reports such as that by Madhusudhan et al. (2012) have suggested that entire exoplanets could be made of diamonds. Exoplanets are planets that orbit another sun and are detected as they pass in front of their home star, blocking out some of that star's light and allowing them to be observed by telescopes here on Earth. Some of these "diamond exoplanets" are thought to have once been stars themselves, but have had their atmospheres and upper surfaces ripped away, leaving behind only their cores (Bailes et al. 2011). Little is known about these far-away objects, but scientists are able to model their compositions using sophisticated computer models and information about the composition of the host star. Further discoveries about worlds around other suns are likely with more observation.

The study of diamonds within extraterrestrial materials can help us to understand much about their history, from impacts on asteroids and Earth to possible conditions on other planets. Thus, with the help of diamonds, we can look back to a time before our Solar System was born.

Dr. Emma Bullock obtained her B. Sc (Hons) in Geochemistry from the University of Manchester in 2001 and her Ph. D. in the field of Meteoritics in 2006 from the Open University and the Natural History Museum in London. In 2006 she moved to the National Museum of Natural History, Smithsonian Institution in Washington, D.C., where she continued her research into meteorites. Emma presently works at the Geophysical Laboratory at the Carnegie Institution in Washington, D.C.

Diamond Heists

by M. Tyler Funk

There is something about diamond, something that has struck the interest and stoked the imaginations of human beings since it first appeared in the written record some 3,000 years ago in India. Diamonds were used then as talismans or amulets to keep evil spirits at bay or to provide their owners with protection in battle. Then, as Christianity began to spread over Europe and Asia, diamond was used in the treatment of wounds and diseases. In the first century CE, Pliny the Elder (Eichholz 1962) stated regarding the diamond: "[It] prevails also over poisons and renders them powerless, dispels attacks of wild distraction and drives groundless fears from the mind." In modern mythos, Saint Hildegarde is said to have professed that making the sign of the cross while holding a diamond unlocked the stone's curative powers and aided in recovery from sickness and injury (Knuth 1999). Indeed, the physician of Pope Clement VII prescribed that Clement ingest fourteen spoonfuls of ground diamond in an attempt to cure him of his various ailments but which may instead have been the death of him (Raumer 1835). While the pope did not survive, the mystical qualities of diamond have.

Even in modern times when diamond was discovered to be much more common than ever imagined, the stone has retained its cultural value as a symbol of eternal love and its currency as a portable, universal vehicle of wealth. Diamond is thus pursued in a way that few other valuables are, and diamonds have been the targets of some of the most incredible heists the world has ever seen.

Diamond heists large and small have been planned and executed for as long as there has been a diamond industry and probably for as long as diamonds have been mined. As far back as the Middle Ages, owners of diamond mines are thought to have encouraged rumors that diamonds were poisonous or otherwise dangerous in order to discourage miners from swallowing the precious stones and smuggling them out of the mines (Cavey 1992). This is hardly a reach given that ingesting diamond fragments, or diamond dust, is much like eating broken glass. In spite of efforts by mining companies to deter theft by workers such losses continue on what is estimated to be a relatively small-scale.

Because of their high value to weight ratio, transportability, and fungibility, diamonds are an attractive commodity to all brands of bad guy from smash-and-grab thieves to crime syndicates to terrorist organizations and rogue governments. In a matter of moments, a thief can steal millions of dollars in gems from displays in retail or private settings.

A large, loose syndicate of Serbian and Montenegrin bandits, the "Pink Panthers" have pulled off numerous brazen, high-dollar thefts of diamonds and other gemstones from ultra-lux establishments. The group acquired its moniker in 1993 after a diamond stolen from a London jeweler was hidden

Upper right: A rare circa 1906 photo depicting a naked South African miner, who was allegedly caught stealing diamonds. Some miners apparently wore mitts to prevent them from palming their finds. Private collection.

Lower right: Some of the jewelry recovered from the 2008 Heist at Harry's. Francois Guillot/AFP photo.

Facing page: Unusual in that it lacks a pavilion but was cut with two back-to-back crowns, the 55.23-carat, pale yellow Sancy was found in India and first documented in Europe in the late sixteenth century, when Nicolas de Harlay, seigneur de Sancy owned it. France's King Henry IV borrowed the stone to use as collateral to secure financing for his army, and de Sancy dispatched it with a trusted courier, who was ambushed and murdered en route. Legend has it that the Sancy was found in the faithful messenger's stomach (Williams 1906).

The slave-miner who found the rough that would become the 141-carat, colorless, flawless *Regent* (pictured on page 43), secreted the 410-carat stone out of a mine in India concealed in the bandages applied to a self-inflicted wound in his calf. An English Sea Captain agreed to share the proceeds from the sale of the rough in exchange for safe passage for the man to a free country. While at sea, the good captain took possession of the diamond and tossed its finder overboard (Streeter 1882).

The *Sancy* and *Regent* were among the French crown jewels when Louis XV was coronated in 1722. The *Regent* was the centerpiece of his coronation crown (**facing page**), placed at the front just above the row of pearls; the Sancy is at the top of the arches of the *fleur-de-lis*. In 1792, during the French Revolution, the crown jewels, including the *Sancy*, *Regent*, and *Hope* diamonds were stolen, and were later recovered. Louis the XV's crown (the diamonds have been replaced by glass replicas) along with the Sancy and Regent diamonds are on display at the Musée du Louvre, Paris. Matt Lee photo.

in a jar of face cream — an apparent homage to the *Pink Panther* film (1963), which starred Peter Sellers as Inspector Clouseau. A report by Bob Simon which aired on the news show *60 Minutes* (Mar 23, 2014) credited the group with more than 370 heists over the last 20 years that have netted more than $500 million in gems, mostly diamonds, the majority of which have never been recovered. Interpol believes there are several hundred Pink Panthers, who work in small teams and fence their takes through networks in the Balkans.

Like the *Pink Panther* films, many of the bands' heists have been set on the French Riviera, although they have pulled off spectacular thefts in places such as Dubai, Tokyo, and London. The Pink Panthers are believed to be behind Japan's greatest robbery: the 2004 theft from a boutique Tokyo jeweler of the *Comtesse de Vendôme*, a necklace composed of 116 diamonds, including the 125-carat centerpiece and worth an estimated 31 million US dollars at the time of the theft. The thieves were eventually caught, claiming, as they frequently do, that they had been hired by the shop owners to stage the heist as part of an insurance scam; the necklace has yet to be recovered.

The infamous Pink Panthers were blamed for a bold robbery in Paris on December 5, 2008, in which four men, three of whom were disguised as women, were buzzed into

Harry Winston jewelers just before closing time. The thieves rolled a bag into the posh inner showroom, waved a gun and a hand grenade, smashed display cases, specifically requested access to secret stores, and took off with what was described in *The New York Times* (Doreen Carvajal, Dec. 12, 2008) as "sacks of emeralds, rubies and chunky diamonds the size of tiny bird eggs valued at more than 80 million euros, or $105 million." The crooks, who turned out to be unrelated to the Pink Panthers, were caught in 2009 when they contacted an Israeli to purchase the stolen jewels. Some of the gems were recovered at that time, and in 2011 another cache, worth an estimated $20 million, was found hidden in a drainpipe in the home of the suspected mastermind.

The "Heist at Harry's" was surpassed as the world's largest retail diamond theft on a Sunday afternoon in July 2013, when a lone thief snuck into a privately hosted diamond show at the Carlton Intercontinental Hotel in Cannes, France, ironically a location for Alfred Hitchcock's 1955 classic *To Catch a Thief*.

According to James Keaton of the *Associated Press* (July 29, 2013), the masked gunman took a bag containing $136 million in diamonds and ran out a side door. That same value in $100 bills would weigh some 1,357 kilograms (2,992 pounds), and with the price of gold in the neighborhood of US $1,200 per troy ounce, $136 million in gold would weigh 3,525 kilograms or 7,771 pounds. Emerald can be worth more per carat than diamond, but the former is far less common; thus large quantities are generally not concentrated in a single location. From a logistics standpoint, nothing else provides such an efficient and attractive target for thieves, a fact that is not lost on those who own or work with high value diamonds. The security around these targets tends to be top notch, but thieves have nonetheless successfully pulled off some incredible robberies.

Probably the most impressive diamond heist of all time occurred on the night of December 1st (or 2nd), 2002 at the Museon museum of science and culture in The Hague, Netherlands. The exhibition entitled *The Diamond — From Rough Stone to Gem*, included diamonds on loan from other museums and private collectors, and well-known pieces of royal jewelry.

Security was thought to be tight. Every valuable diamond in the Museon that night was housed in a cabinet made of reinforced glass and there were motion detectors throughout the exhibit area. Both human and automated security monitors were on guard 24 hours a day: security cameras covered every nook and cranny of space within the exhibit area, and the guards patrolled every conceivable entrance or exit. Nevertheless, of the 28 display cases in the exhibit, the 6 that contained the most important diamonds were empty when the Museon (which was closed on Monday) reopened on Tuesday, December 3rd. Those six cases contained the most valuable pieces, many of historic significance. The museum eventually stated that the combined value of stolen diamonds was approximately 12 million US dollars.

Now for a dose of the unbelievable: the display cases, though empty, were found closed and unbroken when the museum reopened on Tuesday morning. There was in fact no sign whatsoever that the cases had been tampered with — they were simply empty. The guards claimed to have not seen a thing; the motion sensors never went off; and the recorded video footage revealed not a single clue; they in fact showed no sign that the robbery had ever taken place. If not for the empty display cases and the single broken window by which the thieves gained entry to the museum, there would have been no evidence at all of the heist.

While security at the Museon would certainly be considered tight, it was neither as high tech nor as redundant as it might have been. But even locations with an amazing number of security redundancies have proven to be vulnerable.

The Antwerp World Diamond Centre in Belgium was considered one of the most secure buildings in the world, and for good reason: some 85 percent of the world's rough diamonds and 20 percent of its cut stones pass through the city (Tagliabue 2012) on their way to the retail markets where they will eventually be sold. The Diamond Centre holds many of these treasures, often for just a day or two while brokers negotiate trades. Many of the most valuable diamonds are kept in the building at some point prior to coming onto the market.

In 2003 the Diamond Centre featured 10 layers of security including security cameras, motion detectors, light detectors, infrared heat detectors, Doppler radar, and a 3-ton steel vault door with its own security measures: a lock with 100 million possible combinations, a nearly impossible-to-copy foot long key, a seismic sensor inside the door to detect any drilling, banging or other attempts to forcibly enter, and a magnetic field around the vault door that would trigger an alarm if it was broken without being properly disabled.

In spite of all the bells and whistles, in February 2003 a group of five Italian thieves connected to the "La Scuola di Torino" (School of Turin) broke into the center's underground vault. The burglars opened and ransacked the safe deposit boxes, making off with a reported $100 million in diamonds, gold, and other gems; they left behind a pile of jewels, watches, and money that police surmise was more than they could carry.

Below: Among the pieces stolen from the Museon exhibition were six treasures on loan from the National Palace in Ajuda, Portugal. One of these was this ornate gold and diamond cane handle, the top of which (**left**) was set with a large faceted diamond. The cane was made in Paris circa 1760 for King Joseph I of Portugal.

Right: It took 8 men just 3 minutes to pry open the cargo hold of a commercial airliner and make off with some US $50 million in diamonds. Yves Logghe/AP photo.

Below: The vault at the Antwerp World Diamond Centre in Antwerp, Belgium, had clearly been devastated by the February 2003 robbery in which thieves got away (temporarily) with an estimated US $100 million in diamonds, gold, and other valuables. Politie Antwerpen photo.

When detectives arrived on the scene of what has since been deemed *The Robbery of the Century*, lead investigator Agim De Bruycker called police headquarters to request a nationwide alert. Then, according to Joshua Davis' report in *Wired* (April 17, 2009), he dialed the vault's alarm company:

"What is the status of the alarm?" He asked. "Fully functional," the operator said, checking the signals coming in from the Diamond Center. "The vault is secure." "Then how is it that the door is wide open and I'm standing inside the vault?" De Bruycker demanded, glancing at the devastation all around him.

Although the crime itself went off without a hitch, the thieves made critical mistakes in the immediate aftermath that led to their arrests. After divvying up the loot and heading back to Italy, they haphazardly left evidence including receipts with identifying information, the stolen surveillance tapes, and a half-eaten sandwich contaminated with the ring leader's DNA in a wooded lot outside of town.

Leonardo Notarbartolo, who for years had rented space and stored stones in the Antwerp World Diamond Centre, was arrested for the crime a week after it was committed. While serving a 10-year sentence for the crime, Notarbartolo told his story to Joshua Davis of *Wired* (April 17, 2009). He claimed that a Jewish diamond dealer hired him to put a team together to perform the robbery. Notarbartolo told Davis that the actual value taken from the vault was in the neighborhood of $20 million, far less than reported. Many of the stones the group had expected to find in the vault were not there, which led them to believe that the dealer who hired him had tipped off some friends, who had removed their valuables but probably claimed them as missing to their insurance companies. If Notarbartolo's account is true, then the Antwerp World Diamond Centre heist of 2003 was not one of the world's largest diamond heists but was instead one of the world's largest insurance scams.

Professional diamond thieves naturally look for security weaknesses at all points of production from mine to trading and cutting centers to sales outlets to clients, and some have exploited vulnerabilities observed when diamonds are being shipped. Some of the world's most infamous and impressive diamond heists have thus targeted airliners contracted to transport stones.

One such robbery took place on the tarmac of the Brussels National airport on Monday, February 18, 2013. Brinks security personnel had just finished loading €38 million in diamonds onto the target plane when eight men dressed as police officers and armed with machine guns drove up to the plane in a Mercedes van and Audi sedan, each with flashing blue lights. Four men jumped out of each vehicle and holding the Brinks' guards at gunpoint, pried open the cargo hold and took possession of the diamonds. The team was back out through the hole that they had cut in the airport fence within 5 minutes. No shots were fired and none of the passengers on board the plane saw anything. In May of that year, police in 3 countries arrested 31 people in connection with the theft.

In a similar strike eight years earlier in February 2005, thieves dressed in uniforms stolen from Royal Dutch Airlines (KLM) and driving a stolen KLM van managed to hijack an armored vehicle carrying $118 million of cut and uncut diamonds. The thieves remain at large; their bounty has never been recovered.

Recognizing that diamonds are at the root of conflicts such as those in Angola, Liberia, and Sierra Leone, government and diamond industry leaders developed the Kimberley Process Certification Scheme (see below) to provide law enforcement in the 81 participating countries a means of identifying a diamond's source and restricting trade in uncertified, so-called *conflict* or *blood diamonds*. The Kimberley Process, however, does little to address diamonds purchased through legitimate channels that are used as a means to hide, trade, and transport assets for criminal or terrorist networks. In a 2004 article in *The Washington Post* (July 14, 2004; Page A19), Douglas Farah and Richard Shultz wrote:

> *Hezbollah has been using diamonds from West Africa to finance its activities since its inception, successfully embedding its financial structure in the diamond trade. Al Qaeda operatives plugged into the same network, bridging the divide between Shiite and Sunni Muslims.*

While Farah claims that the US Central Intelligence Agency

Left: A young miner working in the Tongo Field, Sierra Leone. The miners in this area are paid for their work and the diamonds, in theory, go through the Kimberley Process; thus their finds are not technically "blood diamonds." However, Shiite Lebanese, with rumored ties to Hezbollah and other militant groups, are the primary buyers of the fruits of their labors. Adam Cohn photo, March 2008.
Facing page: A shop window is broken with a sledgehammer in a 2007 smash-and-grab robbery in New York's Diamond District.

THE KIMBERLEY PROCESS FOR COLLECTORS

by John H. Betts

Mineral collectors who purchase rough, uncut diamond crystals should be aware of the Kimberley Process Certification Scheme (KPCS), and how it affects their collection and record-keeping requirements. In 2002 the United Nations and major diamond producing countries formulated the Kimberley Process to prevent conflict diamonds ("blood diamonds") from entering the marketplace. The scheme became effective in the beginning of 2003 and requires all non-faceted rough diamonds, including cleaved and sawn diamonds, to be sealed in tamperproof containers and transshipped with Kimberley Process Certificates (KPC). Currently 81 nations are participating in the program which has largely prevented the supply of rough diamonds from being tainted with conflict diamonds.

In the United States, the incoming KPC is filed with the Department of Commerce, and every transaction between sellers and buyers is accompanied by a detailed receipt listing carat weight to $1/100^{th}$ of a carat (0.01 carat) and a *Warranty of Kimberley Process*. These receipts provide a paper trail back to the original KPC on file with the Department of Commerce.

All uncut diamonds shipped across international borders must have a KPC; this includes diamonds from non-conflict countries such as Brazil, Australia, Canada as well as the United States. Currently diamonds from the Marange area of Zimbabwe and from Cote d'Ivoire are banned from international trade, and Venezuela has voluntarily suspended participation in the KPCS, making diamonds from those countries illegal to import or export.

When buying uncut diamond crystals, collectors should require the seller to provide a detailed receipt with *Warranty of Kimberley Process*. The buyer should ensure the receipt details the weight of the diamond to $1/100^{th}$ of a carat. This receipt should be kept on file to provide evidence of legitimate acquisition.

Anyone selling diamonds must issue a similar receipt to buyers, and a new KPC must be issued when selling a diamond. For diamonds acquired prior to the 2003 implementation of the KPCS, diamonds should also be accompanied with an affidavit explaining precise history of how the diamond crystal was acquired to provide a paper trail back to its original source. The Department of Homeland Security, Customs Enforcement Division is responsible for enforcing these laws and these paperwork requirements are designed to protect diamond buyers from prosecution.

(CIA) has denied all of his reports on the subject, the Financial Action Task Force (FATF), an international policy making body charged with combating money laundering, terrorist financing and other threats to the international financial system, concluded in a 2013 report that the diamond trade is subject to considerable vulnerabilities and risks:

> *The closed and opaque nature of the diamonds markets and the high value of diamonds combined with a lack of expertise in this area on the part of the authorities have left this industry susceptible to abuse by criminals.*

As long as diamonds are a valuable and liquid commodity and until the industry adopts "fingerprinting" technologies that can positively identify individual stones, people will endeavor to steal them. From smash-and-grabs at neighborhood jewelry stores, to mission-impossible style robberies, to white collar insurance scams, and politically-motivated actions, thefts have long been part of the legacy of diamonds and will likely remain so in the future. Heists may always be a part of the story of the world's most recognizable precious stone.

Tyler Funk is a freelance writer and a researcher and social media coordinator at Lithographie, Ltd. Tyler has entertained a fascination with the natural world since childhood; his primary academic interest is in permaculture, an environmentally restorative method of growing food that builds topsoil rather than depleting it. Tyler is also the proud father of a 5-year-old, who inspires him to make the world a better place for future generations.

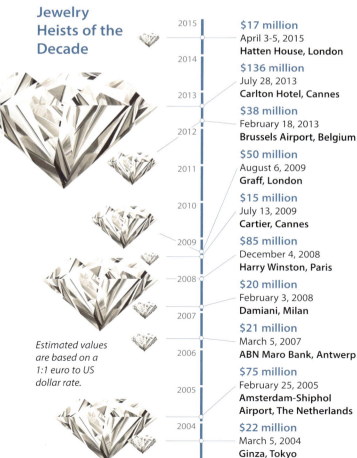

Jewelry Heists of the Decade

Estimated values are based on a 1:1 euro to US dollar rate.

- **$17 million** — April 3-5, 2015 — **Hatten House, London**
- **$136 million** — July 28, 2013 — **Carlton Hotel, Cannes**
- **$38 million** — February 18, 2013 — **Brussels Airport, Belgium**
- **$50 million** — August 6, 2009 — **Graff, London**
- **$15 million** — July 13, 2009 — **Cartier, Cannes**
- **$85 million** — December 4, 2008 — **Harry Winston, Paris**
- **$20 million** — February 3, 2008 — **Damiani, Milan**
- **$21 million** — March 5, 2007 — **ABN Maro Bank, Antwerp**
- **$75 million** — February 25, 2005 — **Amsterdam-Shiphol Airport, The Netherlands**
- **$22 million** — March 5, 2004 — **Ginza, Tokyo**

What Is GIA

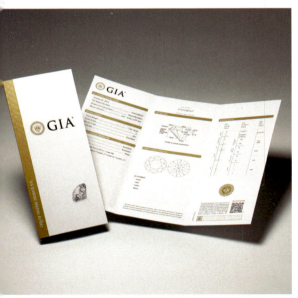

THE WORLD'S FOREMOST AUTHORITY ON DIAMONDS, COLORED STONES AND PEARLS

With objectivity and independence as its hallmark, GIA is recognized as the leader in gemological research, education and impartial gem laboratory services.

GIA sets the standard for determining the qualities of diamonds, colored gemstones and pearls. As the creator of the 4Cs, the International Diamond Grading System™ and the 7 Pearl Value Factors™, GIA provides all who buy or sell gems with a common language. And it continues its role as the leading research institute with its peer-reviewed journal, *Gems & Gemology*.

THE LEADING EDUCATOR FOR THE GEM AND JEWELRY INDUSTRY

More than 365,000 students — many holding important and influential positions throughout the industry — received their education at GIA. The Institute offers a comprehensive gemology and jewelry manufacturing arts curriculum and its Graduate Gemologist diploma program is widely regarded as the most prestigious professional credential in gems and jewelry.

GIA operates in 13 countries with 10 campuses, 9 grading laboratories and 4 research centers around the world. As an independent nonprofit organization, all of GIA's activities are governed by its mission to protect the public trust in gems and jewelry.

For more information, contact us today.
GIA.edu

CARLSBAD   NEW YORK   LONDON   ANTWERP   DUBAI   GABORONE   JOHANNESBURG
MUMBAI   RAMAT GAN   BANGKOK   HONG KONG   TAIPEI   SEOUL   TOKYO

Diamonds, to 8.01 carats.
Argyle Mine, Kimberley Division, Western Australia, Australia.
C & J Cubbison, Jeff Scovil photo

LITERATURE AND CITED WORKS

Albuquerque, L. d. 1989. *Notícia do Brasil* [in Portugese]. Lisbon: Alfa.

Arzamastsev A. A., B. V. Bialiatski, A. V. Travin, L. V. Arzamastseva, S. E. Tsarev. 2005. "Dyke Rocks from the Khibina Massif: Relations with the Plutonic Series, Age, and Characteristics of the Mantle Source" *Petrology* T13:295–318.

Asiedu, D. K., B. Dampare, P. A. Sakyi, and D. Boamah. 2007. "Major and Trace Element Geochemistry of Kimberlitic Rocks in the Akwatia Area of the Birim Diamondiferous Field, Southwest Ghana." *African Journal of Science and Technology* 8 (2):81–91.

Bailes, M., S. D. Bates, V. Bhalerao, et al. 2011. "Transformation of a Star into a Planet in a Millisecond Pulsar Binary." *Science* 333:1717–1720.

Bain & Company. 2016. *The Global Diamond Report 2016.*

Balfour, I. 1987. *Famous Diamonds.* London: William Collins Sons.

Ball, S. H. 1929. "Historical Notes on Diamond Mining in Minas Gerais." *Mining and Metallurgy* 10 (270):282–285.

Balmer, R. S., J. R. Brandon, S. L. Clewes, et al. 2009. "Chemical Vapour Deposition Synthetic Diamond: Materials, Technology and Applications." *Journal of Physics: Condensed Matter* 21 (36):364221.

Banks, D. 2008. *John Huddleston (1862-1941): The Man Behind the Myth of "Diamond John,"* 14. Self-published.

Bardet, M. D. 1965. "The Diamond Deposits of the USSR." *Bureau de Recherches Géologiques et Minières* Special Pub. 71.

Beard, M. 2015. *SPQR. A History of Ancient Rome.* London: Profile Books Ltd.

Bedini, A., S. Ehrman, S. N. Cesaro, M. Pasini, I. A. Rapinesi, and D. Sali. 2012. "The Vallerano Diamond from Ancient Rome: A Scientific Study." *Gems & Gemology* 48 (1):39–41

Benson, S. 1990. "USSR, Special Report. Mystery of Soviet Industry Unraveling but Questions about its Future Still Remain." *Diamond World Review* 59:38, 40, 42.

Berman, R. 1992. "Thermal Conductivity of Isotopically Enriched Diamonds." *Physical Review B*45 (10):5726–5728.

———. 1992b. "Thermal Conductivity of Vapour Deposited and Isotopically Enriched Diamonds." In *The Properties of Natural and Synthetic Diamond.* Edited by E. J. Field, 291–300. London: Academic Press.

Beveratos, A., R. Brouri, T. Gacoin, A. Villing, J. P. Poizat, and P. Grangier 2002. "Single Photon Quantum Cryptography." *Physical Review Letters* 89 (18):187901.

Beveridge, A. S., trans. 1912. *The Bābur-nāma in English (Memoirs of Babur)*, vol. 2, p. 33. London: Luzac & Co.

Bhat, Ramakrishna, M. 1987. *Varahamihira's Brahat Samhita*, 2nd ed. Dehli: Motilal Banarsidass Publishers Pvt. Ltd.

Bogatikov, O., V. K. Garanin, and V. Kononova. 1999. *The Arkhangelsk Diamond Province: Geology, Petrography, Geochemistry and Mineralogy* [in Russian]. Moscow: Moscow State University Press.

Bogatikov, O., V. A. Kononova, A. A. Nosova, A. V. Kargin. 2009. "Polygenetic Sources of Kimberlites, Magma Composition, and Diamond Potential Exemplified by the East European and Siberian Cratons." *Petrology* 17 (6): 606–625.

Bosshart, G. 1989. "The Dresden Green." *Swiss Watch and Jewelry Journal* 2:513–519.

Bowen, D. C., R. D. Ferraris, C. E. Palmer, and J. D. Ward. 2009. "On the Unusual Characteristics of the Diamonds from Letšeng-la-Terae Kimberlites, Lesotho." *Lithos* 112S:767–774.

Bragg, W. H. and W. L. Bragg. 1913. "The Structure of the Diamond." *Proceedings of the Royal Society of London, Series A* 89 (610):277–291.

Bundy, F. P. 1980. "The P, T Phase and Reaction Diagram for Elemental Carbon." *Journal of Geophysical Research* 85 (B12):6933.

Burgess, R., G. B. Kieviets, and J. W. Harris. 2004. "Ar-Ar Age Determinations of Eclogitic Clinopyroxene and Garnet Inclusions in Diamonds from Venetia and Orapa Kimberlites." *Lithos* 77:113–124.

Burton, Sir R. F. 1869. *Explorations in the Highlands of Brasil; with a Full Account of the Gold and Diamond Mines.* Volume II, 125–154. London: Tinsley Bros.

Butler, J. E., M. Geis, K. E. Krohn, J. Lawless, Jr., S. J. Deneault, T. M. Lyszczarz, D. Flechtner, R. Wright. 2003. "Exceptionally High Voltage Schottky Diamond Diodes and Low Boron Doping." *Semiconductor Science and Technology* 18 (3):S67–S71.

Butler, J. E., A. Cheesman, and M. N. R. Ashfold. 2009. "Recent Progress in the Understanding of CVD Growth of Diamond." In *CVD Diamond for Electronic Devices and Sensors*, edited by R. S. Sussmann, 103–124. Chichester, UK: John Wiley & Sons.

Butler, J. E. and R. L. Woodin. 1993. "Thin-Film Diamond Growth Mechanisms." *Philosophical Transactions of the Royal Society of London Series A — Mathematical Physical and Engineering Sciences* 342 (1664):209–224.

Byrne, K. S., J. D. Anstie, J. G. Chapman, and A. N. Luiten. 2012. "Infrared Microspectroscopy of Natural Argyle Pink Diamond." *Diamond & Related Materials* 23:125–129.

Canales, D. G. 2005. "The Akwatia Diamond Field, Ghana." Master's Thesis, New Mexico Institute of Mining & Technology.

Carrington, W. A., L. M. Hanssen, K. A. Snail, D. B. Oakes, J. E. Butler. 1989. "Diamond Growth in $O_2 + C_2H_4$ and $O_2 + C_2H_2$ Flames." *Metallurgical Transactions A* 20 (7):1282–1284.

Caspi, A. 1997. "Modern Diamond Cutting and Polishing." *Gems & Gemology* 33 (2):102–121.

Cattelle, W. R. 1911. *The Diamond*, p. 177–204. New York: John Lane, Company.

Cavey, C. 1992. *Gems & Jewels, Fact & Fable.* London: Studio Editions Ltd.

Celii, F. G. and J. E. Butler. 1991. "Diamond Chemical Vapor-Deposition." *Annual Review of Physical Chemistry* 42:643–684.

Censier, C. 1996. "Alluvial diamonds in the Central African Republic." *African Geoscience Review* 3 (2):217–230.

Chapman, J., G. Brown, and B. Sechos. 1996. "The Typical Gemmological Characteristics of Argyle Diamonds." *Australian Gemmologist* 19:339–346.

Chaves, M. L. S. C., J. Karfunkel, A. Hoppe, and D. B. Hoover. 2001. "Diamonds from the Espinhaco Range (Minas Gerais, Brazil) and Their Redistribution through the Geological Record." *Journal of South American Earth Sciences* 14 (3):277–289.

Chronic, J., M. E. McCallum, and C. S. Ferris. 1965. "Lower Paleozoic Rocks in Diatremes in Southern Wyoming and Northern Colorado." *Geological Society of America Special Paper* 87:280.

Clackson, S. G. and M, Moore. 1992. "An X-ray Study of Some Argyle Diamonds." *Industrial Diamond Review* 52:192–194.

Clayton, D. D. and L. R. Nittler. 2004. "Astrophysics with Pre-Solar Star Dust." *Annual Review of Astronomy and Astrophysics* 42:39–78.

Cohen, E. 1872. "Geological Notes on the Occurrence of Diamonds in South Africa" [in German]. *Neues Jahrbuch für Mineralogie* 1872:857–861.

Collins, A. T. 1980. "Vacancy Enhanced Aggregation of Nitrogen in Diamond." *Journal of Physics C: Solid State Physics* 13 (14):2641–2650.

———. 1982. "Colour Centres in Diamond." *Journal of Gemmology* 18 (1):37–75.

———. 2003. "The Detection of Colour-Enhanced and Synthetic Gem Diamonds by Optical Spectroscopy." *Diamond and Related Materials* 12 (10/11):1976–1983.

Collins A. T., and A. W. S. Williams. 1971. "The Nature of the Acceptor Centre in Semiconducting Diamond." *Journal of Physics C: Solid State Physics* 4 (13):1789–1799.

Collins, A. T., and K. Mohammed. 1982. "Optical Studies of Vibronic Bands in Yellow Luminescing Natural Diamonds." *Journal of Physics C: Solid State Physics* 15 (1):147–158.

Coopersmith, H. G., R. H. Mitchell, and W. D. Hausel. 2003. *Kimberlites and Lamproites of Colorado and Wyoming, USA.* Ottawa: Geological Survey of Canada.

Corbett, I. B. 1996. "A Review of the Diamondiferous Marine Deposits of Western Southern Africa." *African Science Review* 3 (2):257–274.

Cornejo, C., and A. Bartorelli. 2009. *Minerals and Precious Stones of Brazil*, 176-225. São Paulo: Solaris Cultural Publications.

Correns, C. W., J. Zemann, and S. Koritnig. 1969. *Introduction to Mineralogy: Crystallography and Petrology* translated by W. D. Johns. New York: Springer-Verlag.

Cunningham, D. 2011. *The Diamond Compendium*. London: NAG Press.

Currie, C. A. and C. Beaumont. 2011. "Are Diamond-Bearing Cretaceous Kimberlites Related to Low-Angle Subduction Beneath Western North America?" *Earth and Planetary Science Letters* 303 (1/2):59–70.

Custers, J. F. H. 1952. "Unusual Phosphorescence of a Diamond." *Physica* 18 (8/9):489–493.

———. 1954. "Letter to the Editor: Type IIb Diamonds." *Physica* 20 (4):183–184.

———. 1955. "Semiconductivity of a Type IIb Diamond." *Nature* 176 (4473):173–174.

Dana, J. D., 1850. *A System of Mineralogy, Comprising the Most Recent Discoveries*, 3rd ed. New York and London: George P. Putnam.

Danilov, B. 1982. *Diamonds and People* [in Russian]. Moscow: Moscow Worker.

Davies, G. 1977. "The Optical Properties of Diamond." In *Chemistry and Physics of Carbon* 13:115.

———. 1984. *Diamond*, 1–143. Bristol: Adam Hilger, Ltd.

Davies, G. R., P. H. Nixon, D. G. Pearson, and M. Obata. 1993. "Tectonic Implications of Graphitized Diamonds from the Ronda, Peridotite Massif, Southern Spain." *Geology* 21 (5):471–474.

Davy, H. 1840. *The Collected Works of Sir Humphry Davy, Vol. 5.* London: Smith, Elder and Co. Cornhill.

Delitsky, M. L., and K. H. Baines. 2013. "Diamond and Other Forms of Elemental Carbon in Saturn's Deep Atmosphere." *American Astronomical Society DPS Meeting #45*. Abstract 512.09.

Delville, R. 1980. "Angola." In *Diamonds, Myth, Magic and Reality*, 137–141. New York: Crown Publishers.

Demaiffe, D., M. Fieremans, and C. Fieremans. 1991. "The Kimberlites of Central Africa: A Review." In *Magmatism in Extensional Structural Settings. The Phanerozoic African Plate*, edited by A. B. Kampuzu and R. T. Lubala537–559. New York: Springer.

De Corte, K., A. Korsakov, W. R. Taylor, M. Cartigny, M. Ader, and P. De Paepe. 2000. "Diamond Growth During Ultrahigh-Pressure Metamorphism of the Kokchetav Massif, Northern Kazakhstan." *The Island Arc* 9:428–438.

De Wit, M. C. J. 1999. "Post-Gondwana Drainage and the Development of Diamond Placers in Western South Africa." *Economic Geology* 94 (5):721–740.

Dobrzhinetskaya, L. 2012. "Microdiamonds — Frontier of Ultrahigh-Pressure Metamorphism: A Review." *Gondwana Research* 21 (1):207–223.

Dundek, M. 2009. *Diamonds*. London: Noble Gems Publications.

Dunn, Dennis P. 2000. "Erosion Diamond Distribution at the Prairie Creek Lamproite Pipe, Murfreesboro, Arkansas" (abst.) *2000 Abstracts with Programs GSA South-Central Section* A9.

Dunn, E. J. 1874. "On the Mode of Occurrence of Diamonds in South Africa." *Quarterly Journal of the Geological Society* 30:54–60.

Eaton-Magaña, S., J. E. Post, P. J. Heaney, R. A. Walters, C. M. Breeding, and J. E. Butler. 2007. "Fluorescence Spectra of Colored Diamonds Using a Rapid, Mobile Spectrometer." *Gems & Gemology* 43 (4):332–351.

Earl Marshal of England (i.e., Henry Howard). 1677. "A Description of the Diamond Mines (of India)." *Philosophical Transactions of the Royal Society of Great Britain.* 12:907–917.

Eaton-Magaña, S., and R. Lu. 2011. "Phosphorescence in Type IIb Diamonds." *Diamond & Related Materials* 20 (7):983–989.

Eichholz, D. E., trans. 1962. *Pliny Natural History*, volume X, book 37, section XV. Cambridge: Harvard University Press.

Eggert, J. H.; D. G. Hicks, P. M. Celliers, D. K. Bradley, et al. 2010. "Melting Temperature of Diamond at Ultrahigh Pressure." *Nature Physics* 6 (1):40–43.

El Atrassi, F., F. Brunet, M. Bouybaouene, C. Chopin, and G. Chazot. 2011. "Melting Textures and Microdiamonds Preserved in Graphite Pseudomorphs from the Beni Bousera Peridotite Massif, Morocco." *European Journal of Mineralogy* 23 (2):157–168.

Escher, B. G. 1942. "On a Remarkable Composite Diamond." *Leidse Geologische Mededelingen* 13 (1):63–69.

Farges, F., S. Sucher, H. Horovitz, and J-M. Fourcault. 2009. "The French Blue and the Hope: New Data from the Discovery of a Historical Lead Cast." *Gems & Gemology* 45 (1):4–19.

Fazakerly, V. W. 1990. "Bow River Alluvial Diamond Deposit." In *Geology of the Mineral Deposits of Australia and Papua New Guinea*, Monograph 14, edited by F. E. Hughes, 1659–1664. Australasian Institute of Mining and Metallurgy.

Fedorovskiy N. M. 1936. *The Country of Diamonds and Gold: Travel to South Africa* [in Russian]. Leningrad-Moscow: ONTI.

Field, E. J., ed. 1992. *The Properties of Natural and Synthetic Diamond.* London: Academic Press.

Field, E. J. 1992b. "Strength, Fracture and Erosion Properties of Diamond." In *The Properties of Natural and Synthetic Diamond*, edited by E. J. Field, 473–515. London: Academic Press.

Fisher, D., S. J. Sibley, and C. J. Kelly. 2009. "Brown Colour in Natural Diamond and Interaction Between the Brown Related and Other Colour-Inducing Defects." *Journal of Physics: Condensed Matter* 21 (36):364213–364223.

Frank, F. C. and A. R. Lang. 1965. "X-ray Topography of Diamond." In *Physical Properties of Diamond*, edited by R. Berman, 69–115, 425–6. Oxford: Clarendon Press.

Franklin, J. 1829. "On the Diamond Mines of Panna in Bundelkhand." *Asiatic Researches* 18:100–122.

Fritsch, E. 1998. "The Nature of Color in Diamonds." In *The Nature of Diamonds*, edited by George E. Harlow, 23–47. Cambridge: Cambridge University Press.

Fritsch E., and K. Scarratt. 1989. "Optical Properties of Some Natural Diamonds with High Hydrogen Content." In *Diamond Optics II, Society for Photo-Optical Instrumentation Engineers*, edited by A. Feldman and S. Holly, 201–206.

———. 1992. "Natural-Color Nonconductive Gray-to-Blue Diamonds." *Gems & Gemology* 28 (1):35–42.

———. 1993. "Gemmological Properties of Type Ia Diamonds with an Unusually High Hydrogen Content." *Journal of Gemmology* 23 (8):451–460.

Fritsch, E., K. Scarratt, and A. T. Collins. 1991. "Optical Properties of Diamonds with an Unusually High Hydrogen Content." In *Materials Research Society International Conference Proceedings, Second International Conference on New Diamond Science and Technology, Washington, DC, Sept. 23–27*, 671–676. Pittsburgh, PA: Materials Research Society.

Fritsch, E., T. Hainschwang, L. Massi, and B. Rondeau. 2007a. "Hydrogen-Related Optical Centers in Natural Diamond: An Update." *New Diamond and Frontier Carbon Technology* 17 (2):63–89.

Fritsch, E., L. Massi, G. R. Rossman, T. Hainschwang, S. Jobic, and R. Dessapt. 2007b. "Thermochromic and Photochromic Behaviour of 'Chameleon' Diamonds." *Diamond & Related Materials* 16 (2):401–408.

Frolov, A. A., A. V. Lapin, A.V. Tolstov, et al. 2005. *Carbonatites and Kimberlites (Relations, Metallogeny, and Forecasting)* [in Russian]. Moscow: NIA-Priroda.

Fryer, C. W., ed. 1997. "GIA Gem Trade Lab Notes" In *Gems & Gemology.* 33 (1) :54.

Gaillou, E., W. Wang, J. E. Post, J. M. King, E. Butler, A. T. Collins, and T. M. Moses. 2010a. "The Wittelsbach-Graff and Hope Diamonds: Not Cut from the Same Rough." *Gems & Gemology* 46 (2):80–88.

Gaillou, E., J. E. Post, N. Bassim, M. Fries, T. Rose, R. Stroud, and J. E. Butler. 2010b. "Spectroscopic and Microscopic Characterization of Color Lamellae in Natural Pink Diamonds." *Diamond & Related Materials* 19 (10):1207–1220.

Gaillou, E., J. E. Post, and J. E. Butler. 2012a. "Boron in Natural Type IIb Blue Diamonds: Chemical and Spectroscopic Measurements." *American Mineralogist* 97 (1):1–18.

Gaillou, E., J. E. Post, T. Rose, and J. E. Butler. 2012b. "Cathodoluminescence of Natural, Plastically Deformed Pink Diamonds." *Microscopy and Microanalysis* 18 (6):1292–1303.

Garanin, V. K., G. P. Kudryavtseva, and A. J. A. Janse. 1993. "Vertical and Horizontal Zoning of Kimberlites." In *Proceedings of the Eighth Quadrennial IAGOD Symposium, held Ottawa, Canada, August 1990,* edited by Y. T. Maurice, 435–443. Stuttgart: Schweizerbart Science Publishers.

Garvie, L. A., P. Németh, and P. R. Buseck. 2014. "Transformation of Graphite to Diamond by Topotactic Mechanism." *American Mineralogist* 99 (2/3):531–538.

Gilbertson, A. 2007. *American Cut: The First Hundred Years.* Carlsbad, CA: Gemological Institute of America.

Giuliani, G., M. Chaussidon, H. J. Schubnel, D. H. Piat, C. Rollion-Bard, C. France-Lanord, D. Giard, D. de Narvaez, B. Rondeau. 2000. "Oxygen Isotopes and Emerald Trade Routes since Antiquity." *Science* 287 (5453):631-633.

Glinnemann, J., K. Kusaka, and J. W. Harris. 2003. "Oriented Graphite Single-Crystal Inclusions in Diamond." *Zeitschrift für Kristallographie* 218 (11):733–739.

Goldschmidt, V. 1916. *Atlas der Krystallformen,* vol. 3. Heidelberg: Carl Winters Universitätsbuchhandlung. Facsimile reprint: Rochester Mineralogical Symposium, Rochester, New York, 1986.

Goodwin, D. G. and J. E. Butler. 1997. "Theory of Diamond Chemical Vapor Deposition." In *Handbook of Industrial Diamonds and Diamond Films.* edited by M. A. Prelas, G. Popovici, and L. K. Biglow, 527–581. New York: Marcel Dekker, Inc.

Gonzaga, G. M., N. A. Texeira, and J. C. Gaspar. 1994. "The Origin of Diamonds in Western Minas Gerais, Brazil." *Mineralium Deposita* 29 (5):414–421.

Greenhalgh, P. 1985. *West African Diamonds 1919–1983,* 306. Manchester: Manchester University Press.

Gübelin E. J. and J. I. Koivula. 2008. *Photoatlas of Inclusions in Gemstones,* vol. 3. Basel, Switzerland: Opinio Verlag.

Gunn, C. B. 1968. "A Descriptive Catalogue of the Drift Diamonds of the Great Lakes Region, North America." *Gems & Gemology* 12 (10):297–303, 333–334.

Gurney, J. J., H. H. Helmstaedt, S. H. Richardson, and S. B. Shirey. 2010. "Diamonds Through Time." *Economic Geology* 105 (3):689–712.

Gurney, J. J., P. R. Hildebrand, J. A. Carlson, Y. Fedortchouk, and D. R. Dyck. 2004. "The Morphological Characteristics of Diamonds from the Ekati Property, Northwest Territories, Canada." *Lithos* 77 (1/4):21–38.

Haggerty, S. E. 1999. "A Diamond Trilogy: Superplumes, Supercontinents, and Supernovae." *Science* 285 (5429):851–860.

———. 2014. "Carbonado: Physical and Chemical Properties, a Critical Evaluation of Proposed Origins, and a Revised Genetic Model." *Earth Science Reviews* 130:49–72.

Hainschwang, T., D. Simic, E. Fritsch, B. Deljanin, S. Woodring, and N. DelRe. 2005. "A Gemological Study of a Collection of Chameleon Diamonds." *Gems & Gemology* 41(1):20–35.

Hainschwang, T., F. Notari, E. Fritsch, L. Massi, B. Rondeau, C. M. Breeding, and H. Vollstaedt. 2008. "HPHT Treatment of CO_2 containing and CO_2-related brown diamonds." *Diamond & Related Materials* 17 (3):340–351.

Hall, A. and Smith, C. B. 1984. "Lamproite Diamonds — are they different?" In *Kimberlite Occurrence and Origin: A Basis for Conceptual Models in Exploration,* edited by J. E. Glover and P. G. Harris, 167–212. University of Western Australia Publication 8.

Hall, P. K. 1970. "The Diamond Fields of Sierra Leone." *Geological Survey of Sierra Leone Bulletin* 5:133.

Harlow, G. E. and R. M. Davies, guest editors. 2005. "Diamonds." *Elements* 1.

Harpending, A. 1913. *The Great Diamond Hoax and Other Stirring Incidents from the Life of Asbury Harpending*. Norman, OK: University of Oklahoma Press.

Hausel, W. D. 1997. "Prospecting for Diamonds in Wyoming and Colorado." *International California Mining Journal* 67 (3):55–56, 67 (4):17–20, 60–62.

Hazen, R. 1993. *The New Alchemists: Breaking Through the Barriers of High Pressure*. New York: Times Books.

Heaney, P. J., E. P. Vicenzi, and S. De. 2005. "Strange Diamonds: The Mysterious Origins of Carbonado and Framesite." *Elements* 1 (2):85–89.

Helgren, D. M. 1979. "River of Diamonds. An Alluvial History of the Lower Vaal River Basin, South Africa." *Department of Geography, University of Chicago, Research Paper* 185:389.

Hill, M. 1972. *Hunting Diamonds in California*. Revised from 1959 edition, originally published as *Pages of History*. Healdsburg, CA: Naturegraph Publishers.

Hill, J. R. and W. S. Blatchley. 2005. *Gold and Diamonds in Indiana: An Update*. Bloomington: Indiana Geological Survey.

Hobbs, W. H. 1899. "The Diamond Fields of the Great Lakes." *Journal of Geolog* 7 (4):375–388.

Holland, J. R. 2007. *Diamonds are Waiting for You: Crater of Diamonds, Where Dreams Can and Do Come True*. Boston: Bit of Boston Press.

Hough, R. M., I. Gilmour, C. T. Pillinger, J. W. Arden, K. W. R. Gilkess, J. Yuan, and H. J. Milledge. 1995. "Diamond and Silicon Carbide in Impact Melt Rock from the Ries Impact Crater." *Nature* 378 (6552):41–44.

Howard, J. M. 1999. Summary of the 1990s Exploration and Testing of the Prairie Creek Diamond-Bearing Lamproite Complex, Pike County, Arkansas, with a Field Guide." In *Contributions to the Geology of Arkansas, vol. IV*. Edited by J. M. Howard, 57–73. Arkansas Geological Commission Miscellaneous Publication 18D.

Howell, D. 2009. "Quantifying Stress and Strain in Diamond." PhD Thesis, University College, London.

———. 2012. "Strain-Induced Birefringence in Natural Diamond: A Review." *European Journal of Mineralogy* 24 (4):575–585.

Howell, D., C. J. O'Neill, K. J. Grant, W. L. Griffin, S. Y. O'Reilly, N. J. Pearson, R. A. Stern, and T. Stachel. 2012. "Platelet Development in Cuboid Diamonds: Insights from Micro-FTIR mapping." *Contributions to Mineralogy and Petrology* 164:1011–1025.

Hutchkinson, M. 1988. *The Poisoner's Handbook*. Port Townsend, WA: Loompanics Unlimited.

Iakoubovskii, K., and G. J. Adriaenssens. 1999. "Photoluminescence in CVD Diamond Films." *Physica Status Solidi A* 172 (1):123–129.

Isberg, J., J. Hammersberg, E. Johansson, T. Wikström, D. J. Twitchen, A. J. Whitehead, S. E. Coe, G. A. Scarsbrook. 2002. "High Carrier Mobility in Single-Crystal Plasma-Deposited Diamond." *Science* 297 (5587):1670–1672.

Janse, A. J. A. 1994. "Is Clifford's Rule Still Valid? Affirmative Examples from Around the World." In *Proceedings of the Fifth International Kimberlite Conference 2, Diamonds: Characterization, Genesis and Exploration*, edited by H. O. A. Meyer and O. Leonardos, 215–235. Brazil: Departamento Nacional da Produção Mineral.

———. 1995. "A History of Diamond Sources In Africa: part I." *Gems & Gemology* 34 (4):228–255.

———. 1996. "A History of Diamond Sources In Africa: part II." *Gems & Gemology* 35 (1):2–30.

———. 2007. "Global Rough Diamond Production Since 1870." *Gems & Gemology* 43 (2):98–119.

———. 2012. "Diamond Production and Discoveries During the Last Fifteen Years." Extended abstracts no 357. 10th International Kimberlite Conference, held February 2012, Bangalore, India.

Janse, A. J. A. and P. A. Sheahan. 1995. "Catalogue of Worldwide Diamond and Kimberlite Occurrences: A Selective and Annotative Approach." In *Diamond Exploration: Into the 21st Century*, edited by W. L. Griffin, 73–111. Special volume 53 (1/3), *Journal of Geochemical Exploration*.

Jaques, A. L., J. D. Lewis, and C. B. Smith. 1986. "The Kimberlites and Lamproites of Western Australia." *Bulletin of the Geological Survey of Western Australia* 138:1–268.

Jerofejev, M., and P. Lachinov. 1888. *Zapiski Mineralogicheskoe Obshchestvo* [in Russian] 24:263–294.

Kangle, R. P., trans. and ed. 1997. *Kautiliya Arthasastra*, Part 2. Delhi: Motilal Banarsidass Publishers Pvt. Ltd.

Kania, D. R., et al. 1993. "Diamond Radiation Detectors." *Diamond and Related Materials* 2(5–7):1012–1019.

Kargin, A., L. Sazonova, A. Nosova, E. Kovalchuk, E. Minevrina. 2015. Metasomatic Processes in the Mantle Beneath the Arkhangelsk Province, Russia: Evidence from Garnet in Mantle Peridotite Xenoliths, Grib Pipe. *Geophysical Research Abstracts*, vol. 17.

Kennedy, T. A., F. T. Charnock, J. S. Colton, J. E. Butler, R. C. Linares, P. J. Doering. 2002. "Single-Qubit Operations with the Nitrogen-Vacancy Center in Diamond." *Physica Status Solidi B Basic Research* 233 (3):416–426.

Kharkiv, A. D., N. N. Zinchuk, A. I. Kryuchkov. 1998. *Primary Diamond Deposits of the World* [in Russian]. Moscow: Nedra.

Kjarsgaard, B. A. 2007. "Kimberlite Pipe Models: Significance for Exploration." In *Proceedings of the 5th Decennial International Conference on Mineral Deposits, Ore Deposits and Exploration Technologies*, 667–677. Edited by B. Milkereit.

King, J. M., ed. 2006. *Gems & Gemology in Review: Colored Diamonds*. Carlsbad, CA: Gemological Institute of America.

King, J. M., R. H. Geurts, A. M. Gilbertson, J. E. Shigley. 2008. "Color Grading 'D-to-Z' Diamonds at the GIA Laboratory." *Gems & Gemology* 44 (4):296–321.

King, J. M., T. M. Moses, J. E. Shigley, and Y. Liu. 1994. "Color Grading of Colored Diamonds in the GIA Gem Trade Laboratory." *Gems & Gemology* 30 (4):220–242.

King, J. M., T. M. Moses, J. E. Shigley, C. M. Welbourn, S. C. Lawson, and M. Cooper. 1998. "Characterization of Natural-Color Type IIb Blue Diamonds." *Gems & Gemology* 34 (4):246–268.

King, J. M., J. E. Shigley, S. S. Guhin, T. H. Gelb, and M. Hall. 2002. "Characterization and Grading of Natural-Color Pink Diamonds." *Gems & Gemology* 38 (2):128–147.

King, J. M., J. E. Shigley, T. H. Gelb, S. S. Guhin, M. Hall, and W. Wang. 2005. "Characterization and Grading of Natural-Color Yellow Diamonds." *Gems & Gemology* 41 (2):88–115.

Knuth, B. G. 1999. *Gems in Myth, Legend and Lore*, 9–10. Self-published.

Koivula J. I., ed. 1987. "Gem News." *Gems & Gemology* 23 (4): 238.

Koivula J. I. 2000. *The Microworld of Diamonds*. Northbrook, IL: Gemworld International, Inc.

Koivula, J. I. and E. A. Skalwold. 2014. "The Microworld of Diamonds: Images from Earth's Mantle." *Rocks & Minerals* 89 (1):46–51.

Kononova, V. A., Golubeva, Y. Y., Bogatikov, O. A. et al. 2007. "Diamond Resource Potential of Kimberlites from the Zimny Bereg Field, Arkhangel'sk Oblast." *Geology of Ore Deposits* 49 (6):421–441.

Kriulina G. Y. 2012. "The Constitutional Characteristics of the Diamond Deposits of the Arkhangelsk and Yakutian Diamond Provinces" [in Russian]. PhD Thesis, Lomonosov Moscow State University.

Kriulina G. Y., V. K. Garanin, A. J. Rotman, O. E. Kovalchuk. 2011. "Features of Diamonds from Commercial Deposits of Russia" [in Russian]. *Moscow University Geology Bulletin Series* 66 (3):171–183.

Kriulina, G. Y., V. K. Garanin, E. A. Vasilyev, V. O. Kyazimov, O. P. Matveeva, and P. V. Ivannikov. 2012. "New Data on the Structure of Diamond Crystals of Cubic Habits from the Lomonosov Deposit." *Moscow University Geological Bulletin* 67 (5):282–288.

KRISTALLE
Est. 1971

Wayne and Dona Leicht

WE ARE CASH BUYERS FOR SINGLE SPECIMENS AND ENTIRE COLLECTIONS!

875 North Pacific Coast Highway
Laguna Beach, CA 92651-1415, USA
949.494.5155; fax: 949.494.0402
e-mail: info@kristalle.com
www.kristalle.com

Kunz, G. F. 1913. *The Curious Lore of Precious Stones*. New York: Halcyon.

Kunz, G. F. and H. S. Washington. 1907. "Occurrence of Diamonds in Arkansas." In *Mineral Resources of the United States*, 1250. Washington: GPO.

Laiginhas, F. A. 2008. "Diamonds from the Ural Mountains: Their Characteristics and the Mineralogy and Geochemistry of Their Inclusions." PhD Thesis, University of Glasgow.

Laiginhas, F., D. G. Pearson, D. Phillips, R. Burgess, and J. W. Harris. 2009. "Re-Os and ^{40}Ar-^{39}Ar Isotope Measurements of Inclusions in Alluvial Diamonds from the Ural Mountains: Constraints on Diamond Genesis and Eruption Ages." *Lithos* 112S, 714–723.

Larson, L. M. and D. C. Rex.1992. "A Review of the 2500 Ma Span of Alkaline-Ultramafic, Potassic and Carbonatitic Magmatism in West Greenland." *Lithos* 28:367–402.

Laufer, B. 1915. "The Diamond, A Study in Chinese and Hellenistic Folk-lore." *Field Museum of Natural History Anthropological Series* XV (1): 43-44.

Law, B. and W. Wang. 2016. "CVD Synthetic Diamond Over 5 Carats Identified by GIA." *Gems & Gemology* 52 (4). In Press.

Le Guillou, C., J. N. Rouzard, L. Remusat, A. Jambon, and M. Bourot-Denise. 2010. "Structures, Origin and Evolution of Various Carbon Phases in the Ureilite Northwest Africa 4742 Compared with Laboratory-Shocked Graphite." *Geochimica et Cosmochimica Acta* 74 (14):4167–4185.

Leipunski, O. I. 1939. "About Synthetic Diamonds." *Uspekhi Kim* 8 (10):1518–1534.

Lenzen, G. 1970. *The History of Diamond Production and the Diamond Trade*. Translated by F. Bradley. London: Barrie & Jenkins Ltd.

Lewis, H. C. 1888. "The Matrix of the Diamond." *Geological Magazine* 5:129–131.

Lewis, R. S., T. Ming, J. F. Wacker, E. Anders, and E. Steel. 1987. "Interstellar Diamonds in Meteorites." *Nature* 326 (6109):160–162.

Liddicoat, R. T., ed. 1993. *The GIA Diamond Dictionary*, 3rd ed. Santa Monica, CA: Gemological Institute of America.

Linares, R. and P. Doering. 1999. "Properties of Large Single Crystal Diamond." *Diamond and Related Materials* 8 (2–5):90–915.

Madhusudhan, N., K. M. Lee Kanani, and O. Mousis. 2012. "A Possible Carbon-Rich Interior in Super-Earth 55 Cancrie." *The Astrophysical Journal Letters* 759:L40.

Malzahn, H. ed. 2000. "Diamant — Der Extreme Edelstein, Das Geniale Werkzeug" [in German]. *extraLapis* 18.

Martineau, P. M., et al. 2004. "Identification of synthetic diamond grown using chemical vapor deposition (CVD)." *Gems & Gemology* 40 (1):2–25.

Masaitis, V. L. 1995. "The Origin and Distribution of Diamond-Bearing Impactites." *Meteoritics* 30:541.

Massi, L., E. Fritsch, A. T. Collins, T. Hainschwang, and F. Notari. 2005. "The 'Amber Centres' and Their Relation to the Brown Colour in Diamond." *Diamond and Related Materials* 14 (10):1623–1629.

Mawe, John. 1812. *Travels in the Interior of Brazil*, ch. 13, p. 219–237. London: Longman, Hurst, Rees, Orme, and Brown.

McEnaney, B. 1999. "Structure and Bonding in Carbon Materials." In *Carbon Materials for Advanced Technologies*, 1–33. Edited by T. D. Burchell. Amsterdam: Pergamon.

McSween, H. Y. 1999. *Meteorites and Their Parent Planets*, 2nd ed. Cambridge: Cambridge University Press.

Meyer, H. O. A, and A. Seal. 1997. "Natural Diamond." In *Handbook of Industrial Diamonds and Diamond Films*. Edited by M. A. Prelas, G. Popovici, & L. K. Bigelow, 481–526. New York: Marcel Dekker, Inc.

Mildren, R. P., J. E. Butler, and J. R. Rabeau. 2008. "CVD-Diamond External Cavity Raman Laser at 573 nm." *Optics Express* 16 (23):18950–18955.

Millar, Howard. 1976. *It Was Finders-Keepers at America's Only Diamond Mine*. New York: Carlton Press.

Mineeva, R. M., S. V. Titkov, and A. V. Speransky. 2009. "Structural Defects in Natural Plastically Deformed Diamonds: Evidence from EPR spectroscopy." *Geology of Ore Deposits* 51 (3):233–242.

Miser, H. D. and A. H. Purdue. 1929. "Geology of the DeQueen and Caddo Gap Quadrangles" *USGS Bulletin* 808.

Mitchel, R. H. 1986. *Kimberlites: Mineralogy, Geochemistry and Petrology*. New York: Plenum Press.

———. 1995. *Kimberlites, Orangeites and Related Rocks*. New York: Plenum Press.

Mitchell, R. H. and S. C. Bergman 1991. *Petrology of Lamproites*. New York: Plenum Press.

Mitchell, R. H. and A. J. A. Janse. 1982. "A Harzburgite-Bearing Monchiquite from Wawa, Ontario." *Canadian Mineralogist* 20 (2):211–216.

Mizukami, T., S. Wallis, M. Enami, and H. Kagi. 2008. "Forearc diamond from Japan." *Geology* 36 (3):219–222.

Moor, G. G. 1940. "Potential Diamond Occurrences in the North of Central Siberia, USSR" [in Russian]. *Doklady Academy of Science USSR New Series* 31 (4):363–365.

Moses, T. M., I. M. Reinitz, M. L. Johnson, J. M. King, and J. E. Shigley. 1997. "A Contribution to Understanding the Effect of Blue Fluorescence on the Appearance of Diamonds." *Gems & Gemology* 33 (4):244–259.

Moses, T. M., M. L. Johnson, B. Green, T. Blodgett, K. Cino, R. H. Geurts, A. M. Gilbertson, T. S. Hemphill, J. M. King, L. Kornylak, I. M. Reinitz, and J. E. Shigley. 2004. "A Foundation for Grading the Overall Cut Quality of Round Brilliant Cut Diamonds." *Gems & Gemology* 40 (3):202–228.

Mugumbate, F. 2012. "Report on the Geological Society Field Trip to the Marange and Chimanimani Diamond Fields — 1 & 2 December 2012." *Geological Society of Zimbabwe Newsletter* February 2013: 12–14.

Nailer, S. G., M. Moore, J. Chapman, and G. Kowalski. 2007. "On the Role of Nitrogen in Stiffening the Diamond Structure." *Journal of Applied Crystallography* 40 (6):1146–1152.

Nasdala, L., D. Grambole, M. Wildner, A. M. Gigler, T. Hainschwang, A. M. Zaitsev, J. W. Harris, J. Milledge, D. J. Schulze, W. Hofmeister, and W. A. Balmer. 2013. "Radio-Colouration of Diamond: A Spectroscopic Study." *Contributions to Mineralogy and Petrology* 165 (5):843–861.

Németh, P., L. A. J. Garvie, T. Aoki, N. Dubrovinskaia, L. Dubrovinskaia, and P. R. Buseck. 2014. "Lonsdaleite is Faulted and Twinned Cubic Diamond and Does Not Exist as a Discrete Material." *Nature Communications* 5:5447.

Newton, I. 1704. *Opticks: Or a Treatise on the Reflexions, Refractions, Inflexions, and Colours of Light. Also Two Treatises on the Species and Magnitude of Curvilinear Coordinates*. London: Sam Smith and Benjamin Walford.

Newton, M. G., C. E. Melton, and A. A. Giardini. 1977. "Mineral Inclusion in an Arkansas Diamond." *American Mineralogist* 62 (5/6):583–586.

Ogasawara, Y. 2005. "Microdiamonds in Ultrahigh-Pressure Metamorphic Rocks." *Elements* 1 (2):91–96.

Olson, D. W. 2014. "Diamond, Industrial." *U.S. Geological Survey Minerals Yearbook*. http://minerals.usgs.gov/minerals/pubs/commodity/diamond/myb1-2012-diamo.pdf.

Orlov, Y. L. 1977. *The Mineralogy of the Diamond*. New York: John Wiley & Sons.

Overton, T. W., and J. E. Shigley. 2008. "A History of Diamond Treatments." *Gems & Gemology* 44 (1):32–55.

Pantaleo, N. S., M. G. Newton, S. V. Gogineni, C. E. Melton, and A. A. Giardini. 1979. "Mineral Inclusions in Four Arkansas Diamonds: Their Nature and Significance" *American Mineralogist* 64 (9/10):1059–1062.

Partoens, B. and F. M. Peeters. 2006. "From Graphene to Graphite: Electronic Structure around the K Point." *Physical Review B* 74:075404.

Pearson, D. G., G. R. Davies, P. H. Nixon, and H. J. Milledge. 1989. "Graphitized Diamonds from a Periodotite Massif in Morocco and Implications for Anomalous Diamond Occurrences." *Nature* 338 (6210):60–62.

Pearson, D. G. and P. H. Nixon. 1996. "Diamonds in Young Orogenic Belts: Graphitized Diamond from Beni Bousera, N. Morocco, A Comparison with Kimberlite-Derived Diamond Occurrences and Implications for Diamond Genesis and Exploration." *African Geoscience Review* 3 (2):296–316.

Pearson, D. G., S. B. Shirey, J. W. Harris, and R. W. Carlson. 1998. "Sulphide Inclusions in Diamonds from the Koffiefontein Mine, South Africa: Constraints on Diamond Ages and Mantle Re-Os Systematics." *Earth and Planetary Science Letters* 160 (3):311–326.

Peters, N. 2010. *Diamond Inclusions*. Deerfield Beach, FL: American Institute of Diamond.

Phillips, D., J. W. Harris, and G. B. Kiviets. 2004. "^{40}Ar/^{39}Ar Analyses of Clinopyroxene Inclusions in African Diamonds: Implications for Source Ages of Detrital Diamonds." *Geochimica et Cosmochimica Acta* 68 (1):151–165.

Phillips, D., and J. W. Harris. 2009. "Diamond Provenance Studies from ^{40}Ar-^{39}Ar Dating of Clinopyroxene Inclusions: An Example from the West Coast of Namibia." *Lithos* 112S:793–805.

Pidgeon, R. T., C. B. Smith, and C. M. Fanning. 1989. "Kimberlites and Lamproite Emplacement Ages in Western Australia." In *Kimberlites and Related Rocks*, vol 1. Edited by J. Ross. et al. Geological Society of Australia Special Publication 14, 369–381. Australia: Blackwell Scientific Publications.

Pierson, H. O. 1993. *Handbook of Carbon, Graphite, Diamond and Fullerenes: Properties and Processing*. Ridge Park, NJ: Noyes.

Polutoff, N. 1965. "The Siberian Diamond Deposits." *Gems & Gemology* (11):342–349, 351, (12):377–379.

Poon, T., and W. Wang. 2016. "Blue HPHT Synthetic Diamond Over 10 Carats." *Gems & Gemology* 52 (4). In Press.

Prawer, S. and R. J. Nemanich. 2004. "Raman Spectroscopy of Diamond and Doped Diamond." *Philosophical Transactions of the Royal Society of London A* 362 (1824):2537–2565.

Rachminov, E. 2009. *The Fancy Color Diamond Book*. Tel Aviv: Diamond Odyssey Ltd.

Rakovan, J., E. Gaillou, J. E. Post, J. A. Jaszczak, and J. H. Betts. 2014. "Optically Sector-Zoned (Star) Diamonds from Zimbabwe." *Rocks and Minerals* 89 (2):173–178.

Read, G. H., and A. J. A. Janse. 2009. "Diamonds: Exploration, Mining and Marketing." *Lithos* 112S (1):1–9.

Reyburn, S. W., and S. H. Zimmerman. 1920. "Diamonds in Arkansas" *Engineering and Mining Journal* 109 (17):983–986.

Richardson, S. H. 1986. "Latter-Day Origin of Diamonds of Eclogitic Paragenesis." *Nature* 322 (6080):623–626.

Ritter, C. 1836. *Die Erdkunde von Asien*, Band IV [in German]. Berlin: G. Reimer.

Robinson, D. N. 1980. "Surface Textures and Other Features of Diamonds." PhD Thesis, University of Cape Town.

Robinson, D. N., J. A. Scott, A. van Niekirk, and V. G. Anderson. 1989. "The Sequence of Events Reflected in the Diamonds of Some Southern African Kimberlites." In *Kimberlites and Related Rocks*, vol 2. Edited by J. Ross. et al. Geological Society of Australia Special Publication 14, 990–1000. Australia: Blackwell Scientific Publications.

Rogers, J. A. 1985. "Kimberlite Exploration, Red Feather Area, and Petrology of the Chicken Park Diatreme, Northern Colorado." M.S. Thesis, Colorado State University.

Roskin, G. 1994. *Photo Masters for Diamond Grading*. Northbrook, IL: Gemworld International.

Rotman A. Y., N. N. Zinchuk, et al. 2003. *Geological Aspects of Minerals Base Stock Company "ALROSA": Current Status and Perspectives, Solutions*, 152–169 [in Russian]. Voronezh (Russia): Voronezh State University.

Rubanova, E. V., O. V. Palazhchenko, V. K. and Garanin. 2009. "Diamonds from the V. Grib Pipe, Arkhangelsk Kimberlite Province, Russia." *Lithos* 112:880–885.

Russell, S. S., C. T. Pillinger, J. W. Arden, M. R. Lee, and U. Ott. 1992. "A New Type of Meteoritic Diamond in the Enstatite Chondrite Abee." *Science* 256 (5054):206–209.

Scarratt, K. 1987. "Notes from the Laboratory—10." *Journal of Gemmology* 20 (6):356–361.

Scott-Smith, B. H., and Skinner, E. M. W. 1984. "A New Look at Prairie Creek, Arkansas." In *Kimberlites I; Kimberlites and related rocks*, edited by J. Kornprobst, 255–283. Amsterdam: Elsevier.

Sewell, R., F. Nunes, D. Paes. 1900. *A Forgotten Empire: (Vijayanagar) a Contribution to the History of India*. London: Swan Sonnenschein & Co., Ltd.

Shiell, T. B., D. G. McCulloch, J. E. Bradby, B. Haberl, R. Boehler, and D. R. McKenzie. 2016. "Nanocrystalline Hexagonal Diamond Formed from Glassy Carbon." *Scientific Reports* 6:37232. www.nature.com/articles/srep37232.

Shigley, J. E., ed. 2005. *Gems & Gemology in Review: Synthetic Diamonds*. Carlsbad, CA: Gemological Institute of America.

Shigley, J. E., ed. 2008. *Gems & Gemology in Review: Treated Diamonds*. Carlsbad, CA: Gemological Institute of America.

Shigley, J. E., B. H. Laurs, A. J. A. Janse (Bram), S. Eden, and D. M. Dirlam. 2010. "Gem Localities of the 2000s." *Gems & Gemology* 46 (3):188–216.

Shigley James E., Christopher M. Breeding, and Andy Hsi-Tien Shen. 2004. "An Updated Chart on the Characteristics of HPHT-Grown Synthetic Diamonds." *Gems & Gemology* 40 (4):303–313.

Shigley, J. E., J. Chapman, and R. K. Ellison. 2001. "Discovery and Mining of the Argyle Diamond Deposit, Australia." *Gems & Gemology* 37 (1):26–41.

Shipley, R. M., and R. T. Liddicoat Jr. 1941. "A Solution to Diamond Color Grading Problems." *Gems & Gemology* 3 (11):162–168.

Shirey, S. B. and J. E. Shigley. 2013. "Recent Advances in Understanding the Geology of Diamonds." *Gems & Gemology* 49 (4):188–222.

Shirey, S. B., P. Cartigny, D. J. Frost, S. Keshav, F. Nestola, P. Nimis, D. G. Pearson, N. V. Sobolev, and M. J. Walter. 2013. "Diamonds and the Geology of Mantle Carbon." *Reviews in Mineralogy and Geochemistry* 75:355–421.

Shor, R. 2013. "Auction Houses: A Powerful Market Influence on Major Diamonds and Colored Gemstones." *Gems & Gemology* 49 (1):2–15.

Shumilova, T. G., Y. V. Danilova, M. V. Gorbunov, and S. I. Isaenko. 2011. "Natural Monocrystalline α-Carbyne." *Doklady Earth Sciences* 436 (1):152–154.

Slodkevich, V. V. 1983. "Graphite Paramorphs after Diamond." *International Geology Review* 25 (5):497–514.

Smith, E., H. Helmstaedt, and R. Flemming. 2010. "Survival of Brown Colour in Diamond During Storage in the Subcontinental Lithospheric Mantle." *Canadian Mineralogist* 48 (3):571–582.

Smith, P. P. K. and P. R. Buseck. 1985. "Carbyne Forms of Carbon: Evidence for their Existence." *Science* 229 (4712):486–487.

Sobolev, V. S. 1936. "Petrology of Trap Rocks of the Siberian Plateau" [in Russian]. *Proceedings of the Arctic Institute* 43.

Spetsius, Z. V. and L. A. Taylor. 2008. *Diamonds of Siberia: Photographic Evidence for their Origin*. Lenoir City, TN: Tranquility Base Press.

Stachel, T. 2014. "Diamond." In *Geology of Gem Deposits*, 2nd ed. Edited by L. A. Groat, 1–28. Mineralogical Association of Canada.

Stachel, T. and J. W. Harris. 1997. "Syngenetic Inclusions in Diamonds from the Birm Field (Ghana) — A Deep Periodotite Profile with a History of Depletion and Re-enrichment." *Contributions to Mineralogy and Petrology* 127 (4):336–352.

———. 2008. "The Origin of Cratonic Diamonds — Constraints from Mineral Inclusions." *Ore Geology Reviews* 34 (1/2):5–32.

———. 2009. "Formation of Diamond in the Earth's Mantle." *Journal of Physics: Condensed Matter* 21 364206.

Stachel, T., J. W. Harris, and K. Muehlenbachs. 2009. "Sources of Carbon in Inclusion-Bearing Diamonds." *Lithos* 112S:625–637.

Stachel, T., J. W. Harris, L. Hunt, K. Muehlenbachs, A. Kobussen, and EIMF. 2017. "Argyle Diamonds – How Subduction Along the Kimberley Craton Edge Generated the World's Biggest Diamond Deposit." *Economic Geology* Special Edition. In Press.

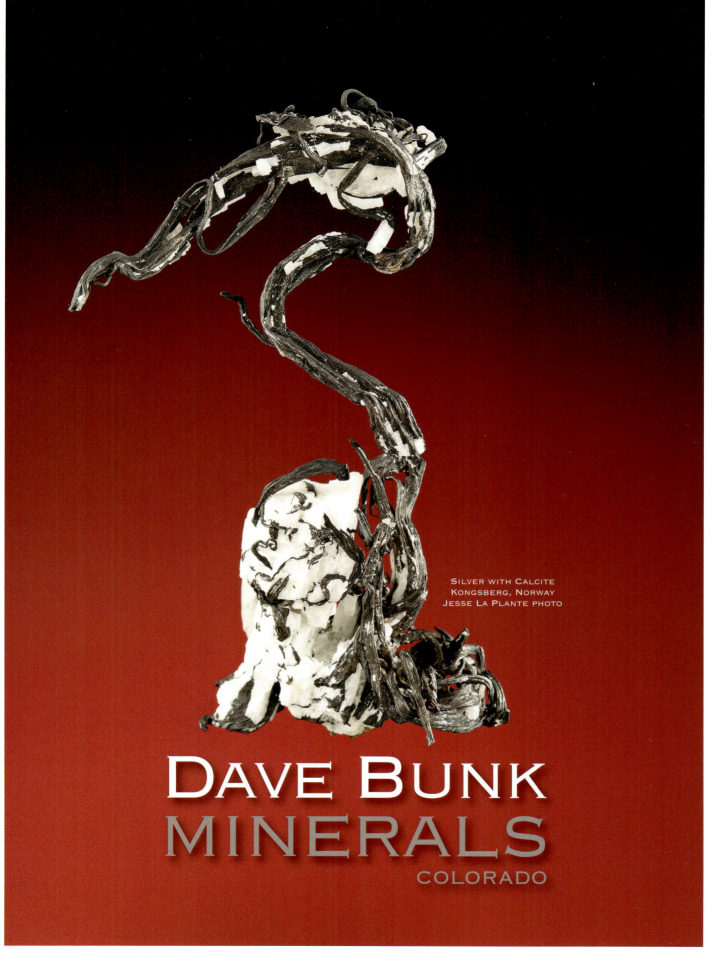

Steenfelt, A., S. M. Jensen, T. F. D. Nielsen, and K. K. Sand. 2009. "Provinces of Ultramafic Lamprophyre Dykes, Kimberlite Dykes and Carbonatite in West Greenland Characterised by Minerals and Chemical Components in Surface Media." *Lithos* 112:116–123.

Stoneham, A. M. 1992. "Diamond: Recent Advances in Theory." In *The Properties of Natural and Synthetic Diamond*, edited by E. J. Field, 3–34. London: Academic Press.

Strnad, J. 1991. "The Discovery of Diamonds in Siberia and Other Northern Regions: Explorational, Historical, and Personal Notes." *Earth Science History* 10 (2):227–246.

Streeter, E. W. 1882. *The Great Diamonds of the World: Their History and Romance*. 2nd ed. Edited and annotated by J. Hatton and A. H. Keane. London: George Bell & Sons.

———. 1898. *Precious Stones and Gems, Their History, Sources and Characteristics*, 6th ed. London: George Bell & Sons.

Sucher, S. D. 2009. "A Crystallographic Analysis of the Tavernier Blue Diamond." *Gems and Gemology* 45 (3):178–185.

Sunagawa, I. 1984. "Morphology of Natural and Synthetic Diamond Crystals." In *Materials Science of the Earth's Interior*, edited by I. Sunagawa, 303–331. Tokyo: Terra Scientific Publishing Company.

Sussex, J. R. 1990. "Mining In and Near the Arctic Circle: A Tale of Foxes and Permafrost." *Diamond World Review* 59:44–60.

Suwa, Y., and A. Coxon. 2010. *Diamonds: Rough to Romance*. Tokyo: Sekai Bunka Publishing.

Tagliabue, J. 2012. "An Industry Struggles to Keep Its Luster." *The New York Times*, November 5.

Tappert, R., T. Stachel, J. W. Harris, K. Muehlenbachs, and G. P. Brey. 2007. "Placer Diamonds from Brazil: Constraints on the Composition of the Earth's Mantle and the Distance to the Kimberlite Sources." *Economic Geology* 101 (2):453–470.

Tappert, R., J. Foden, T. Stachel, K. Muehlenbachs, M. Tappert, and K. Wills. 2009. "The Diamonds of South Australia." *Lithos* 112S:806–821.

Tappert, R. and M. C. Tappert. 2011. *Diamonds in Nature: A Guide to Rough Diamonds*. Berlin: Springer.

Tavernier, J. B. (1678). *The Six Voyages of John Baptista Tavernier*. Translated by John Phillips. London: R. L. and M. P.

Tennant, S. 1797. "On the Nature of Diamond." *Philosophical Transactions of the Royal Society* 87:123–127.

Tillander, H. 1995. *Diamond Cuts in Historic Jewellery 1381-1910*. London: Art Books International.

Titkov, S. V., J. E. Shigley, C. M. Breeding, R. M. Mineeva, N. G. Zudin, and A. M. Sergeev. 2008. "Natural-Color Purple Diamonds from Siberia." *Gems & Gemology* 44 (1):56–64.

Titkov, S. V., S. V. Krivovichev, and N. I. Organova. 2012. "Plastic Deformation of Natural Diamonds by Twinning: Evidence from X-ray Diffraction Studies." *Mineralogical Magazine* 76 (1):143–149.

Trueb, L. F. and C. S. Barrett. 1972. "Microstructural Investigation of Ballas Diamond." *American Mineralogist* 57 (11/12):1664–1680.

Turkevich, J. 1963. *Soviet Men of Science: Academicians and Corresponding Members of the Academy of Sciences of the USSR*, 364–365. Princeton: D. Van Nostrand Company.

Vance, E. R., J. W. Harris, and H. J. Milledge. 1973. "Possible Origins of α-damage in Diamonds from Kimberlite and Alluvial Sources." *Mineralogical Magazine* 39 (303):349–360.

van der Bogert, C. H., C. P. Smith, T. Hainschwang, and S. F. McClure. 2009. "Gray-to-Blue-to-Violet Hydrogen-Rich Diamonds from the Argyle Mine, Australia." *Gems & Gemology* 45 (1):20–37.

van der Laan, H. L. 1965. *The Sierra Leone Diamonds: An Economic Study Covering the Years 1952-1961*. London: Oxford University Press.

von Raumer, F. 1835. *Historisches taschenbuch*, I Ser., vol VI [in German]. Leipzig: F. A. Brodhaus.

Vernadsky, V. 1908. *Essays on Descriptive Mineralogy. Vol 1 "Native Elements."* St. Petersburg: Imperial Academy of Sciences.

Verzhak, V. V. 2001. "Geological Structure, Material Composition, Conditions of Formation and Methodology of Prospecting the M. V. Lomonosov Diamond Deposit" [in Russian]. PhD Thesis, Lomonosov Moscow State University.

Vierthaler, A. A. 1961. "Wisconsin Diamonds." *Gems & Gemology* 10 (7):210–215.

Wang, W. 2007. "HPHT-Annealed Yellow-Orange Diamond with a Strong 480 nm Absorption Band." *Gems & Gemology* 43 (1):49–50.

———. 2008. "Natural Type Ib Diamond with Unusual Reddish Orange Color." *Gems & Gemology* 44 (3):255–256.

Wang, W., T. Moses, R. C. Linares, J. E. Shigley, M. Hall, and J. E. Butler. 2003. "Gem-Quality Synthetic Diamonds Grown by Chemical Vapor Deposition (CVD) Method." *Gems & Gemology* 39 (4):268–283.

Welbourn, C. M., M. L. T. Rooney, and D. J. F. Evans. 1989. "A Study of Diamonds of Cube and Cube-Related Shape from the Jwaneng Mine." *Journal of Crystal Growth* 94:229–252.

Whittaker, A. G. 1985. "Carbyne Forms of Carbon: Evidence for their Existence." *Science* 229 (4712):485–486.

Wilks, E. M. and J. Wilks. 1965. "The Hardness and Wear of Diamond During Grinding and Polishing." In *Physical Properties of Diamond*, 221–250, 428–429. Edited by R. Berman. Oxford: Clarendon Press.

Wilks, J. and E. M. Wilks. 1992. "Wear and Polishing of Diamond." In *The Properties of Natural and Synthetic Diamond*, edited by E. J. Field, 573–604. London: Academic Press.

Williams, G. F. 1906. *The Diamond Mines of South Africa*, 24. New York: B. F. Buck & Company.

Williams, J. F. 1891. "The Igneous Rocks of Arkansas" *Arkansas Geological Survey Annual Report for 1890* 2:457.

Wilson, A. C. 2006. "Unusual Archean Diamond-Bearing Rocks of the Wawa Area." *Institute on Lake Superior Geology 52nd Annual Meeting Sault Ste Marie, Ontario* 52 (3):31.

Wilson, A. N. 1982. *Diamonds from Birth to Eternity*, 295–301. Los Angeles: Gemological Institute of America.

Wilson, L., and J. W. Head. 2007. "An Intergrated Model of Kimberlite Ascent and Eruption." *Nature* 447 (714):53–57.

Wilson, M. G. C., H. McKenna, and M. D. Lynn. 2007. *The Occurrence of Diamonds in South Africa*. Pretoria: Council for Geoscience.

Wirth, R. and A. Rochol. 2003. "Nanocrystalline Diamond from the Earth's Mantle Underneath Hawaii." *Earth and Planetary Science Letters* 211 (3/4):357–369.

Woods, G. S. 1986. "Platelets and the Infrared Absorption of Type Ia Diamonds." *Proceedings of the Royal Society A* 407 (1832):219–238.

Yacoot, A. and M. Moore. 1993. "X-ray Topography of Natural Tetrahedral Diamonds." *Mineralogical Magazine* 57 (387):223–230.

Yaxley, G. M., V. S. Kamenetsky, G. T. Nichols, R. Maas, E. Belousova, A. Rosenthal, and M. Norman. 2013. "The Discovery of Kimberlites in Antarctica Extends the Vast Gondwana Cretaceous Provinces." *Nature Communications* 4:2921. www.nature.com/articles/ncomms3921.

Zaitsev, A. 2001. *Optical Properties of Diamond: A Data Handbook*. Berlin: Springer.

Zinchuk, N. N., V. I. Koptil. 2003. "Mineralogy of Diamonds from the Yubileinaya Pipe (Yakutia)." *Geology of Ore Deposits* 46 (2):135–149.

Zhu, Q., A. R. Oganov, M. Salvado, P. Pertierra, A. O. Lyakhov. 2011. "Denser than Diamond: Ab initio Search for Superdense Carbon Allotropes." *Physical Review B* 83:193410.

Drawing of a pseudo-five-fold diamond from Victor Goldschmidt's 1916 *Atlas der Krystalformen*, vol. 3, fig. 360.

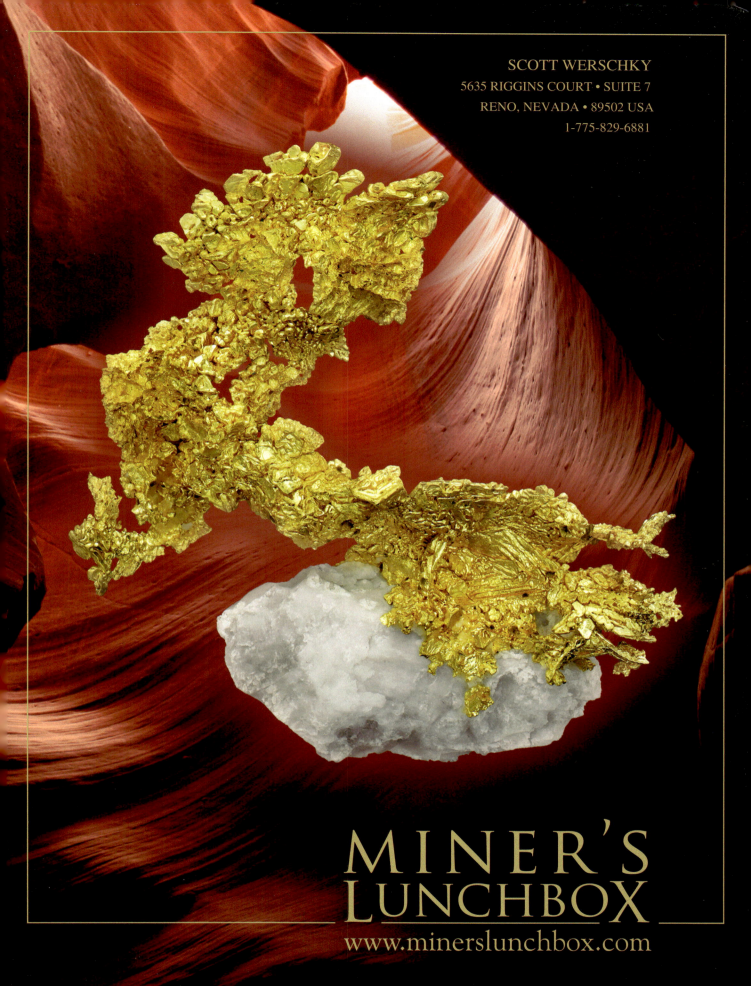

Polish your knowledge

Are these diamonds or synthetic moissanites?* If you're not sure, sign up for our world-famous **Diamond Diploma**, one of the most comprehensive and valuable diamond qualifications worldwide.

You will gain a thorough understanding of diamonds and how the diamond market operates; learn about diamond grading, the 4Cs and the other factors that influence value; study the factors that affect a diamond's appearance and properties; and will learn how to identify and recognise imitations, synthetics and treatments. Our Diamond Diploma graduates can apply for Membership, entitling them to use the prestigious **DGA post-nominal letters** — a mark of excellence in the trade.

For more information or to sign up contact **education@gem-a.com.**

* They're diamonds.

Creating gemmologists since 1908

Join us.

The Gemmological Association of Great Britain, 21 Ely Place, London, EC1N 6TD, UK. T: +44 (0) 20 7404 3334 F: +44 (0) 20 7404 8843. Registered charity no. 1109555. A company limited by guarantee and registered in England No. 1945780. Registered Office: 3rd Floor, 1-4 Argyll Street, London W1F 7LD.